Total Project Control

Wiley Operations Management Series for Professionals

Other published titles in this series are:

Harnessing Value in the Supply Chain: Strategic Sourcing in Action, by Emiko Banfield

The Valuation of Technology: Business and Financial Issues in R&D by F. Peter Boer

Logistics and the Extended Enterprise: Best Practices for the Global Company by Sandor Boyson, Thomas M. Corsi, Martin E. Dresner, and Lisa H. Harrington

Internet Solutions For Project Managers, by Amit K. Maitra

Total Project Control

A Manager's Guide to Integrated
Project Planning, Measuring,
and Tracking

Stephen A. Devaux

WILEY

John Wiley & Sons, Inc.

New York • Chichester • Weinheim • Brisbane • Singapore • Toronto

To my darling,
Deb,
who gave me the love, strength, and encouragement without which
this would never have been written,
and to
my two most important and successful projects, my wonderful sons,
A.J. and Eric Devaux

Designations used by companies to distinguish their products are often claimed as trademarks. In all instances where John Wiley & Sons, Inc., is aware of a claim, the product names appear in initial capital or all capital letters. Readers, however, should contact the appropriate companies for more complete information regarding trademarks and registration.

This text is printed on acid-free paper.

Copyright©1999 Stephen A. Devaux
Published by John Wiley & Sons, Inc.
All rights reserved. Published simultaneously in Canada.

This publication is designed to provide accurate and authoritative information in regard to the subject matter covered. It is sold with the understanding that the publisher is not engaged in rendering legal, accounting, or other professional services. If legal advice or other expert assistance is required, the services of a competent professional person should be sought.

Library of Congress Cataloging-in-Publications Data:
Devaux, Stephen A., 1949–
    Total project control : a manager's guide to integrated project planning, measuring and tracking / Stephen A. Devaux.
        p.   cm. — (Wiley operations management series for professionals)
        Includes index.
      ISBN 0-471-32859-6 (cloth : alk. paper)
      1. Industrial project management.   I. Title.   II. Series.
HD69.P75D48   1999
658.4'04—dc21   98-54154
                                                                      CIP

10 9 8 7 6 5 4 3 2

Contents

List of Figures

Acknowledgments

There have been so many people who have assisted me during my professional career that to list them all would be as long as the book itself. I am sure I shall omit many to whom I owe a great deal. However, I shall limit my acknowledgments here to those on this list. Without any one of them, this book would never have been possible:

Debra Alpern
Tony Blaize
Deborah and Robert
Bloomberg
Peter Bottjer
Ed Breslin
Francine Davis
Christine Eyre
Jeanne Glasser
Barbara and Ian Griffin
Wayne Halverson
Jamie Katz
William Kelleher
Chico Khan

Sam Miller
PageMasters & Company
Russ Phillips
E.C. Queree
Susan Rodburg
Julie Wittes Schlack
Harold Sullivan
Larry Tapper
David Wamback
Julie Winston
Linda Witzling
All the members of The
Group

Preface

The term *project management* has a multitude of meanings. The head of a construction company erecting a downtown skyscraper, the pharmacologist overseeing clinical trials for a new drug, the account manager supervising the development of a database for a Fortune 100 client—all three are engaged in project management. Yet chances are that the things they do are very different. And doesn't that make sense? After all, aren't their projects very different?

Well, yes and no. It is true that varied types of work will require different knowledge bases for each of the project managers. But outside of the work itself, all these projects actually have a great deal in common.

➤ Each has a schedule, limited either by a strict deadline or an "as soon as possible" requirement.

➤ Each has resources, usually in limited quantities, that must be targeted, scheduled, and tracked.

➤ Each has a budget that must be planned and tracked, either in workhours or in dollars, preferably in both.

➤ Each is going to run into unforeseen circumstances, to which the manager's ability to react and adapt is likely to be a key factor in the success or failure of the project.

Most important of all, each has a scope of work to be accomplished. But for the three projects listed above, and for every one of the millions of other projects that industry must undertake, each work scope is very different. Traditional project management has always understood this. Unfortunately, its methodologies, which can address the scheduling, resourcing, budgeting, and tracking needs of any project regardless of type, are unable to deal with work scope in an acceptably quantifiable manner. As a result, traditional project management "factors out" work scope from the management process by assuming it to be a "prerequisite" to the process. The traditional approach is: "Once you determine your work scope, we can provide you with a multitude of quantitative techniques for planning, scheduling, resourcing, budgeting, and tracking your project." All these techniques are based on a defined and constant work scope.

There are, of course, recommended approaches for defining work scope. Some project management consultants offer scope templates for certain projects. In software development, systems life cycle methodologies are used as a check list for defining the scope and making sure that nothing of importance is omitted. However, the work itself is never quantified in a way that can support decision making. As a result, project decisions affecting scope (or alternatively the way that scope should affect project decisions) remain a shot in the dark. The hundreds upon hundreds of project management software packages that have been developed over the years provide zero assistance in this regard.

Other than saying "Scope definition is important," modern project management is silent.

■ THE TPC APPROACH

Total Project Control (TPC) views the entire project process, from initial concept through delivery to the customer, as a coherent whole. It offers a major improvement over traditional project management, by providing the entire organization with quantitative data and analysis throughout.

Even if work scope were only a minor part of the project picture, it would still be crucial to deal with it effectively. As Peter Senge demonstrated in his book *The Fifth Discipline*, it is vital to address every piece of a complex process as part of the whole. Separating an integral process into independent phases is fraught with pitfalls, which can exacerbate the very problem the project was undertaken to solve.

But work scope is not a minor part of the project. In fact, it is the most important part. It is the raison d'etre of the project, the reason for the investment of millions of dollars. Without the work scope, as represented by the ultimate deliverable, there would be absolutely no reason to undertake the project. No reason to expend resources or to take up time. The work scope is what every project is about, whether to build a warehouse, refuel a nuclear reactor, or bring a new consumer product to market. And yet it is this crucial area that traditional project management has neglected.

In this neglect, the project manager (and by proxy the entire organization) is analogous to a poker player who has no idea how much money is in the pot. How can any investment decision be made, on a quantified basis, unless there is at least some sense of what value awaits a successful outcome? And, as the game progresses, and the size of the pot changes, the good poker player must constantly reassess his risk in deciding on future investment. Yet once again, the project manager, with millions at stake, shuts his eyes to the dynamic forces of the business world, which dictate that work scope should be a constantly changing variable, even if the project management methodology (and software) say it's not.

Precisely because work scope varies greatly from project to project, and even, over time, within a single project, the ability to manage that changing work scope is vital:

➤ To ensure a satisfactory level of quality for acceptable cost.

➤ To select the best elements of scope to cut when forced to do so in order to meet schedule and/or budgetary requirements.

➤ To increase scope where the project's return on investment (ROI) can be enhanced by the additional deliverable(s).

➤ To determine which of many possible project work scopes should be undertaken as part of the multiproject portfolio.

■ "TOTAL SYSTEMS" THINKING

Total Project Control addresses the need to manage every project in its totality: all of its parameters and data, all of its resources and areas of responsibility. It also provides a means of managing a project, and an entire project portfolio, as a single, integrated system, in a way that allows an occurrence in one project, activity, or data item, to be reflected in all the other affected projects, activities, and data items. This reflection is visible in quantifiable, measureable, and comparative terms, so that decisions can be made not on subjective and tunnel vision-slanted criteria, but on the basis of the one underlying criterion that motivates all businesses to operate: What is best for overall profitability?

This total systems approach of *Total Project Control* unites the macro- and micro-levels of work and management. It allows decisions regarding a single project or activity to be driven by criteria and data generated on the basis of overall corporate benefit. Without micromanaging, senior management can provide quantified data which point the way for detailed project decisions. Then the entire organization can sing from the same hymnbook, with optimized profits as the guiding, and verifiable, principle.

This is what *Total Project Control* offers. It builds, in crucial and dramatic ways, on such traditional project management tools as work breakdown structures, critical path method, and activity-based costing. But it guides them all with a unifying theme: quantified decision-making data, without which no corporation that is dependent on revenue-generating projects can ever function efficiently. Further, it examines the organizational and structural issues involved in such a total systems approach to project management.

■ ABOUT THIS BOOK

This book is not intended as a text guide to traditional project management. Yet, to explain the techniques of TPC fully, it is sometimes necessary to delve into fundamental aspects of work breakdown structures, critical path method, activity-based costing, resource scheduling, earned value, and other basic techniques. A baseline of understanding in traditional project management is essential to the appreciation of *Total Project Control*.

Let nothing in this book seem to disparage the work of those project management theorists who developed the traditional methods. They are wonderful and creative tools, and the business world would be much better off today if it had only embraced them all to a far greater extent than it has. Indeed, any reader who is not familiar with these techniques would be well advised to obtain a text on basic project management.

Nevertheless, it is the contention of this book that traditional project management methods omit key data items, which are crucial not only for managing projects efficiently, but also for making the utilization of all project management methods more universal. The goal of management is to conduct business profitably. Therefore the more directly project management is tied to profit forecasting and generation, the greater the enthusiasm for its implementation, across not just each project, but the entire organization. TPC provides this direct link.

Introduction

Every project, no matter what the industry or work type, is a compromise among three variables: scope, time, and cost. It may be pictured as a triangle, as shown in Figure I.1.

Scope is the total amount of work to be conducted, the sum of the activities that will lead, at the end of the project, to the "deliverable" or "product." Cost is sometimes referred to as "budget," the total resource usage required to accomplish the work scope. Time is the total elapsed time, from concept to completion, that it takes to perform the work scope. I recommend getting used to this triangle; it will be a recurring motif in Total Project Control (TPC), a paradigm for thinking about all project-related matters.

Traditional project management deals with the two vertical sides. Indeed, project management software packages often boast of their ability to handle cost/schedule integration, that

Figure I.1 The Project Triangle

is, to show the effect of a change in schedule on cost and vice versa. But what about the foundation on which the whole project rests? The work scope? The bottom line? Surely we need to be able to make decisions across all three variables? And to be able to see the impact of any change across all three?

■ THE DEVELOPMENT OF TRADITIONAL PROJECT MANAGEMENT

Most of the literature on project management nominates either 1957 or 1958 as the date of its birth. The reason these two dates are mentioned is that these are the years in which project management's greatest and most beneficial techniques were documented: The Critical Path Method (CPM) in the construction industry in 1957 and Program Evaluation and Review Technique (PERT) by the consulting company Booz-Allen & Hamilton on the U.S. Navy's Polaris missile program the following year.

Thus, right from conception, project management was perceived as a scheduling tool. Increasingly, it became identified *as* scheduling. As the years passed, other project management techniques were superimposed on the original CPM. In 1964, IBM enhanced CPM with the precedence diagram methodology (PDM), which allowed greater and easier scheduling flexibility; activity-based resource assignments (ABRA, without the cadabra) led to resource scheduling, which led to activity-based costing (ABC, *with* the cadabra), which led to cost scheduling, which led to earned value tracking and analysis. That, basically, represents the current state of the art. Prior to TPC, there hadn't been a major methodological enhancement in almost 20 years.

Almost since the start of commercially used computers, corporations have been loading the hundreds of commercially available project management software packages onto mainframe, mini, or network systems; putting project managers in charge of projects; creating program offices with schedulers and accountants reporting to a program manager; and, with varying degrees of discipline, holding the project manager accountable for bringing the project in on time and on budget. (The project manager defending late delivery on the grounds of insufficient resources, enhanced quality, or additional scope has had his work cut out, often literally!)

To this end, project management techniques have worked with differing degrees of success, in different industries, different companies, and on different projects. However, it should be noted here that many, many times, apparent success on schedule and cost was only achieved through major sacrifices in work scope, in both specific features and in quality. These sacrifices were often invisible due to the lack of an integrated scope plan, and they have often come back to haunt American industry. But what is undeniable is that industry has been much more successful when these techniques have been used than when they have been ignored. The more thoroughly these techniques have been applied, the better the chances of success.

Yet four decades after CPM was codified, these techniques are still largely ignored by corporate America. Often, they are regarded as the bailiwick of a plastic-pocket-protector-type lead engineer who manages the project in his copious spare time. Senior management, as often as not, takes a "hear no evil" approach: "I don't care how you do it, just get it done on time. I have more important things to worry about than these project things." If schedules start slipping, or falling apart, the call goes out: "Leadership! That's what we need from our project managers!" Napoleon was a great leader whose soldiers would follow him anywhere. They froze to death on the Russian steppes.

Senior management is correct; leadership is needed—but throughout the system, not just at the project management level. Senior management must take the steps necessary to embed project management within the organization. And, alas, more often than not, they haven't. And even if they wanted to, traditional project management doesn't show them how.

Of course, project management should have been a key ingredient in those corporate total quality management (TQM) programs of the eighties and early nineties. Any company that says it is committed to TQM, yet has no procedures to ensure the vigorous application of CPM schedule optimization to all its large and medium-sized projects is fooling itself, and, in the process, wasting millions of dollars (see Chapters 6 and 7). Any department that does not know its cost of leveling with unresolved bottlenecks (CLUB) for each project, and across all projects per fiscal year, is almost certainly not staffed at its optimum level. Any CEO who does not demand a regular earned value report on the CPI and SPI (not to mention TPC's DIPP) of all major projects should seek a job more in keeping with his preferred level of involvement.

■ REACTION TO COMPETITION FROM OVERSEAS

Meanwhile, through the application of project management methods developed in this country, overseas competitors consistently reach market faster and cheaper than their U.S. equivalents. It should be no mystery why this happens: Product development speed is dependent on project scheduling, and the primary tool for project scheduling is CPM, still an esoteric technique in much of American industry but standard operating procedure in Japan, for instance.

A few years ago, it took Detroit 5 years to produce a new automobile—to go, as Ford Motor Company phrased it, from concept to customer. Despite high profile programs to shorten that all-important time-to-market, the delay has barely been reduced.[1] Japanese automakers require little more than half that time, between 30 and 36 months. What does this mean, in the very real terms of the marketplace? The typical Japanese car:

➤ Incorporates technology that is 2 years newer.

➤ Is assembled using technology that is 2 years newer.

➤ Is based in market research that is 2 years newer.

To be sure, the programs that Detroit introduced to try to cut their time to market included certain project management methods. But these were applied without full comprehension of the effort necessary to use the tools. Software programs were loaded onto mainframes, Gantt chart schedules were drawn, and reports printed. As milestones were missed, and schedules became further and further removed from reality, project management methods were, for the most part, abandoned.

"No computer's going to tell me how to schedule work," one plant manager, responsible for thousands of workers, responded to the attempt at automated scheduling. "I've been making cars for over 30 years, and the schedules we draw up in my plant are the best that anyone can do."

Maybe they are. Maybe each scheduler (of the dozens of schedulers) placing each activity (of the thousands of activities) on each project (of the hundreds of projects) was divinely inspired. In that case, the plant schedule can be expected to be as good (but no better) than an optimized CPM schedule leveled for resource availability through a competent software algorithm. Even then, certain very useful TPC data items, such as the exact amount of delay for each project due to resource shortages (the CLUB), will be invisible.

Even more important, all project managers should keep one thing in mind: On projects, what even God proposes, man all too often disposes. God's schedule may be divine at the outset, but some Adam or Eve is sure to come along and upset the applecart: A just-in-time delivery is going to be delayed; a labor union is going to start a work action; or those Lucifers in Washington are going to mandate back-seat airbags on all new models. Now what? The manager with the CPM schedule loaded into the computer inputs the delays, performs a little what-if analysis, and determines the best alternative; the manager with the divinely revealed schedule has to start sacrificing goats in hope of more inspiration. And if none is forthcoming, I'll guarantee he or she doesn't know of how to optimize a critical path schedule so that resources can be targeted to the right activities, future delays can be forecast and workarounds planned, and days and weeks can be shaved from the now all-too-corpulent schedule.

When consumer costs rise and workers lose their jobs, corporate leaders too often look not to improved management, but to legislative protections, designed to raise prices even higher for the American consumer while protecting the very inefficiencies that helped generate our competitive handicap in the first place.

■ PROJECT MANAGEMENT AND THE SOFTWARE INDUSTRY

An oft-heard excuse for not using project management techniques is the work type or industry. This theory holds that project management may be very useful on someone else's type of project, but not on mine.

At a party in Cambridge, Massachusetts, a few years ago, a conversation took place with the head of information systems for an international management consulting firm. After politics and the Red Sox had been exhausted, the topic drifted to consulting in general, and then to project management. "Look," said the CIO, "that stuff may work when you're dealing with manufacturing, or construction or something, where there's a tangible product at the end and everybody knows what to do. But it just wouldn't work in software. The best programmers work by building the system as they go, and you never know until the end how long things are going to take. Stuff like critical path and all that other lingo are out the window before you even start."

I replied: "You mean, because you don't know for sure how long the project is going to take, there's no point in trying to figure out how long the project's going to take?"

The response was a further elaboration of the complexities of the software development world, the variations in programmer ability, the vagueness of technical specifications, and all the other crutches that corporate America has been leaning on for years to explain its resistance to planning and controlling projects in a businesslike and systematic fashion.

Two things are notable about this CIO's response:

1. That project management is inappropriate in "soft" projects, such as software development.

2. That project management is appropriate and common in "hard" projects (presumably, those with clearer definition, and a greater wealth of historical data for estimating task durations), such as construction or manufacturing.

In fact, while certainly more common than in the software field, manufacturers and construction companies are often equally unaware of the benefits of traditional project management tools. Even when they utilize them, they often do so halfheartedly and haphazardly, with limited knowledge and less benefit. Almost invariably, certain management levels and departments that should be key players in the process are omitted.

What about other soft industries? Entertainment? Publishing? Pharmaceuticals? Advertising? Commercial banking? Is project management making a meaningful impact?

The truth is, as tardy as software development has been in adopting project management methods, that field is still often ahead of these other multibillion dollar industries. Indeed, when one takes corporate America as a whole, there can be no doubt that billions of dollars are wasted every year on projects of all sizes, in all industries; dollars that our overseas competitors save through their more consistent and disciplined use of project management methodologies.

➤ The Software Industry and Project Management Software

One of the biggest problems in the implementation of project management is the misconception that once you buy a software package and put it online, you'll derive the full range of benefits from project management methodology. All these manufacturers, engineers, and construction people are relying on project management tools that a bunch of software people (who, as I pointed out earlier, are often among the least sophisticated project management users) design, develop, and market.

There are hundreds of different project management software packages on the market. Prices run from six figures down, and the functionality of each tends to reflect that range. Many of them are severely limited by the lack of project management knowledge of the software designers who created them. Yet even the most sophisticated functionality does nothing to actually manage the project; it merely computes data on the basis of information fed into it. The decisions still have to be made by human beings. It would help if those individuals understood what the data meant, and why it was important. But all too often, user and management ignorance result in an initial investment in project management methods and software being abandoned because the immediate result is not on-time and under-budget delivery.

A few years ago, I was delivering an executive-level seminar at the Virginia headquarters of a major government contractor. The topic was the implementation of a high-end project management software package.

"The trouble with project management systems," someone said, "is, garbage in, garbage out."

The executive responsible for the implementation, a highly respected individual who had been a major player in the *Apollo* program, immediately replied:

"Oh, no, Fred, it's much worse than that! The trouble with these systems is: 'Garbage in, Gospel out!'"

Not only does the project manager making decisions on the basis of the data need to understand what's coming out, but those people who are feeding in the data need to know what to put in. And that's asking for an awful lot in a company whose CEO thinks that project management knowledge and skills are beneath his notice, something that should be taken care of two or three levels down.

➤ Integrating Projects and Profits

As long as project management is perceived as a "project" tool, and as long the project is confined to schedule and cost (which is, after all, what the project management software deals with), then senior management will *not* involve itself. "We're too busy worrying about profitability to concern ourselves with inconsequentials such as how to actually *meet* those deadlines we set." Thus project management becomes confined to the "trenches." The project manager knows that informing senior management about slippage will lead not to additional resources but to harassment and/or replacement. Therefore rather than planning for an optimized schedule that might enhance profitability (the very goal that senior management is after), the project manager works to develop

1. A padded schedule, with delayed deadline.
2. An inflated budget.
3. A nebulous work scope that can be trimmed invisibly to meet the deadline. (Who cares if the result is a

product that breaks if you look at it? Or one whose post-launch support costs rapidly devour the profit margin?)

4. A "black hole" project from which no information escapes.

This is the trap of the "limited" approach (however well-intentioned) of traditional project management. Rather than a total systems approach, it builds in a disconnect between the project's goals and those of the organization. Senior management wants profitable projects, but is only able to quantify its wishes in terms of the two sides of the triangle that traditional project management addresses: schedule and cost. To operate smoothly, the entire organization must be:

1. Driven by the single goal of profitability.

2. Quantified and measured on contributions to that goal.

3. Willing to make *and accept* decisions based on quantified analysis of profitability.

These are the enhancements that the TPC method offers to traditional project management, in the form of such new profitability-based data items as the DIPP, DRAG cost, NVA, and CLUB. The impact of their widespread implementation is likely to be far-reaching. Not only will good management decisions at both the project and executive levels be supported by quantitative data, but bad decisions will also become harder to justify. The universal corporate downsizing of the past decade was frequently undertaken without considering its ultimate impact on profitability. How can I say this? Because I worked with many clients who underwent downsizing, and I know that there were absolutely zero metrics in place to determine what the impact on project performance would be of reducing resources. Only TPC, as epitomized by the CLUB, could provide such data for a project-driven organization. Undoubtedly, many horrendous decisions were made that seriously damaged corporations, careers, and lives.

When it is demonstrably clear that: (1) Shortening a task from 4 weeks to 2 will allow product delivery to occur 2 weeks earlier; (2) Such shortening relies on five workers working 16-hour days, including weekends; and (3) Such an early delivery would add $2 million to the product's return on investment (a not-unreasonable projection), then the decisions of all concerned parties (executives, project managers, labor unions and individual workers) regarding appropriate incentives are likely to be shaped in a manner that makes such an efficiency possible. This and other aspects of TPC are likely to greatly alter the way that project business gets done over the next few years.

Notes

1. On National Public Radio's *Talk of the Nation* program, I once asked Ford Motor Company's CEO, Alexander Trotman, why this was so, and why efforts to impose rigorous project management discipline had been abandoned, as my contacts at Ford assured me was the case. Trotman informed me that while my information may have been true 5 years ago, it was no longer valid. He pointed to the new Mustang, which he claimed took 35.5 months to develop, as a program that typifies the new Ford approach, one which utilized strict CPM and other project management methods, and one that is now being incorporated into all Ford programs.

   When I played a tape of Trotman's comments to several of my Ford contacts (who have been thoroughly frustrated in the failure of their attempts to institute project management methods), they laughed, and pointed out:

   ➤ The Mustang was not a whole new car, just a new body. Thirty-five-and-one-half months for a new body is nothing to brag about.

➤ The Mustang was an off-line, or skunk works, program, nearly cancelled several times.

➤ Maybe the Mustang took under 3 years, and maybe it didn't. Trotman obviously has a vested interest in minimizing the elapsed time. But he is also the timekeeper, and if he says 35.5 months, who's going to argue?

➤ If the Mustang program utilized project management methods, it did so in great secrecy. None of my contacts was aware of its using rigorous CPM.

➤ If the Mustang program used PM methods, there is no indication of any carryover to other Ford programs. Working with Ford suppliers over the past 4 years, I have seen the Ford-generated time lines for new vehicle development: 54 to 62 months, in every case.

Is Trotman deliberately lying when he says that project management has come to Ford? Perhaps not. This may be just another case of an executive who is so out of touch with the middle levels of his corporation that he has no awareness of their methods or culture. And probably not much idea about what "a rigorous project management discipline" would entail, either.

2. The DIPP was first formulated in the author's September 1992 issue of *Project Management Journal*, in an article titled "When the DIPP Dips: A P&L Index for Project Decisions." It has since become the basis for the entire TPC approach.

The Nature of a Project

The seed of the business world's problem with projects lies in the very essence of project work itself. It's different from the day-to-day work of traditional businesses. Different from the deal-with-each-issue-as-it-arises approach that the current corporate structure is designed to handle.

The tsunami of projects that has swamped the business world in the past 30 years has forced the creation of new strategies for dealing with this type of work effort. Project teams, matrix structures, temps and freelancers, worker empowerment, activity-based costing, project templates, paradigms, post mortems, and management information systems are just some of the strategies being implemented to deal with the exigencies of project work. Yet each of these innovations tends to be considered, and implemented or rejected, piecemeal. There is little understanding as to the precise characteristics of a project that each of these strategies is designed to address, nor recognition of the relationship that each has with all of the others. The strategy will be improperly used and will likely either fail or, worse, backfire without such an understanding.

I attended a meeting many years ago when working for the Information Resources division of Citicorp. The systems we were installing were complex, and the process was a nightmare of obfuscation and political wrangling among the many departments involved (customer service, programming, network communications, quality assurance, documentation, and training). A new director of installations was hired, and one of his first actions was to announce the creation of three installation teams. Each of these would be supervised by an installation manager, yet each team member would continue to report to his or her old manager. Naive to project management concepts, I was very confused. After leaving the meeting, I turned to my colleague Jim and whispered, "I don't understand. Who's our boss now, Phil or Vera?"

"Ah, Steve," said Jim sagely, "this is what's called matrix management." This was my first exposure to the term.

"What's that? How does it work?," I asked.

Jim scratched his head.

"I don't know." Then he brightened, "But I know that's what it's called!"

Looking back on this episode, it is now clear that the new installation director's solution, implementing project teams, was absolutely correct. However, the way it was done, with no training and little explanation of what the problems were and how the new structure was designed to resolve them, proved disastrous. Rather than ending the turf wars, the new structure introduced yet another tier of combatants, and the result was more system bugs, greater inefficiency, slower problem resolution, and the resignations of some of the best employees.

The millions who have been subjected to the matrix management solution over the past few decades will have no trouble recognizing the above scenario. The result has been that matrix management is now identified with chaos and political mayhem. It needn't be that way. But it will be, as long as both managers and employees fail to understand the intrinsic nature of project work, the stresses it puts on the traditional hierarchy, and the way that the political and communications issues, which invariably arise, must be addressed.

The truth is that a project is a total system, and must be dealt with in its totality to achieve the best results. And that totality requires a full comprehension of the intrinsic nature of a project.

■ THE DEFINITION OF A PROJECT

The very fact that work is unified under the penumbra of a single project has implications for the intended results and for the difficulties that are likely to be encountered. These affect the way in which the effort should be managed. But why is work unified as a project?

For many years, I began my management seminars with the following commonly accepted definition of the word. A project, I would write on the whiteboard,

1. Is a group of related work tasks,
2. To be performed within a definable time period, and
3. To meet a specific set of objectives.

I would then ask the attendees which of the three defining parameters was the one that caused companies to implement project management. They would invariably come up with the correct answer, no. 2. I would then explain how this was absolutely correct, that project management provided tools such as CPM (critical path method) scheduling and resource leveling that were specifically designed to help managers deal with issues of deadlines and schedules. But why *was* it that project management was implemented primarily to deal with schedules? Is that definable time period really the most important aspect of a project? Clearly not!

The purpose of a project, its very raison d'être, is the specific objectives that it is undertaken to achieve: the outcome, or product, or service, or deliverable, that justified investment of resources to that end. Clearly, project management techniques and software are helpful in dealing with the specific objectives of a project: The work breakdown structure (WBS) is especially helpful in defining and controlling the work scope. But then why isn't project management implemented for this reason? Because there is nothing quantifiable about the WBS. On the other hand, project management's scheduling techniques are extremely quantified. Not only is the old saying, that what can be measured can be improved, true; but also, *what is quantified is what will be implemented.*

However, this created a paradox. Project management is the technique for managing projects; yet its greatest benefit, its most valuable metrics, concern scheduling, only a secondary concern of the project manager. But about the *thing* itself, the very reason to do the project, the item the customer wants to buy, project management remained remarkably silent. If it's the most valuable aspect of the project, surely our techniques and the project management software should address this. And if it's valuable, then surely we can value it!

I soon realized that I had hit upon a crucial omission in my tri-cornered definition of the project: What was it about the activities that caused them to be a group, anyway? It was more than the simple fact that a single project manager had decided to "do" them. It was even more than a chronological relationship, based on scheduling dependencies to determine which activities must precede others. *It was the fact that their value was related; that each added to the value of the others, so that the total value of the project "deliverable" could not be achieved until all of the work scope was finished!*

As a result, the total project control (TPC) definition of a project was formulated:

1. As a group of related work tasks,
2. To be performed within a definable time period,
3. Meeting a specific set of objectives, and
4. Whose value is interdependent.

In other words, a project is a *total system*, and needs to be managed as such. To do otherwise is to risk setting up a shell game, in which product features, schedules, resources, budgets, cash flow, and work performance are modified willynilly, on the basis of short-term benefit, without ever referencing the impact on the most important aspect of the big picture: project value, and its impact on profit.

All this might actually seem commonplace were it not for the fact that projects are managed like shell games. The throw-it-over-the-fence syndrome is a long-recognized problem in corporate multifunctional projects, where individual functional departments are often excluded from any role in the planning process until the partially completed product comes crashing over the cubicle wall. The waste of time and resources to do the remediation required to make the product fit the new department's specifications is enormous; the reduction in the value of the ultimate deliverable due to inadequate multifunctional input during the design phase is often even greater, yet less visible.

Project managers, the matrix organization, and multifunctional project planning teams, are corporate adaptations intended to overcome a project's incompatibility with the traditional hierarchical corporate structure and they have certainly helped. But key departments in a project's work are often still ignored, or uninformed until the last minute. This is usually due to an oversight. But much more troubling, and costly, are two aspects of the shell game that have become endemic to the very way we do projects. They are indicative of our failure to recognize the true nature of a project: *that the value of the project's objectives, and the work tasks required to achieve them, are inextricably interdependent!*

The following is an all-too-common example of this problem:

> *A software product is being developed for the commercial market. (Actually, it could be any kind of product, but this particular problem is especially common in the software industry.) Problems have plagued the development process, and the project manager is about to be called on the carpet for late delivery and budget overruns, even though they are not her fault. Faced with this predicament, she acts quickly. By making the user interface less intuitive, reducing the number of help screens, and cutting back on the accompanying documentation, she can now ship the product without the kind of delay or cost overruns that senior management deems unacceptable. Crowned a heroine for her quickstepping, she moves on to manage another project. A few months later she leaves the company, shortly before it goes Chapter XI due to the failure of its sales force to sell a software product that had rapidly acquired a reputation for user hostility, poor documentation, and a lack of adequate telephone support.*

The first aspect of the shell game in the above case is quite easy to see: The project manager was responsible and the project budgeted for a user-friendly interface and both online and printed documentation. But when push came to shove, the time and money for those features got applied to fix the software development problems. The job of dealing with the inadequate interface and documentation was shoved over to two areas that the company did not identify as part of the project: telephone support and, most important, sales and marketing.

Both these areas are almost invariably omitted from project calculations and project accounting. This provides a glorious opportunity to participate in the shell game, as well as the chance to obfuscate the shortcomings of any of the involved departments or individuals through pointless finger–pointing (pointless because there is seldom a clear paper trail to show where the fault lies). Instead, everyone can happily blame someone else while both the product and the company lose money. But that's not a project manager's issue, is it? After all, her job was just to bring the project in on time and within budget, right?

And this brings us to the second aspect of the shell game, one which occurs in almost every corporate project performed in the United States: There is a *total* disconnect between the performance of the work and the process by which a project's value is generated (whether that process is called marketing, sales, or delivery). The project manager's mandate is to complete the project work to specification, in a timely and economical fashion: it is *not* to increase the profit generated by the deliverable. That is marketing's concern. The metrics to which the project manager works are project duration and budgetary costs. Indeed, there *is* no metric, in traditional project management, for product profitability.

This is what the total in TPC means: The scope of work, as represented by the deliverable, is the most important part of the project. It is the motivating force behind the project, the "thing" that is desired by the all-too-often-forgotten customer. As such, it must be tied, in its totality, to traditional project management responsibilities: schedule and cost. In the TPC methodology, this is accomplished through a new data metric, the DIPP. Precisely how DIPP works is described in Chapter 2. Suffice it to say, for the moment, that the DIPP measures project profitability.

In the TPC approach, the true nature of the project, as a collection of interdependent work items that provide value, has to be comprehended fully so that the project can be managed accordingly.

■ THE MULTI-PROJECT PORTFOLIO

Just as the purpose of the individual project is to generate value, the purpose of all the projects within the organization's multi-project portfolio is to generate value, to enlarge the company's bottom line. The total value minus total costs of all of the corporate projects often represents the profit margin of project- or product-driven organizations. To this end, project information must be visible at a summary level in order to ensure that decisions made on one project are not so detrimental to another project (or projects) as to reduce the profitability of the overall portfolio.

Frequently, two projects within the same organization may be in need of the same resource at the same time. This is precisely the problem that the multi-project resource leveling function of traditional project management software was developed to handle. Unfortunately, the traditional methodology has no means of dealing with project value. Therefore, even when the software tells the users that there is a problem, and even when it alleviates that problem to the best of the software algorithm's resource leveling capability, the software may actually be doing more harm than good, blindly resolving the bottleneck in a way that reduces the organization's profit. And because there are no metrics, the revenues disappear without a trace.

There are thousands of corporate organizations that depend on projects for more than 90 percent of their revenues. Yet, other than intuitively, they have no way of tying the projects they do to their profits. That means that they cannot measure precisely each project's profits, and they have only guesswork on which to base such decisions as resource targeting, hiring, staff downsizing, project scope reductions, and critical path crashing. There is no data to help senior management maximize profits on a multi-project basis. This can lead to such unfortunate situations as the following.

Imagine that a product development company has a portfolio of four products: A, B, C, and D. Each has a planned delivery date as shown in Figure 1.1, and each is expected to generate revenues, as shown in the column marked EMV (expected monetary value). The column labeled Cost ETC shows the cost estimate-to-complete, or the amount of

Project Name	EMV (000)	Current Completion Date	Cost ETC
A	$1,000	Aug. 1	$200
B	$2,000	Oct. 1	$1,000
C	$5,000	Nov. 25	$2,000
D	$10,000	Jan. 30	$3,000

TOTAL PORTFOLIO: Expected Monetary Value:		$18,000
Cost ETC:		$6,200
Expected Net:		$11,800

Figure 1.1 Portfolio Report Displaying Traditional Project Management Data

money budgeted to bring each project from its current status to completion.

These data are the *absolute minimum* that the senior manager in charge of these four projects should have available to him or her. If the organization is doing a good job of *even traditional* project management, the senior manager should in fact have this information. (Whether or not revenue information is up to date, or whether it is ever juxtaposed against the project cost data, is another issue.) However, even these data are inadequate. To see why, let us now imagine that another product is proposed.

Imagine this new product is expected to be extremely profitable, generating 67 percent of the revenues of the other four products *combined*. When a detailed plan of the project (Project E) to create the new product is assembled, its budget shows the revenues generated will be 400 percent of the anticipated costs (see Figure 1.2).

What vice president could resist such an opportunity? Who could possibly eschew such a profitable new product? And yet, there is not enough information here to make an informed decision, one way or another, about undertaking Project E! Why? Because nowhere are there data that show how this new project, and its need for resources, will affect the schedules, the

Project Name	EMV (000)	Target Completion Date	Cost ETC
E	$12,000	Feb. 10	$3,000

Figure 1.2 Traditional Project Management Data for Additional Project

delivery dates, and thus *the expected revenues* of the other four projects. The only way the senior manager could undertake Project E with confidence would be by staffing it with an entirely new set of resources. (This may indeed be the best decision but how often does this happen? Almost invariably, the same pool of resources are required simply to shoulder the burden of the additional work and perform whatever miracles are necessary.)

Without access to TPC data, the vice president will almost certainly elect to take on what appears to be a profitable new project. When the organization's profits decrease, it will be blamed on bad luck, or poor project management, rather than the lack of adequate data.

What data should the vice president have available? In Chapter 3, we shall see that the TPC Business Case recognizes and quantifies the way that the EMV of a project changes according to completion date. Total Project Control mandates that these project data must be available and analyzed not only at the project level but also across the entire portfolio. The senior manager should have the TPC Portfolio Summary Report available as shown in Figure 1.3.

Similar data for the new project, Project E, is shown in Figure 1.4.

The TPC reports do not treat EMV as a constant, but instead show how each project's value will be impacted by delay or acceleration. Additionally, they show the Simple DIPP, the index of profitability per cost dollar. Project E has a DIPP of 4.0, representing 400 percent return on each dollar, but *only* if it is completed on February 10. Any delay will result in an EMV reduction of $2.4 million per week.

Project Name	EMV (000)	As Of	Current Completion Date	Loss Per Week Late (%)	Gain Per Week Early (%)	Cost ETC	Simple DIPP
A	$1,000	Aug. 1	Aug.1	5	5	$200	5.0
B	$2,000	Oct. 1	Oct. 1	10	5	$1,000	2.0
C	$5,000	Nov. 25	Nov. 25	20	2	$2,000	2.5
D	$10,000	Jan. 30	Jan. 30	10	5	$3,000	3.3

TOTAL PORTFOLIO:

Expected Monetary Value:	$18,000
Cost ETC:	$6,200
Expected Net:	$11,800
Simple DIPP:	2.9

Figure 1.3 The TPC Portfolio Summary Report for the First Four Projects

Expected monetary value is almost invariably dependent on completion date (whether impacted by market window, contractual penalty clause, net present value, or simply delay in the time at which the benefits of the project work start to accrue). The ripples caused by dropping Project E into the resource pool shared by the other four projects must be identified and analyzed, not just in terms of their effect on the completion dates, but, especially, in terms of the effects of such delays on the EMVs of each project and all the projects.

A good project management software package, with resource leveling capability, is indispensable. The vice president needs to be able to perform resource leveling on a multi-project basis, generating schedules for all of the projects that take into account the constraints of limited resources. Such a software package will produce schedules

Project Name	EMV (000)	As Of	Current Completion Date	Loss Per Week Late (%)	Gain Per Week Early (%)	Cost ETC	Simple DIPP
E	$12,000	Feb. 10	—	20	5	$3,000	4.0

Figure 1.4 The TPC Summary Report for Project E

Project Name	EMV (000)	As Of	Current Completion Date	Loss Per Week Late (%)	Gain Per Week Early (%)	New Expected Value	Cost ETC	Simple DIPP
E	$12,000	Feb. 10	Feb. 10	20	5	$12,000	$3,000	4.0
A	$1,000	Aug. 1	Aug. 29	5	5	$800	$200	4.0
B	$2,000	Oct. 1	Oct. 29	10	5	$1,200	$1,000	1.2
C	$5,000	Nov. 25	Dec. 16	20	2	$2,000	$2,000	1.0
D	$10,000	Jan. 30	Mar. 13	10	5	$4,000	$3,000	1.3

TOTAL PORTFOLIO:		
Expected Monetary Value:	$20,000	(+$2,000)
Cost ETC:	$9,200	(+$3,000)
Expected Net:	$10,800	(−$1,000)
Simple DIPP:	2.2	(−0.7)

Figure 1.5 The TPC Portfolio Summary Report for All Five Projects, with Project E's Completion Date Fixed

that reflect the impact of Project E, showing that each of the other projects' completion dates will have to be delayed. But what even a *good* software package, offering traditional functionality, will produce is a schedule that fails to take into account, or even reflect, the impact of such delays on the organization's revenues and/or profit. And is not that precisely the information that the portfolio manager desperately seeks? Figure 1.5 shows what might happen when resources for the five projects are scheduled through the resource leveler, but with Project E's completion date fixed at February 10.

The inclusion of Project E with a rigid completion date has so delayed the other four projects that both the DIPP and the net profit of the organization across the portfolio have shrunk.

Resource leveling algorithms are programmed to level (i.e., resolve bottlenecks) in the same way that projects are typically managed in traditional project management—by seeking to reduce costs or shorten project durations. But neither of these should be the main goal of project management. The main goal should be to *increase profits*. But traditional software has no functionality that incorporates such data. This becomes even more costly when making resourcing decisions on a multi-project basis.

If the full range of TPC data is available, the senior manager can at least be aware of the negative impact of Project E, and can manually change the parameters to try to generate a more profitable portfolio profile. Perhaps E should be discarded because its delay penalty will be so great. Perhaps C should be terminated, and its resources cannibalized for A, B, and D. Perhaps approving the hiring of a few additional key resources can change the entire context, increasing ETC but also boosting EMVs sufficiently to increase net profit. Or perhaps a change of project priorities in leveling the resources can help. All of these should be tried, with the TPC Portfolio Summary Report reflecting the results so that the best solution can be adopted. Figure 1.6 shows one possible solution.

The new TPC Portfolio Summary Report shows that this particular targeting of resources will generate a schedule in which the net profit will increase by $8.2 million. Even though such modifications may have to be performed manually, the benefits to the bottom line are immense. This technique should allow resource leveling algorithms to level

Project Name	EMV (000)	As Of	Current Completion Date	Loss Per Week Late (%)	Gain Per Week Early (%)	New Expected Value	Cost ETC	Simple DIPP
A	$12,000	Feb. 10	*Jan. 13*	20	5	*$14,400*	$3,500	4.1
B	$1,000	Aug. 1	*Sept. 12*	5	5	*$700*	$200	3.5
C	$2,000	Oct. 1	*Oct. 15*	10	5	*$1,600*	$1,000	1.6
D	$5,000	Nov. 25	*Nov. 25*	20	2	*$5,000*	$2,000	2.5
E	$10,000	Jan. 30	*Feb. 27*	10	5	*$8,000*	$4,000	2.0

TOTAL PORTFOLIO:

Expected Monetary Value:	$29,700	(+$9,700)
Cost ETC:	$10,700	(+$1,500)
Expected Net:	$19,000	(+8,200)
Simple DIPP:	2.8	(+0.6)

Figure 1.6 The TPC Portfolio Summary Report for All Five Projects, Adjusted to Optimize Profit

resources for "right-sized" staffing levels and maximum profit.

CONCLUSION

➤ The purpose of a project is not to be short or inexpensive, but to make a profit. It should be managed in such a way as to maximize that profit.

➤ All the work, and all aspects of the project that impact its profit should be analyzed together, in an integrated way that shows the effect of the various alternatives on the project profit.

➤ Each project that is managed in a context with other projects should be analyzed in an integrated way that shows the effects of each (ostensibly internal) project decision on all the other projects, and, specifically, on the multi-project profit.

➤ Insofar as projects are managed without regard to profit, bad (profit-reducing) decisions will be made, both randomly and systematically, throughout the organization.

Chapter

An Overview of TPC Planning

How do projects get planned? The sad truth is that they barely get planned at all. Like Topsy, a terrifying number of projects, in all industries, just grow. This is not the case in all cultures. In Japan, for instance, it would be unthinkable to start work on a major corporate project without spending many hours on team meetings to discuss schedules, scope, resources, and other issues. But U.S. culture is very different. Americans worship the television hero who, often through his own lack of foresight, finds himself surrounded and imperiled. A blazing .44 Magnum is a lot more exciting than avoidance of danger by proper anticipation. The project manager who acquires the reputation as a wizard at firefighting tends to get more credit than the one who quietly and efficiently removes all combustibles before the conflagration.

Projects of any significant size and/or complexity, which have not been planned, rapidly descend into chaos. In a multi-project organization, they often bring other projects crashing down also.

For the unplanned project, there are at least six pitfalls that can be enumerated:

1. The Throw-It-over-the-Fence Syndrome. In this syndrome the project is tossed from one functional area of responsibility to the next with no previous communication, commitment or buy-in on features, schedule, resources, or budget.

2. The 50-to-1 Life Cycle Correlation. In this instance, work is performed out of order, or is performed inadequately the first time around, so that it has to be repeated. The result is that completed work often has to be undone and redone. The penalty for doing project work out of order is said to be $50 for every one dollar it would have cost if done correctly. But this is only an average—the premium, especially in product development, can be hundreds of thousands of dollars. Imagine the cost of a minivan recall to replace the little latch on the rear seat.

3. Resource Bottlenecks. I am constantly astounded by the number of organizations where projects generate more than 90 percent of the revenues; almost all resources are shared and multi-projected, with individuals working on four or five separate projects in a week; and no effort is made to assemble and maintain a resource database (resource library) that reflects usage across time and that allows bottleneck identification and resolution. In such organizations, projects are being thrown into chaos *daily* because of the large number of bottlenecks. The excuse seems to be:

> *What's the point in trying to plan my project schedule? When it gets to the drafting department (or contracts, or testing, or manufacturing or programming, or documentation, or packaging), it's going to be delayed anyhow until someone is put on it.*

The resource manager's only reasonable response to such a situation is to turn his or her department into a black hole, from which not even information can escape. ("No, I can't tell you when your work will be ready, or who will be working on it. We'll call you when it's done.")

It never seems to dawn on anyone that the lack of project planning and scheduling is *precisely* what ensures that there will be delays in each department. First, this makes it impossible for resource managers to plan to have resources available as soon as a project arrives. Second, in such multi-project situations departments will always be under-resourced because there is no way of justifying additional resources without identifying, measuring, and monetizing the precise impact of bottlenecks on each and every project through the cost of leveling with unresolved bottlenecks (CLUB).

This is one of the great benefits of TPC methodology, and will be discussed in detail in Chapter 9. However, let me add the good news: You'll get to identify those bottlenecks even if you make no attempt to foresee them—when the project hits them face-first, and everything is thrown into chaos. Identify them now or identify them when you're making excuses during the project post-mortem—take your pick.

4. Resource Underutilization. Efficient use of resources in a project situation has less to do with how organized or hardworking those resources are, and much more to do with the project context. Resources must be utilized on the right project work and, in a multi-project environment, on the right project. Targeting the resources to the right work requires the employment of the critical path method (CPM) in scheduling, on each project and all projects in the organization's portfolio. If CPM is not used, resources will be expended on work of a less critical nature (from a scheduling viewpoint); in that sense, they will be underutilized.

5. Abandoned Projects. The number one reason that corporate projects are abandoned before completion is that planning was either totally inadequate or nonexistent. Frequently, project management consultants are called upon to act as "project doctors": They are hired to make a sick project well. This author has *never* been summoned to the bedside of a project for which even the most rudimentary WBS had been developed. As a result, no one on these projects realizes what work remains to be done, or even what work has already been completed. Good consultants know exactly what to do: They go back to square one and, with the help of the subject matter experts on the project, develop a detailed WBS.

What do senior managers do, if they don't bring in a consultant? "Heck, this project's a turkey! No one can even tell me where we are on it. Spending any more on this thing would just be throwing good money after bad. Time to pull the plug!" And who's to say they're wrong?

But by far the most important pitfall of inadequate planning is the following.

6. Lack of Direction when Responding to Change. We are about to explore this idea in great depth, for herein lies the entire philosophical basis for project management. For the moment, it is enough to say that the project plan is like a roadmap—its purpose is not only to show you the best route to where you want to go, but also, if you get lost, to show you the best way to get back on course. Without it, you are truly lost.

■ THE BENEFITS OF PROJECT PLANNING

[One] area that technologically superior companies emphasize is the quality of their product planning. In most walks of life where planning is possible, people will tell you that good planning is absolutely crucial and necessary. However, almost no one does it. We have wondered why, and can only surmise that they don't know how to, don't have time, or can't see the benefits.

—Dr. P.R. Nayak,
Managing Rapid Technological Development
Arthur D. Little Co., Cambridge, MA 1990

Dr. Nayak's paper went on to demonstrate, quite conclusively and quantitatively, the vast array of benefits that accrue from good project planning. Projects that are well planned become shorter and cheaper, products function better and longer, and project managers' blood pressures go down.

But all this just makes the lack of planning even more puzzling—why *don't* companies plan their projects? Nobody likes to be wrong. And if one's job is on the line, it is particularly important not to be wrong. Being wrong when planning or providing estimates for a project can be very painful. The results can be overwork, underpay, blame, and unemployment. Yet project estimates are extremely dodgy; project requirements and information are constantly changing, making the best laid plans of mice and managers inaccurate. But there's no use complaining about this—it's simply the nature of project work. If you can't handle this, you shouldn't be in the project business.

Unfortunately, this dodginess often makes project workers extremely reluctant to make estimates or predictions about their project. They are often afraid that when things change, they will be blamed for the inaccuracies of their predictions, and their toes will be held to the fire. To avoid that happening, project leaders will often resist committing their expectations to paper. "Sure I've planned it," they say. "I've got it all in my head." But that doesn't allow them to manage a complex project, with requirements and schedules constantly changing, and other team members needing to understand just what *is* in their heads.

Yet one must have sympathy for these project leaders. Because they are in fact correct—they will be blamed, and their toes will be held to the fire if their predictions turn out to be wrong! And so they do what any reasonable person would do when placed in such an unreasonable position: They pad their estimates. Then, of course, Parkinson's Law (Work expands to fill time available!) takes over, and two of the primary reasons for project planning, namely, shorter durations and more efficient resource usage, are torpedoed right up front.

The root of the problem is suggested by Dr. Nayak: neither the project leaders nor the senior managers really understand the purpose of project planning. They are assuming that planning is performed in order to generate an accurate prediction of the future. Unfortunately, on projects of any significant size and/or complexity, an accurate prediction of the future is just about impossible. Things change. While an accurate estimate is certainly preferred over an inaccurate one, from a project point of view, an inaccurate prediction is a lot better than no prediction at all.

This brings us to the heart of the philosophy behind project management, and it is crucial that this be understood. Projects can be large, complex, and expensive efforts. A failure can cause corporate bankruptcy, lost fortunes, and long waits in unemployment lines for thousands of people. Project management methods can greatly reduce the likelihood of such a disaster. But only if the understanding of those asked to employ such methods is not such that it makes them sabotage the effort.

■ THE PURPOSE OF A PROJECT PLAN

What precisely should planning do? What are the features of a good product plan that will generate the desired benefits? If that is known, planning techniques can be improved.
Traditional project management consists of a toolbox of different techniques discovered by project managers over the years. These techniques were developed, and their use spread, precisely because they were helpful. What characteristics of projects do project managers have to wrestle with? There are two that seem particularly significant:

1. Typically, projects consist not of one type of work or discipline, but of many, all interrelated and interdependent, some dodgier and more nebulous than others.

2. All projects are subject to change, and managing those changes is one of the most difficult parts of a project manager's job.

These two realities of project managers' lives lead to two generalizations about the techniques they have developed:

1. They are likely to be universally useful, without regard to the nature of the project work involved.

2. They are likely to be of particular assistance in managing change, the greatest bugbear of the project manager's existence.

Having discovered many years ago that projects change, project managers have developed a methodology replete with techniques for managing those changes. How ironic, therefore, that the awareness of project uncertainty is often used as an excuse to avoid planning. "Heck," says the harried project leader, "this work is so nebulous, and so cutting edge, that who knows *what* we're going to find once we start in! Whatever we plan now is bound to change, so there's no point in planning at all!" This is roughly analogous to a medical school student saying, "Heck, there's no point in studying normal anatomy because all the people I see are going to be sick."

Thus, what is the project manager going to want to do when a change occurs? What would be the main characteristics of a technique that would help a project manager manage the unforeseen events that cause changes? The process that she will go through necessitates having a project plan in the first place. If she does, she will then follow seven steps. These seven steps provide us, quite serendipitously, with the happy acronym: "A-I-M F-I-R-E"!, which seems to be a useful mnemonic.

➤ A-I-M!

When a project change occurs, the project manager, first and foremost, needs to be

1. **Aware** that such an event has occurred. This can only be done by noting a variance between the plan and what has occurred. Some plans are much better at this than others. It

is extremely important that this variance be identified as early as possible, while it can be remedied with the least drastic corrective action. To return to the medical analogy, the project plan works as a diagnostic tool, identifying the abnormality while it is still possible to treat the patient with the least invasive procedures. The earlier that the plan helps identify the variance, and the smaller the variance is when it's identified, the better the plan.

Next, the project manager needs to

2. Isolate the areas of impact. You don't want to go around cutting tissue where there's nothing wrong. The philosophy behind management-by-exception is that it allows the manager's attention to be concentrated only where it's needed. And in those areas, the project manager should then measure the variance.

3. Measure the variance. The variance must be measured in terms of changes in requirements, schedule slippage, or cost overruns, or in TPC, in the expected monetary value (EMV) of the deliverable (perhaps triggered by changed requirements or schedule slippage). All these changes should be analyzed and reported in terms of their impact on TPC's fundamental metric, the DIPP. This not only allows analysis on the basis of profitability, but also hitches the project's wagon to maximizing that metric.

What kind of plan, what kind of qualities in it, will best assist the project manager in meeting her A-I-M? The answer: *granularity,* or *detail,* and *quantification.*

The broader and more general the plan, the longer and more macro the variance can grow before it becomes detectable. For example, a variance in a schedule that is measured in weeks and reported once a month may be as great as four weeks before it becomes evident. A two-week reporting period, on activities measured in days, is likely to turn up schedule slippage much earlier.

Traditionally, quantification is in time units for schedule and in money units for budgetary cost, and variances are reported in these metrics. TPC's DIPP provides a single index that quantifies the impact across all measurable variances, so that decisions can be made on comparative, profit-based data.

➤ F-I-R-E!

Once a variance has been identified, isolated, and measured, the project manager needs to determine if action is needed, and if it is, what is best. Again, the project plan is the crucial tool to assist in this.

The project manager needs to:

4. Forecast the future impact. What will be the effect of the current variance if no changes are made to the plan? Is the current variance a "one-time hit?" Will the one-week delay, or the $1,000 over-spending, remain at that level, or are these variances either the symptoms or the triggers of other problems? What if that 1-week delay means that the resources for a subsequent activity will no longer be available when they'll be needed? What will all these variances add up to by project completion? And what will the impact be on the project DIPP?

5. Investigate alternatives to the current plan. Are there routes to more satisfactory outcomes? Are they practical? What might the ripple effects be of employing such routes? Such analysis is done through "what-if scenarios." Basically, these consist of introducing even more variances to the plan in order to see what beneficial effects there might be. And, again, what does beneficial mean in terms of the project DIPP.

But the project DIPP is only part of the story.

First, what if, after all the alternatives have been investigated, the project manager is unable to avoid taking a huge hit on the project DIPP? Shouldn't this call for immediate escalation to a project review board or senior management?

Second, what if the project manager is able to maintain, or even raise, the original DIPP, but only by diverting resources from another project? Perhaps from the critical path of another project, thus delaying it and perhaps lowering its DIPP? Should the project manager even have the capability to look at such an alternative? Who would approve such a change? And on what data?

Both of these situations should automatically trigger:

6. Review by senior management. A threshold level should be built into each project's DIPP, triggering a review any time that the project's expected profitability declines by more than a certain amount. But senior management should also have its finger on the organizational profitability, as reflected by the multi-project portfolio DIPP. Any change in the DIPP of one or more projects should automatically be uploaded to the multi-project level and reflected in the portfolio DIPP. Senior management should have the ability to check this, through a desktop information system. The profitability data, and delta, as shown in Figure 2.1, should be available and checked each morning.

Any decrease in portfolio DIPP should be immediately traceable to the project change that triggered it. If senior management is uncomfortable with that change, an ad hoc review should take place. This may involve two or more project managers, as well as resource and marketing managers.

Notice again how it is the quantifiable nature of the project management data, especially the DIPP, that triggers the review by showing, in numerical terms, that (1) a change has occurred, and (2) the impact has been detrimental, and by how much.

TOTAL PORTFOLIO:	Expected Monetary Value:	$20,000	(+$2,000)
	Total Cost ETC:	$9,200	(+$3,000)
	Expected Net:	$10,800	(–$1,000)
	Simple DIPP:	2.2	(–0.7)

Figure 2.1 TPC Senior Management Report on Portfolio Profitability

Finally, the project manager must:

7. Execute the new plan. Whatever the modifications (delayed deadline, retargeting resources from another project, hiring new or more expensive resources, trimming features of the deliverable) that resulted in the most satisfactory outcome, not just for the one project but for the organization's entire portfolio, must be incorporated into the new project plan. The project manager must communicate the new plan to all affected parties (team members, suppliers, customer interface) who have not yet been notified.

Again, what sort of plan will aid the project manager in performing the F-I-R-E procedures quickly, accurately, and comprehensively? The primary answer is—flexibility. The more flexible the medium and format in which the plan resides, the easier it is to visualize future impacts, whether triggered by unplanned variances or input as part of the what-if analysis. Also, the faster and easier it is to document and publish the revision(s).

As far as the medium is concerned, the computer is obviously a wonderfully flexible tool. Project management software varies quite considerably in terms of its flexibility, but even the least user-friendly packages represent a giant advantage over the age of pre-computerized project management, when schedules would be drawn in pencil on rolls of meat-wrapping brown paper, then taped up and down the corridors of the engineering department's building. Changes in those days (or during the early days of computers, when punch cards had to be used for every change) were a true nuisance, and what-if analysis all had to be conducted in the human brain.

Perhaps the very inflexibility of the pre-microprocessor medium forced project managers to store their data in formats that had the utmost flexibility. The WBS and the critical path method network diagram (PERT chart) are wonderful formats precisely because it is possible to see the impact of a change almost as soon as it is input to the plan. The WBS holds the scope and budgetary data in a way that allows for easy additions and subtractions, while the CPM network "flows" an initial change early in the schedule through to the end of the project, so that its impact can be measured.

■ CONCLUSION

Managing projects effectively puts a premium on managing the changes that impact every project. These can only be managed through the initial preparation of a project plan that is detailed and is in a flexible format and medium. In other words, you can't A-I-M and F-I-R-E unless, first, you're ready to do so. And that means starting with a good project plan.

Accuracy in planning is always better than inaccuracy. A truly accurate plan would obviate the need to ever manage change. However, the size and complexity of projects means that all but the simplest projects are likely to undergo significant (if not *major*) changes during execution. A plan that was once *thought* to be accurate, and therefore was cast in concrete, becomes worthless with the first change.

A good project plan is one that provides the detail and flexibility to assist in the A-I-M and F-I-R-E process. It is a working document, to be repeatedly updated as the project goes along, and to be used as a tool for managing change.

■ COROLLARY AND PARADOX

The following is an oft-heard refrain from project planners:

> Some of this project is pretty straightforward, and I can give you a real solid plan for doing it. But, heck, some is so nebulous, that who knows what we're going to find once we start in! Whatever we plan now is bound to change, so there's no point in planning at all!

Suppose that the project planner is correct in diagnosing the situation: one portion of the project is simple and straightforward—the other is extremely complex. The $64,000 question is this: If the purpose of a detailed and flexible project plan is to help manage change, where do you most need that plan? Do you most need a plan on a project (or phase, or task) where the work scope is known, the work is straightforward, the resources committed, and the workers are experienced? *Or do you need a plan on a project where the work is nebulous and cutting edge, where we don't know what we're going to find, where we don't control the availability of resources, and where whatever we plan now is bound to change?* Surely it is obvious that, if a project is deemed so simple and straightforward that the plan is not likely to change, then we hardly have to plan it at all. It's the 99 percent of projects that *are* tough and nebulous that need a project plan, as a working document to help manage the *unpredictable* changes that we *predict* are going to occur. It is precisely those parts of a project that are most unclear, the phases and tasks wherein lie the perils, that need the most planning, the most attention, the most detail.

And so we have a paradox: The more likely it is that the plan will turn out to be inaccurate, the more benefit the project manager will get from a plan that is detailed and flexible. The fuzzier the goals, the more important it is to plan. Again, the object of planning is not accuracy so much as a working document that can serve as a tool for dealing with the inaccuracies.

■ HOW AND WHAT TO PLAN

The next question that comes to mind is *how* to plan? Here is where TPC alters the paradigm for even those organizations that currently utilize the full array of traditional project management planning techniques.

The typical way in which a corporate project is undertaken is approximately as follows:

1. Someone gets an idea for a product, or a cost reduction program, or decides to respond to a request-for-proposal from a potential customer.

2. Initial summary planning is conducted, often by the marketing department. This results in a business case that provides a thumbnail sketch of the deliverable, estimates the potential revenue benefits, outlines the resources, and "guess-timates" the budget. The business case frequently also affixes a project duration, or delivery date.

3. The business case is then reviewed, usually by the customer or senior management. Sometimes, the important step of including those who will have primary responsibility for the development project (e.g., project manager, engineering department, manufacturing) is undertaken at this stage. But all too often, that step does not occur until after final commitment to the project has been made. Then those poor workers get saddled with the whole parcel, work scope, budget, and deadline, without ever being allowed to "buy out" of any commitments that seem unreasonable.[4]

4. Once the project is approved (or the contract signed), a project team is assigned to it, with all its concrete-etched commitments. Why is a certain feature included? Why is June 15 the deadline? Why is the budget $3.4 million? Don't be silly. Because it is! Now go find a way to do it!

Such arbitrary project parameters result in two scenarios:

1. On rare occasions, the parameters might be too loose. In that case, Parkinson's Law and whatever its budgetary equivalent might be will surely bubble both

the project plan and its implementation out to their inefficient limits.

2. Much more often, the project will not fit within the pre-set parameters, and one, or more, or all, will slip, whether formally or invisibly. And thus millions of dollars are lost every year through such unmanaged inefficiencies.

To fully understand what is occurring here, it is necessary to return to the project triangle model first discussed in the introduction. Every project, no matter what the industry or work type, is a compromise among three variables: scope, time, and cost, as shown in Figure 2.2.

Again, scope is the total amount of work to be conducted, cost is the "budget" measuring total resource usage, and time is the total elapsed time, from concept to completion.

Traditional project management deals only with the two sloped sides; in other words, the way the project looks after it has been approved and as it is handed to the project manager. Additionally, although the term *cost/schedule integration* is a shibboleth of traditional project management, the two-sided approach offers no such benefit. In order to truly integrate cost and schedule, one would need to be able to translate the one to the other, in order to make decisions involving trade-offs between them. But the two parameters use completely different metrics. Resource usage can be turned into cost and quantified in dollars (or euros, or yen) so as to provide a single unit across all resources. This enables the comparison of nuclear physicist workhours with

Figure 2.2 The Project Triangle

janitor workhours, and also pounds of nails and interest on loans with janitor workhours. However, time is estimated and measured in hours, days, or weeks. Traditional methods are no more capable of comparing cost with schedule than of apples with orangutans.

Indeed, the only way to truly integrate the parameters of a project is to deal with all three sides of the model in a single unit. But in traditional project management, scope is not quantified at all. It is usually documented as a list of the deliverables (in U.S. Government-related work, sometimes called a C-list or contract list, consisting of contract line item numbers or CLINs). But how do you quantify the different forms that work scope on a project can take? What single metric could be used to unite depth charges with propeller blades, with missile telemetry software, with coats of paint, with bulkhead penetration test results, with toilet seats? This is what a true method of quantifying project work scope needs to provide. Further, one should then be able to take these distinct forms of deliverable and work scope, combine them with duration and budget, and come up with a single measurement for each aspect of a project, allowing a ratio for comparison, contrast, and trade-off with all other aspects of the project. This is what TPC offers.

➤ Scope/Cost/Schedule Integration

Work scope is the foundation on which the whole project rests. It is the reason for doing the project—to obtain the value that will accrue from the work, in the form of an additional "thing," or revenue, or savings. In the triangle model, it is the baseline of the triangle. And that is exactly what the work scope is: the bottom line of the project, the value its completion is expected to add to the organization. In a company whose revenue is completely project generated (as is the case with most product development companies, as well as many other types), the total organizational bottom line, its profit, is the sum of the value produced by all the individual projects.

Once we recognize this, two things come into clearer focus:

1. Quantifying scope is important. It is directly related to profitability. In a project-driven company, if you haven't quantified project scope, you *cannot* accurately estimate, or work to increase, profit.

2. The metric used to quantify scope is the dollar. To be precise, the *expected* dollar that measures the value that the project is undertaken to generate.

Now, *how* one goes about estimating the value of a project is a topic of its own, beyond the scope of this book. Obviously, it often relies on experience, research, and guesswork. But this information is the driver of the whole project. And, obviously, *some* estimating of expected value is implicit for any project. Without an estimate that the final product will be worth more than the cost of the work that must be done, no project would ever be justified. In a world of limited resources, no decision between two competing projects could ever be made without assumptions about their comparative expected values.

"But," comes the cry, "such estimates are likely to be inaccurate!"

So try to make them accurate. If the budget for a project is likely to be $5 million, surely it's worth an additional 1 percent, or $50,000, to discover if the expected value is $40 million, $14 million, or $4 million. Then perhaps you can discover how to add a few million by changing the project's work scope or schedule.

Besides, the project's budget and duration are only estimates, but that doesn't get used as an excuse to say it's not worth estimating what they're likely to be. When a good poker player decides on whether to call, raise, or fold, he or she doesn't *know* exactly what is going to happen, or what the size of the pot will be when it's won; but that player *certainly* uses all the available data, including the current size of the pot (the global market?), the cards showing (current competitive products?), and the proclivities of the other players (demand volatility?) to estimate the growth potential of the pot and to determine his or her actions. Poker is reputed to be a game of luck, yet the player who performs this analysis best almost invariably walks out a winner at the end of the evening. Surely a multimillion dollar project is worth more analytical effort than a dollar-ante poker game!

The subject of EMV analysis will resume when we talk about TPC's value breakdown structure (VBS) in the next chapter. But for the moment, we can see that our quantification of scope by EMV gives us metrics for two sides of the triangle, scope and cost, in a single unit: money. Also, EMV minus cost equals anticipated profit. We can analyze scope-adding or cost-cutting measures according to their impact on these two sides, and thereby increase or decrease the anticipated profit. We can compare two potential projects according to their anticipated profits and elect to pursue the more profitable one.

But what about the third side of the triangle, *time*? The answer is that the expected value of a project is based not only on the work scope but also on *when* that work scope is completed. Thus the estimate of expected value is time dependent: deliver your Christmas toy to the stores by November 20, and you'll generate revenues of $20 million; delay delivery until December 20, and you might make $2 million. Almost every project will vary in EMV depending on completion date, even if only because it's that much later before the benefits of the work (e.g., cost savings or decreased personal labor) begin to accrue. On some projects, delay will decrease the EMV at an even rate. Conversely, sometimes the cost of delay can be precipitous. If a satellite is to be launched from a space shuttle, and the shuttle is to be launched from Cape Canaveral on April 15, then the satellite's EMV is constant through that date, and drops to zero after the date of the scheduled launch. In such cases, it is not worth anything to reduce the schedule to earlier than April 15. But if the project slips by so much as 1 day, it's worth the

entire EMV to move the completion date back to the fif-
teenth. How to accomplish this, and what decisions can be
justified in such circumstances, will be covered in later chapters. But all the data regarding each and every project's EMV
across the entire portfolio, must be assembled up front as
part of the TPC Business Case. The EMV then must be
tracked and, if necessary, updated at regular intervals
throughout the project. It doesn't make much sense to have
regular and up-to-date project information, but to allow the
market information that is driving the project to be many
months old. It is senior management's responsibility to
make sure that the following data are collected, and then
used, for every project as soon as it is approved for funding.

1. What is the EMV of the project?
2. As of what date?
3. What is the plus or minus value for each unit of delay
    or acceleration?

If the EMV and delay/acceleration values change, project
analysis needs to reflect that change. The project manager
should immediately be made aware of the changes, and modifications to the project plan should be investigated.

■ PLANNING AND TRACKING THE DIPP

The index for assessing scope/cost/schedule integration for
each project is the DIPP. This key TPC data item needs to be
tracked for every project. First formulated in the September
1992 issue of *Project Management Journal*, the DIPP tracks
project profitability using the formula:

$$\text{DIPP} = \frac{\text{EMV (as of current completion date)}}{\text{Estimate-to-Complete (ETC)}}$$

At the start of the project, the ETC is the project budget. As implementation proceeds and work gets done, the ETC should decrease, and the accrued costs become "sunk" costs, unrecoverable expenditures which, being unalterable, should have little impact on the analysis of future actions. The future profitability of the project is the EMV *minus* the ETC. But the DIPP is an index of the efficiency with which the project resources will be utilized until completion. A DIPP of less than 1.0 means that the project will cost more to complete than its EMV. Such a project should either be changed (increase the EMV by adding valuable work scope items? cut costs by reducing resource use? decrease delay cost by *adding* resources?), or terminated. By analyzing the EMV, ETC, and delay/acceleration cost/value, the project manager should always endeavor to invest the resources at her disposal in the best possible way to maximize the DIPP. Regular project reporting on the DIPP, period by period, should be standard operating procedure.

Additionally, the initial plan should include a forecast of what the DIPP is anticipated to be at each reporting point until the end of the project. (It should of course increase as costs are sunk and the ETC decreases.) A histogram, such as the one in Figure 2.3, should be produced with each report, showing how the DIPP is tracking against both the original and the current plans.

➤ TPC at the Organizational Level

The same sort of analysis that is performed at the project level should also be done at the macro-, or multi-project portfolio level.

The portfolio DIPP indicates the expected profitability across all the projects (provided that overhead burdens are attached to budgetary costs). Senior management should be expected to analyze how current resources might be better spread to take advantage of the diverse project delay/acceleration cost/value factors. Senior management may decide

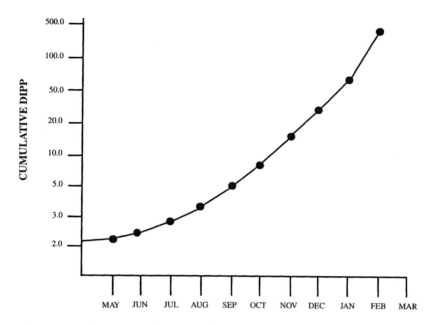

Figure 2.3 Histogram Showing Actual DIPP vs. Planned DIPP Overtime

to delay (or even terminate) some projects and accelerate others to target the resources to the best projects for the purpose of maximizing the DIPP.

The DIPP is *not* identical to organizational profitability. Given fixed costs, the DIPP indicates how much profit those costs are expected to generate. But senior management also has the option of increasing costs by investing in additional resources. In such an event, the organizational DIPP (EMV over ETC) might actually go down even as raw profitability (EMV minus costs) increases.

The decision on whether to increase staffing and other resources, while remaining the responsibility of senior management, can be greatly aided by project-specific and functional department information, namely the CLUB. Additionally, the organizational CLUBs indicate the cost, in terms of delay factors, of each resource summed across all the projects. By working to reduce these, senior management can not only increase organizational profitability, but also can move toward that elusive goal of right-sizing the organization that has been the object of so much blind flailing during the past decade (see Chapter 9).

It has frequently been my misfortune to work with the depressed employees of clients who have recently been undergoing downsizing. This is *not* to say that there are not good reasons for downsizing. But what I don't understand is how any organization engaged in project work can possibly know *where* or *who* to downsize when it's *not* scheduling by CPM, *not* utilizing activity-based resource assignments and costing (ABRA or ABC, respectively), *not* doing resource leveling, and doesn't understand what its organizational CLUBs are. That extra electrical engineer *may* only be needed one week out of every three. But *not* having him there, on staff, precisely when he *is* needed, may, in 1 year, delay 17 projects by 1 week each. Without using CPM, companies are shooting blindly, and are *far* more likely to maim productivity and profitability than anything else. In many product development situations, it is not unreasonable to estimate a cost of $500,000 for each week of delay to market. That's a total cost of $8,500,000, while saving the electrical engineer's annual burdened salary of $100,000.

It is not surprising that within the past two to three years, we have seen somewhat of a turnaround, in that corporations are admitting that they were hurt by their previous ill-advised, and often drastic, downsizing. The executive of a project-driven organization that downsizes staff without first identifying and measuring CLUBs should be the first one out the door.

The following chapters will explore the specific techniques of TPC planning. But two overriding concepts must be kept in mind:

1. The entire organization engaged in project work should at all times be driven by optimization of the multi-project portfolio's profitability.

2. Project profitability is a compromise among work scope, time, and cost. If work scope is quantified as EMV, the project can be measured and optimized by using the DIPP.

Chapter 3

An Overview
of Planning the Work

Every project is a compromise among the three variables of scope, time, and cost and may be pictured as in Figure 3.1. This paradigm drives *so much* about the project context, whether within one project or throughout a project-oriented organization, that it keeps resurfacing as the jumping-off point for further issues and discussion.

Take the project as a whole, or any one of the myriad and diverse work tasks within it: how long will it take, and how much will it cost? How does one go about getting even a ball-park estimate?

Every project is unique, consisting of a unique work scope performed under unique circumstances. Therefore estimates about either time or cost will also be unique, dependent on the project-specific work scope. "Got some work for you to do. How long is it going to take, and how much is it going to cost?" Well, that depends on what the work is. The project leader who provides estimates without an adequate definition of work scope is signing his or her own pink slip.

Thus the first task of the project planner is to define the work scope, in detail. The greater the detail, the more

Figure 3.1 The Project Triangle

accurate the estimates that can be generated. But make no mistake: Defining the work scope is the hardest part of project planning.

However, let us now assume that our scope-defining effort has been successful. What we now have is the total work scope divided into its several components and subcomponents, and the work activities necessary to create them. The work scope may now be pictured as shown in Figure 3.2.

The planning team should now be in a position to generate time and cost estimates for each activity, time being the elapsed time of the activity's duration, and cost being the dollar value of the resources required to complete the activity's work scope. In effect, each activity becomes its own project, with its own little triangle, as shown in Figure 3.3.

Each of these triangles, with their time and cost estimates, is now integrated into a total project plan. This is done by scheduling all the work through CPM and computing the budget through ABRA and ABC.

Imagine we are part of a planning team working for MegaProdux, Inc. We have been assigned to develop a new product and, after many days of effort, we have developed a

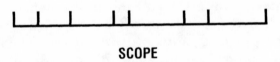

SCOPE

Figure 3.2 The Project Work Scope Base

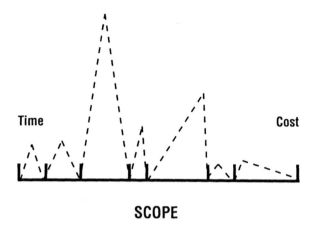

SCOPE

Figure 3.3 The Several Triangles of the Project Activities

plan that includes a schedule of 35 weeks with a budget of $3.5 million. Suppose that this amount of time is deemed unacceptable, by the customer, by senior management, or due to some fixed market window, such as a space shuttle launch or the Christmas shopping season. We must reduce the schedule by, say, six weeks. Utilizing CPM to its fullest functionality, we "crash the critical path" with additional and more expensive resources until there is a 30-week schedule—but now with a budget of $3.8 million. And when we produce our new plan for approval, it is vetoed. We are told that our mandate is to perform the project in 30 weeks for the original budgeted cost of $3.5 million.

If we have *really* done a thorough job of utilizing CPM for scheduling, and done all the "fast tracking" (simultaneous activities) we can, this leaves us but one choice: the third side of the triangle, or work scope. Some of the components, subcomponents, features, quantity, or quality will have to be trimmed from the planned deliverable in order to meet the mandated parameters of time and cost. But where to conduct such pruning? And what will its impact be? Does it make sense that we've been given this mandate in the first place?

Before answering these questions, let us see how TPC addresses this problem.

■ QUANTIFYING THE PROJECT TRIANGLE

This is where traditional project management, even with cost/schedule integration, offers little help, but where the scope/cost/schedule integrated plan of TPC allows for a quantified comparison of the trade-offs involved in different solutions to the problem. If, as suggested in Chapter 2, the EMV of the project has been calculated and incorporated into the project planning process, there is a baseline for determining what impact other changes to the project may have on its most important feature: its profitability.

Profit, of course, is value minus cost. In the project triangle, *cost* (which is really resource usage) is nicely quantified into dollars or some other monetary unit. If we have the EMV of the project *also* monetized, then:

➤ Two of the three sides can be analyzed using the same unit.

➤ One side minus the other will give the expected project profit.

➤ One side divided by the other (EMV divided by ETC) will give the profitability index, the DIPP.

So now we have two sides of the project triangle quantified in the same all-important unit, as shown in Figure 3.4. But what about the third side to the triangle (see Figure 3.5)? How should *time* be quantified on a project? Time always *is* quantified—as weeks, days, hours, minutes. But that does not really help: How do we translate such units into dollars?

It was Benjamin Franklin, more than 200 years ago, who gave the answer: "Time," he said, "is money!" How exactly is *time* money on a project? As discussed earlier, by delaying

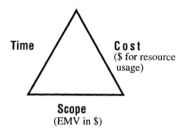

Figure 3.4 Quantifying Two Sides of the Project Triangle

the point at which we start receiving the benefits of the completed work scope, time becomes money.

■ THE TPC BUSINESS CASE

This answer leads to a crucial feature that distinguishes the TPC Business Case from the traditional one. Most business cases for projects (and we must recognize that many corporate projects are embarked upon without ever having *any* kind of business case) will have a paragraph or column discussing the benefits of the project, and will often quantify these into an EMV. But it is crucial to recognize that the EMV of the project is *not* a constant: It is a variable dependent upon, among other things, the delivery date of the final product. That delivery date is determined by the total elapsed time of the project. Therefore the *time* side of the project triangle must be quantified, unit by unit, per its plus or minus

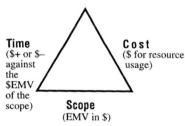

Figure 3.5 Quantifying All Three Sides of the Project Triangle

dollar effect on the EMV of the project. And that quantification belongs right up front, as part of the business case, where it can be used by the project manager and planning team to generate a plan which is as valuable as possible.

➤ Project Delay Curves

Just how this plus or minus impacts the EMV varies from project to project. Delay Curve 1 (Figure 3.6) represents a contracted delivery for a specific customer. The impact of a two-week delay might merely be the net present value (NPV) reduction for the same dollar figure received two weeks later. Earlier completion of such a project would result in a similarly small acceleration premium.

On the other hand, the project may be to launch a satellite from the space shuttle to take close-up photos of a comet

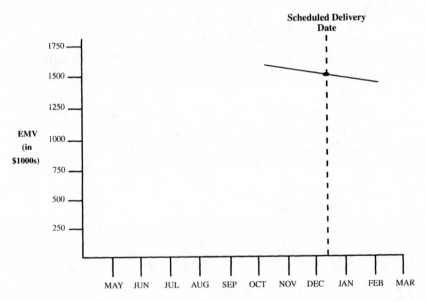

Figure 3.6 Delay Curve 1—EMV Variance on a Fixed Cost Contract Due to Time Value of Money

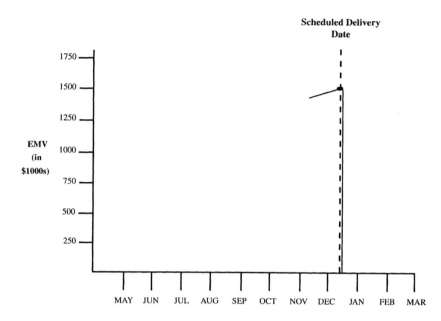

Figure 3.7 Delay Curve 2—EMV Variance Due to Schedule Variance around a Fixed Deadline

passing near Earth. Completing the project early may result in reduced profit, due to having to store the satellite until launch. But a satellite that misses the blast-off date of the shuttle by one day will have its EMV reduced from $20 million to zero. Consider Delay Curve 2, as shown in Figure 3.7.

Delay Curve 3 occurs, for example, in refueling projects at nuclear power plants, or other similar maintenance projects. Each day that the power plant has to be offline for refueling may represent the loss of $1 million. In such a case, *every* day of the project's duration, from cool down to restart, reduces the EMV of the deliverable (i.e., a refueled and working power plant) by $1 million (see Figure 3.8).

Delay Curve 4 is often seen in product development projects for the retail market. Take the example of a game or toy for the holiday shopping season. The product needs to be in U.S. stores the day after Thanksgiving Day. To be one week

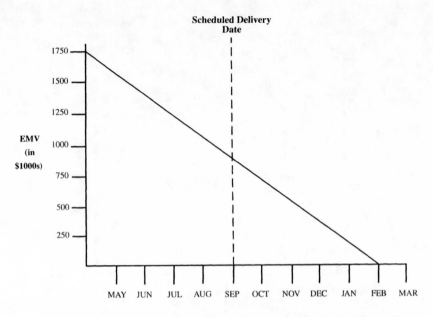

Figure 3.8 Delay Curve 3—EMV Reduction for Unavailability of Revenue-Generating Equipment

late implies a revenue loss of 20 percent. Each additional week the item is late equates to a similar loss until, after five weeks, the shopping season will have been missed and revenues reduced to zero. In addition, there is a small reward to be gained through early delivery; each week that our product is in the stores *before* Thanksgiving will increase our revenues by 4 percent. With an EMV of $20 million, the delay cost is $4 million for each week after Thanksgiving, with an acceleration premium of $800,000 for each week before that date. This type of delay curve is pictured in Figure 3.9.

Delay Curve 5 is the situation fairly typical of pharmaceutical and other R&D-based product development projects, where the first product to market will enjoy a huge boost to revenues, the second to market a smaller share, and so on. The pharmaceutical company developing the product knows that competitors are at work in the same field, but does not know how close to market they are. In such a situation, per

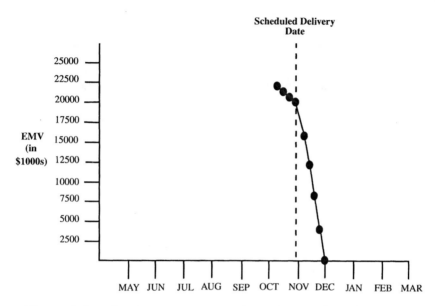

Figure 3.9 Delay Curve 4—EMV Variance in Retail Market Due to Schedule Variance around a Seasonal Market Window

unit delay cost must be estimated on the basis of probability and risk: What will revenues be if our product is first to market, versus second to market; what are the probable dates on which competitors might deliver an identical product to market; and how does that probability change per unit of time.

Our marketing department has researched the situation and estimated that, if our product is first to market, it will result in an EMV (after NPV analysis, of course) of $100 million. Being second to market will lower the EMV to $40 million. It has also determined that there is a 10 percent chance of our competitor reaching market May 1, a further 50 percent by June 1, a further 25 percent chance by the beginning of July, and 5 percent more for each of August, September, and October. Figure 3.10 shows that, based on these numbers, our project's EMV will be $100 million if delivered by the end of April, $94 million in May, $64 million in June, $49 million in July, $46 million in August, $43 million in September, and $40 million in October.

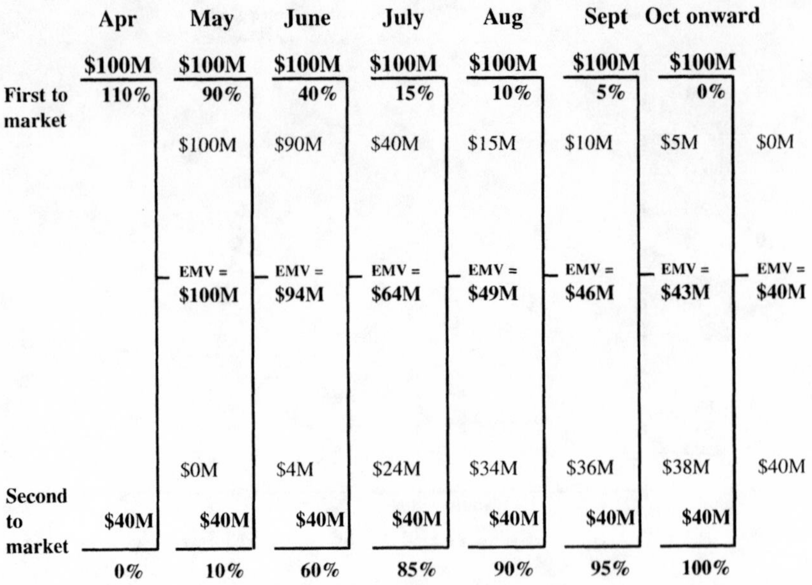

	Apr	May	June	July	Aug	Sept	Oct onward	
	$100M	**$100M**	**$100M**	**$100M**	**$100M**	**$100M**	**$100M**	
First to market	110%	90%	40%	15%	10%	5%	0%	
		$100M	$90M	$40M	$15M	$10M	$5M	$0M
		EMV = $100M	EMV = $94M	EMV = $64M	EMV = $49M	EMV = $46M	EMV = $43M	EMV = $40M
		$0M	$4M	$24M	$34M	$36M	$38M	$40M
Second to market	**$40M**	**$40M**	**$40M**	**$40M**	**$40M**	**$40M**	**$40M**	
	0%	10%	60%	85%	90%	95%	100%	

Figure 3.10 Diagram Calculating EMV Variance Based on Value and Probability of Being First or Second to Market

Based on these data, Figure 3.11 shows the delay cost curve for each month from April through October. The first month is worth $6 million, the second an additional $30 million, the third $15 million, and so on.

Most projects fit into one or another of the five delay curve profiles shown in Figures 3.6 to 3.11. If we know our delivery curve, then, depending on what delivery date our schedule is currently headed for, we can calculate the maximum amount that we should spend on additional resources to accelerate our schedule. Experience shows this amount is almost always much more than the resources would cost (and almost always more than the organization that has *not* had the situation spelled out for them, in TPC terms, is willing to allocate). The constraint tends to be that the needed resources are often unobtainable.

But, in addition to spending more money on resources, there is another way to shorten the schedule: cut the work

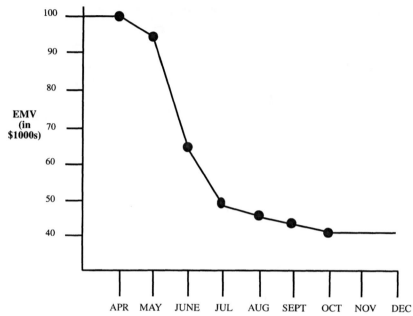

Figure 3.11 Delay Curve 5—EMV Variance Based on Value and
Probability of Being First or Second to Market

scope. Increasing resources tends to reduce profit by increasing cost. Cutting work scope also tends to reduce profit, but by reducing EMV: a product with fewer features, less reliability, or reduced advertising, is likely to generate less revenue. Which should a project manager elect to do, add resources or cut scope? Answer: Whatever leads to a larger DIPP.

■ OPTIMIZING THE DIPP AT THE MICRO LEVEL

Let us now return to the problem on page 40. As a planning team for MegaProdux, Inc., we are being ordered to cut our 35-week MegaMan project down to 30 weeks while maintaining our budget at $3.5 million. Now incorporate into this scenario the information that MegaProdux is a toy company, that week 31 is the start of the holiday shopping season, and that our deliverable, MegaMan, is expected to generate sales of $10 million. Assume that Delay Curve 4 (see Figure 3.9) is applicable. All this information belongs in the TPC Business Case, and can be succinctly summarized in the fashion displayed in Figure 3.12.

If we are to do as ordered and complete the project in 30 weeks for $3.5 million, we need to cut scope. But we want to cut it in the way that reduces the project's value as little as possible. Now, how do we determine which of the little activity triangles is *adding* the appropriate amounts to time and cost such that their *removal* will give us the schedule and budget needed while reducing the value the least?

When we "drill" down to the micro-, or activity, level of the project, the relationships between components and between the work activities required to produce them, are closely intertwined, in terms of both EMV and schedule. The impact that removing a component or activity has on a project depends not only on the component or activity itself, but also on the rest of the product and project.

What, for example, is the value of a staircase in a house? It depends very much on where the staircase leads; if the

---

MegaMan Development Project

EMV: $10,000,000 at end of week 30

Delay penalty: 20% or $2,000,000 per week

Acceleration premium: 4% or $400,000 per week

Target Budget: $3,500,000

Figure 3.12 Summary of the TPC Business Case for the MegaMan Project

house is a one-floor ranch, and the staircase leads nowhere, its value is at most, decorative.[1] On the other hand, if most of the important rooms in the house are on the second floor, then the staircase acquires a value almost equal to the total value of the second floor (unless there is also an elevator). The issue is: How much would the house be worth without the staircase, if it had all the other rooms and features, but no staircase? How much *value* is the staircase *adding* to the house? This is called its *value-added*. We will explore how to compute this value-added in greater detail shortly.

What about the *time* side of the activity's triangle? How interconnected is that? Again, whereas a project's time is its duration, an activity's duration may have no significance whatever when attempting to shorten a project's schedule. It all depends where in the project schedule the activity occurs. If the project is scheduled through the critical path method, *only* critical path activities impact the project schedule. *How much* they impact it depends on far more than simply the activity's duration. This impact is one of the key data items of the TPC methodology, and is called DRAG.

We will cover DRAG in great detail in Chapters 6 and 7. For the moment, let us just say that DRAG is the amount of time an activity is adding to the duration of the total project, or, conversely, the amount of time that could be saved by *removing* an activity from the project schedule.

So far we have only addressed the time of an activity—not the *time* of an activity. You will recall that when we wanted to analyze the project in a scope/cost/schedule manner, we had to deal with time *not* as a duration (in weeks, days, hours, etc.) but as an impact on the EMV of the project. So too the *time* of the activity triangle should be measured not simply in DRAG units, but in DRAG cost: the amount of money by which the project's value is being reduced as a result of having to perform this activity, with X number of units of DRAG.

This is extremely important, because the cost of the time to do a project is usually far larger than the cost of the resources (i.e., *cost*) to do the project. That correlation extends down to the activity level in even more dramatic numbers. A critical path activity may be utilizing $30,000 in resources over its three weeks of duration. But if two of those three weeks represent time added to the project schedule, it is not exaggerating to say that, in a product development project, each week could represent $500,000 in irrecoverable revenues, or a total activity DRAG cost of $1 million.

Activities cannot, then, be managed to maximum profit. Well, they *can*—but it depends on how you define profit. What is the profit on a staircase within a house? What is the profit on the left wing of an airplane? Without the project, the activity may be worth nothing (or very little). The activity gets its value by *adding value* to the rest of the project. But that value is offset by

➤ The cost of resources required to perform that activity.

➤ The reduction in the project's EMV due to the amount of time it is delayed by the performance of that activity.

This leads to the activity's equivalent of profit: net value-added (NVA). The NVA of an activity is its value-added minus the sum of its resource cost and its DRAG cost.

$$NVA = \text{value-added} - (\text{cost} + \text{DRAG cost})$$

The NVA of an activity may change as the project is implemented. An activity that has a value-added of $200,000, a budget of $20,000, and 2 weeks of DRAG may start with an NVA of $180,000 if the initial schedule will meet the deadline and there is no acceleration premium. However, if there is a delay cost of $100,000 per week, and the project's critical path slips 2 weeks, suddenly the NVA will be:

$$\$200,000 - (\$20,000 + \$200,000) = -\$20,000$$

Either this activity should be removed from the project, or another change should take place. But this all requires careful and detailed oversight of the project. Traditional project planning and project management software do not support such data items as EMV, the DIPP, activity value-added, delay cost, acceleration premium, NVA, DRAG cost, or even simple DRAG. Ideal, of course, would be a software package that would not only handle such input and output, but would also send an alert whenever any component or activity declined to a negative value-added (or a value-added below a level preset by the user). Without such software, much project effort on slipping projects is likely to be wasted on work of negative value.

Take the MegaMan project as an example. With a $10 million EMV at 30-weeks duration, and loss of 20 percent for each week longer (see Figure 3.9, Delay Curve 4), the numbers in Figure 3.13 show that senior management is wise to insist on a maximum duration of 30 weeks.

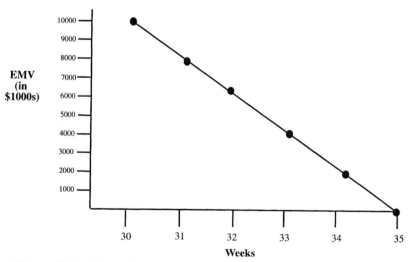

Figure 3.13 Chart of MegaMan Project EMV, Weeks 30–35, Based on Delay Curve 4

However, limiting the budget might not be the wisest idea. The tactic of limiting costs while requiring shorter durations is only successful when projects have been poorly planned. It assumes padded duration estimates and poor application of CPM techniques. However, if senior management really assumes that it can shorten the project by five weeks simply by reducing the inefficiencies of the project manager, it should let the project manager go, and start over. (Of course, senior management is often right in such an assumption, but it must shoulder the blame for project management knowledge and techniques not being standard operating procedure within the organization. Standardized project management procedures, including reporting and oversight, a good project management software package, and training for both its project teams and itself in the intricacies of project management would go a long way toward making projects shorter, cheaper, and more profitable.)

If in the MegaMan project, the planning team has applied the techniques of traditional project management properly, then requesting the additional $300,000 in order to shorten the project by 5 weeks is probably both reasonable and wise. Even at the gut level, without TPC metrics, it doesn't take a genius to figure out that this project needs to be done by the start of week 31, and if the additional $.3 million needed to trim the 5 weeks is enough to reduce the profit drastically, then we probably don't want to be doing this project in the first place.

But, without realizing it, senior management may have made a much more costly decision. Despite all the trouble and care to which our planning team has gone, we find ourselves being told to do a $3.8 million project (given current work scope and deadline) for $3.5 million. Somehow, we have to make this a $3.5 million project. And the only way to do that is to reduce cost by cutting work scope. Out goes MegaMan's elaborate costume and fancy packaging, along with half of the advertising budget. We now have a schedule that will have our toy in the stores on time. As well as a toy guaranteed to be on the shelves, marked down by 90 percent, weeks after the holiday season ends. Even if the retailers take most of the beating *this* year, MegaProdux, Inc. will take the beating *next* year, when the retailers shy away from such a loser. Most of the time, this sort of thing happens without anyone in senior management even being aware of it.

Again, work scope is the ignored stepchild of the traditional project management approach. It is regarded as a constant, which allows managers at all levels to tinker with schedule and budget while pretending that they are leaving work scope unchanged. In the MegaMan example, the changes are pretty drastic and should be extremely visible. But if senior management does not bother to look. . . .

However, the pruning of scope is often much more subtle and much more insidious. Design is rushed, testing is shortened, corrections are not double checked, and quality is thoroughly compromised, all without leaving telltale evidence until the product collapses on the shelves. Or while little Jenny is playing with it, which might be fine, except that Jenny's mom returns the toy, and the store reports it defective.

If MegaProdux, Inc. were using the TPC approach, the entire MegaMan scenario would have been different.

In the first place, our planning team would never have submitted a project plan with a 35-week schedule. The TPC Business Case from which we were working would have guided us by quantifying the lost revenue for each week late. With the DIPP as our guiding star, we would have planned toward maximized profitability, and very likely generated a schedule of 20 weeks, with minimum cost. But even that might have been insufficient. Remember, in addition to the delay cost for the weeks beyond week 30, Delay Curve 4 also offers an acceleration premium of 4 percent per week for each week *less* than week 30. The entire EMV picture is shown in Figure 3.14.

Now, with an additional $400,000 per week to be made, it may be possible to augment MegaMan's profit even more. It is certainly going to be tough to squeeze additional weeks out of an already tight schedule; but with *up to* $400,000 each week to be targeted to just the right activities, something might be possible. Perhaps one could spend an extra $350,000 each week for five weeks and make an additional quarter mil. . . .

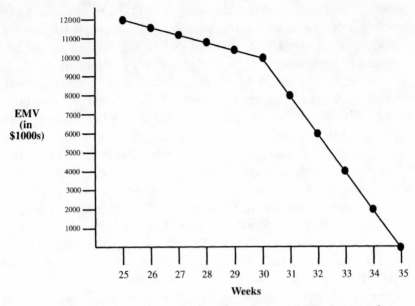

Figure 3.14 Chart of MegaMan Project EMV, Weeks 25–35, Based on Delay Curve 4

The other thing that the TPC approach would do is make it clear that cutting the costume and packaging, and halving the advertising budget, are not smart moves. The value-addeds of those activities guarantee that cutting them would slice deeply into the EMV, which would be immediately apparent through a reduced DIPP.

There *may*, however, be components and activities that could be eliminated without serious penalty. Such candidates would be the ones that the TPC approach would point out as having low NVAs. Again, a software package that lists NVAs in ascending order would be most helpful. But first, such data have to be input to the project plan.

■ CONCLUSION

The reader should by this time have a pretty good idea of what TPC is designed to accomplish: an environment for project work in which everyone, from the level of the smallest activity right up to the CEO, is working toward the goal of maximized value. All project decisions, such as product features, schedule, budget, and staffing levels should be analyzed on the basis of quantified data that should be generated right up front in the business case. These will show, at the project level, what makes the project more profitable, and, at the portfolio level, what makes the organization more profitable (which, of course, may sometimes mean canceling even a profitable project).

At the project and activity level, management should be concerned primarily with using available resources to optimum efficiency, whereas at the organizational, or multiproject level, where decisions regarding staffing levels and cash flow issues tend to be made, profit should be the primary concern. This does not mean that senior management can ignore efficient resource use, nor that project and activity managers should ignore profit. What it does mean is that, whereas senior management should manage toward profit by using the formula

$$\text{projected profit} = \text{EMV} - \text{cost}$$

Project and activity managers should manage for efficient resource use as reflected by the DIPP

$$\text{project DIPP} = \text{EMV} \div \text{ETC}$$
$$\text{activity DIPP} = (\text{value-added} - \text{DRAG cost}) \div \text{ETC}$$

In the following chapters, we will see how these data should be input, analyzed, and put to use.

Note

1. Or negative. Even the most decorative staircase is taking up room that could be occupied by a *more* decorative (or even useful) accessory. This is called *opportunity cost*, and may result in our beautiful riser and banister having negative value. Eliminate!

Planning the Work Scope

Once the TPC Business Case has been developed and reviewed by the customer, product champion, senior management, and/or project management review committee, it reaches the first gate. A *gate* is a decision point in the project process. At this point, it will be either killed, tabled, returned for further information and analysis, or approved for detailed work scope development. Approval should bring with it funding for the necessary resources to complete the entire planning process, including detailed scheduling and costing. Figure 4.1 shows the first three phases, through the completion of the detailed plan.

The first gate approves funding through the end of phase 3 in order to avoid delaying the project. However, the second gate, after phase 2 when the detailed work scope is developed, can close if the work scope document is not approved, thus canceling further funding for phase 3.

With the business case approved, it is time to assemble a planning team. This is essential for a project of any significant size or complexity. The wide range in the types of work involved in a large project underscores the need for

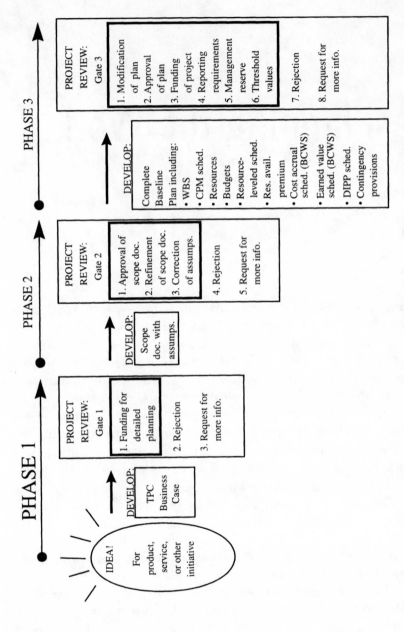

Figure 4.1 The Project Review Process for Gating and Funding

distributed expertise. The precise composition of such a team depends on the nature of the project. However, there are certain functions that are often overlooked. Marketing is probably the most important of these. But others include documentation, training, finance, and maintenance or support, the latter of whom will have to live with the product long after its delivery and the disbanding of the rest of the project team.

The job of the planning team is to develop a document that specifies and describes all the components and sub-components to be developed by the project. This document is variously called the work scope document, the product definition, the technical specifications, or the statement of work (SOW). Often these documents include information other than about work scope, such as target delivery date, target budget, or a list of available or required resources. This is all nice-to-know information; however, none of these is absolutely pertinent to the purposes of this document. The delivery date, budget, and resource information will be worked out later in the planning process. The purpose of the work scope document is simply to define, completely and comprehensively, the ultimate deliverable, and nothing else.

As mentioned before, the work scope is the most important part of the project. It is the reason for doing the project. It is what the customer wants from the project. Thus by emphasizing the work scope to such an extent, TPC is in complete harmony with modern business theory by putting the customer first. If the customer does or does not want the product, or doesn't want a particular component of the product, that should be the driving factor of the work scope definition.

Now, just who the customer is depends on the project. An internal project may have a senior manager as its customer. A fixed price contract for a specific client will have a specific customer. A product for the retail market may have millions of customers. But, in all cases, a specific representative of the customer must be identified, and must have authority over work scope definition and the work scope document. In the case of the retail market product, this individual should be the product manager or the marketing representative.

I have seen this become a problem. A southern California toy company, with which I have done a good deal of work, has always suffered from a tense relationship between the marketing managers and the project people (technically, it does not have project managers in the true sense of the word). The people responsible for doing the work felt that the marketing managers were constantly tinkering with the product definition and work scope, with no accountability for the schedule delays and costs thereby incurred. The marketing managers felt that they were responsible for the final product and wanted to make sure that it conformed to their customers' desires. The problem is a classic one in product development projects when project and product are seen as separate, rather than parts of a whole system.

This is one of the main problems that TPC is designed to solve. The DIPP is a whole system index, incorporating both the market and the project work. If the toy company had been measuring project performance via the DIPP, each change in project plan would have been captured and measured in both schedule and cost, and the DIPP would have declined unless justified by input of data showing an increased EMV. The marketing manager, for whom additional project work and costs are invisible, will naturally insist on any scope change likely to increase EMV. But if he or she can see, and must account for, the cost of the trade-off on schedule and cost (and further the opportunity cost through decreased resources and time for other products), he or she will be less cavalier in calling for enhancements. Marketing managers who don't change will soon be changed.

■ THE SCOPE DOCUMENT

Defining the work scope is by far the most important part of the project planning process. If an organization planned all of its projects' work scope, in detail, and did no other planning, it would still be a huge improvement over the situation that currently exists at most corporations. Companies and project managers omit even this fundamental planning step. They invest millions upon millions of dollars in projects where they have only the sketchiest idea of what they are *going* to do, and, later, of what they *have* done. Why do they omit it? Because it is the hardest and most labor intensive part of the planning process!

And how important it is! Suddenly, the work gets done not by whim but by decision. The scope document can be distributed to the project team, who can ask questions, make improvements, and anticipate what they will need to do. In addition, schedules, resources, and budgets can be computed, improved, and communicated.

The only question is, how *do* you plan the work scope?

Each type of project is different, and each project is different. It is therefore difficult to set hard-and-fast rules for assembling scope documents. The best idea, I have found, is to start with the benefits you want to achieve, incorporate them into the business plan, then move as rapidly as possible to a concrete image of the thing that will provide those benefits. By concrete, I mean a sketch, drawing, blueprint, model, prototype, or any combination thereof. Sometimes the deliverable may be particularly intangible, perhaps a service instead of a product. A sketch or flow chart of how the service would be processed and delivered could be of great help. For a software project, the first question should always be: What are the issues or problems this software is being designed to resolve? Second, what screens, data fields, algorithms, reports, and so forth will help it to resolve those problems? Third, what will the visible manifestation of the product look like? The better defined this becomes, the more efficiently the software can be coded. The scope document should be a detailed, comprehensive, written list of all the deliverables to be generated by the project. It is not until each deliverable has been properly defined that it becomes possible to collect the other necessary data, such as how each component will be designed, developed, assembled, tested, integrated, and whatever else needs to be done; who will be responsible for each phase, component, and activity; how long each activity will take; what resources will be needed to perform each activity; how much each component, subcomponent, and activity will cost; and how much each component and activity is contributing to the EMV of the entire product and project.

The scope document is developed during the initial stages of the project. But it must be updated throughout the project, as work scope is added or subtracted based on the decisions of customer, product manager, senior management, or project manager. The impact of any scope changes during the project should be analyzed, and receive the necessary approval, and then the original scope document amended to reflect the current status. The amended document should then be distributed to all project team members and other interested parties, and adjustments for present and future work, schedule and cost, incorporated into the plan.

➤ The Three Parameters of Scope

In defining each component of the final deliverable, the project manager and planning team should consider three dimensions or aspects:

1. Appearance. What does the component look like? In product development projects, this may even be the most important aspect of the product. A product that looks good, and is nicely packaged, will sell better than one that isn't. The importance of appearance can vary considerably across components in the same project. The appearance of the new automobile's exterior is obviously crucial to its marketability, while the appearance of its carburetor is of minimal importance.

Whatever the importance of a component's appearance, it must be described and defined as closely as possible, in terms which are as quantitative as possible. Anything that can be measured and/or weighed must be defined accordingly, with minimum and maximum values mandated. Such quantification should be generated based on customer desires. It will, in turn, drive work scope to achieve such minimums and maximums, and then to test that they have, in fact, been achieved.

2. Performance. The performance of a product or component is what it must do under what circumstances. The paradigmatic example is the mileage requirements set for automobiles by the U.S. Environmental Protection Agency. The EPA mandates minimum levels for driving mileage per gallon of gasoline on city streets and highways. This is exactly how all performance specs should be stated in the work scope document: what performance level the component must achieve under what circumstances. Again, as in the "appearance" dimension, performance specs should represent a minimum standard to be achieved. Surpassing performance specs is only helpful if it comes for free, without impact to schedule or budget, or if it improves the EMV of the final product. Otherwise, time has been wasted on "creeping elegance."[1]

Response time on a computer system supporting 100 workstations, speed and efficacy of a pharmaceutical product on a 20-year-old female subject, durability of a toy being played with by a 10-year-old boy, number of defective parts per 100,000 in a manufacturing process, and weight that a ladder can support without breaking are all examples of performance specifications.

3. Standards. Scope specification standards are somewhat different from the other two dimensions listed above in that standards are superimposed on appearance or performance specifications. Standards are the requirements that some organization, internal or external to the corporation, has decided are necessary in order to protect itself or the public interest from the project's natural desire to maximize its value. Governments and government agencies are frequently the ones that impose standards, although industry groups and corporations also impose standards on themselves.

The two most important things about scope specification standards are:

➤ They generate mandatory activities. These are activities that must be performed if the project is to be done. As we will see shortly when we get into the topic of the VBS, mandatory activities have the same value as the entire project since the project cannot be completed without performing them. This leads to the second important aspect of scope specification standards.

➤ Scope specification standards should be imposed whenever there is a gap between what is valuable for a project and what is valuable for the organization as a whole, or for the public interest.

For example, a certain pharmaceutical company, which suffered from product tampering almost 20-years ago, has a requirement that all its patent medicines must be packaged in tamper-evident containers. Today, the incident that generated that policy has largely been forgotten, and I suspect that many project and product managers would love to cut their budgets by resorting to cheaper packaging. But the corporation knows that if such a decision led to a new tampering incident, the hit that it would sustain, just from the public relations standpoint, would be devastating. Tamper-evident containers are much more valuable to the company than to the individual project. Many quality control programs are internally mandated for somewhat similar reasons.

In a similar vein, the Nuclear Regulatory Commission has set many standards regarding the refueling of a nuclear power plant. These standards add expensive days and weeks to each refueling outage in the United States, time that outage managers would love to eliminate. After all, the chances of a meltdown occurring on any *one* outage would remain slim. However, the Nuclear Regulatory Commission has some 104 plants to worry about, and that changes its odds considerably. Thus when it discovered that a Connecticut plant was saving time by cooling its reactor for only 60 hours instead of 240, it was not pleased. The fines were substantial.

■ THE ASSUMPTIONS APPENDIX

How do you make plans or estimates, when you're not sure what work is required? This is a quandary in which project workers often find themselves. Under such circumstances, the project worker must tie any estimate of time or cost to the scope of work he or she anticipates will be required. And if he does not know what that scope of work will be, he or she must make assumptions. Assumptions will allow detailed planning and estimating. However, each assumption and its associated estimate(s) must be itemized, so that the fact that there is uncertainty about their inclusion will be underlined, and so that when assumptions turn out to be wrong, the associated time and cost can be eliminated from the plan.

The assumptions appendix should be a standard part of any project scope document. Indeed, it should be the very first item following the main body of the document. Attention should be called to it by whatever means possible, for example, printing the heading in red. It is *the most important* part of the scope document in that, by definition, it is where there is the greatest likelihood of confusion.

As mentioned earlier, defining the scope document is the hardest part of project planning. And the most important. And the most time-consuming. But we don't want it to be any more time-consuming than it has to be. Many project planners abandon the planning process precisely because it seems to take so long to nail down all the requirements. Doing so is both unnecessary and unproductive. Developing the scope document should be accomplished as swiftly as possible, so that the rest of the planning process can begin. An assumptions appendix, documenting all uncertainties regarding scope inclusions and exclusions, can be a tremendous time-saver. It can provide a "straw man" so that others with an interest in the project can refine the work scope.

Once the scope document and attached assumptions appendix have been developed, they must be distributed to those who can check, amend, and delete work scope items that are not wanted and include whatever additional scope is needed. If there is a formal product development process, such as in Figure 4.2, we have now reached gate number 2, requiring formal review and approval of the planned work scope.

■ THE FUSED MEMO

If there is no such formal process, however, it is still crucial to ensure that the correct work scope is being undertaken. The review process must be undertaken by an ad hoc group of reviewers, consisting of the customer, product manager, product champion, senior management, and perhaps, functional managers and vendor representatives. In such a context, the project manager should distribute the work scope document as an attachment to a fused memo. A *fused memo* is one that "goes off" after a certain time. Timing is now crucial. For the project plan to be finalized, we must have a defined work scope. It is impossible to "plan to a moving target." Now, this does not mean that once the work scope document has been finalized, there would be no further scope changes. But it does mean that in order to plan schedules,

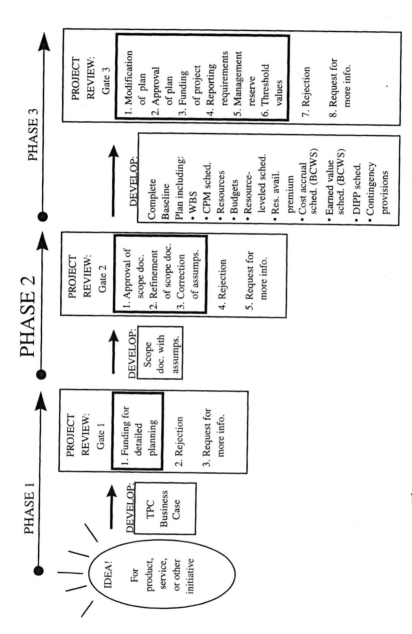

Figure 4.2 Gate 2 of the Project Review Process for Gating and Funding

resources, and budgets, we have to be able to take a snapshot at some point so as to finalize the plan. Changes to the work scope after that point must be understood as changes to the whole project plan, requiring modification of schedule and budget.

The fused memo should call attention to this scope document and assumptions appendix as representing the planned work, and then set a specific date (perhaps 2–3 weeks hence) after which work scope will be frozen and scope changes managed as formal changes to the project baseline plan.

Of course what is likely to happen to our scope document (fused memo or not), is that it will sit for weeks in the *IN* box of 90 percent of the recipients. Therefore the wise project manager will take the time to call the recalcitrant managers a couple of days before the fuse expires. Getting the work scope correct is too important to allow it to be torpedoed by a manager who takes his or her project responsibilities lightly.

Whether subject to a formal or ad hoc scope review process, the project manager and planning team must press ahead in developing the plan as quickly as possible. In the formal product development gating process, funding for the full planning process through gate number 3, was approved at gate number 1 precisely so as to avoid unnecessary delays. Similarly, in the ad hoc process, planning should continue even while the fused memo is smoking in *IN* boxes.

But then the following the rhetorical question arises, "How can you continue planning when you don't even know what the work scope is going to be? Won't that mean we'll wind up undoing a lot of work we've already done?"

There is the beauty of the planning process. For what is the next planning document our team will assemble? The WBS. What is the primary function of the WBS in a project plan? To help in managing work scope changes. The WBS, often omitted from the planning process, is the project document that puts the work scope into a format that is specifically designed to make it relatively easy for the project manager to adjust the plan to changes in the work scope.

So the planning team has a work scope document that is (1) based in substantial part on assumptions, and (2) undergoing review and refinement for the next week or two. So what do we do? We develop precisely the tool we need to manage all the changes that we know we're going to have to make. That tool is the WBS. Great, this project management stuff, ain't it?

Note

1. What is the cure for creeping elegance? Re-eduction for the organization's best people. (Not mediocre workers who want to leave work at 5 o'clock and go home. They might kill you in other ways, but not through creeping elegance!) The best workers, who tend to exhibit great pride of workmanship, need to have a concrete goal to pursue, something to replace the satisfaction they get from a well-built component. Completing their work on time and within budget may give satisfaction to some, but others may be too far removed from the *nature* of their work. The DIPP rolls in the value of their work, through its value-added, and provides a measurable way of judging its quality while incorporating the essential project aspects of schedule and cost. What's the best way to perform your work? The one that helps maintain a high project DIPP.

Developing the Work Breakdown Structure

If I could wish but one thing for every project, it would be a comprehensive and detailed WBS. The lack of a good WBS probably results in more inefficiency, schedule slippage, and cost overruns on projects than any other single cause. When a consultant is brought in to perform in the role of "project doctor," invariably there has been no WBS developed. No one knows what work has been done, nor what work remains to be done. The first thing to do is assemble the planning team and teach them how to create a WBS.

The WBS is the framework or skeleton upon which the whole project rests. Remember, the work scope is the most important part of the project, and the WBS is that work scope organized into a detailed hierarchical format. It is the WBS that ties all three sides of the project triangle (work scope, schedule, and cost) together.

Unfortunately, even when a WBS is assembled on a given project, it is often not done very well, due to the planner(s') lack of knowledge of both the underlying principles and the benefits of a WBS. Often one sees a project manager sitting in front of a computer screen trying to create a list of activities, formatted somewhat haphazardly into a hierarchy. This list, rarely more than 50 to 100 items long, then becomes the WBS for the project, and scheduling data is superimposed upon it. The fact that dozens of activities, representing weeks of work and tens of thousands of dollars, were overlooked by the project manager becomes evident later on, sometimes just soon enough to convince everyone that this project management stuff does not work. The WBS is far too important to trust to the efforts of one individual. Since a project usually consists of a wide variety of types of work, and therefore requires distributed expertise, that expertise has to be assembled during the most important phase of the planning process, right up front when planning the work scope. Capturing all the planned project work in the WBS is crucial. Activities that are omitted will not be planned, scheduled, resourced, or budgeted. One could almost wish that the activities won't be done, either. But chances are that they *have* to be. So the absence of these activities will be discovered at some point when completed work has to be undone in order to fix the omission. The result will be schedule slippage and dramatic extra cost.

The project manager can develop the upper levels of the WBS hierarchy. But ultimately she will get down to a level where greater subject matter expertise than her own is necessary to plan the details of how the work must be done. At that level, the branches of the WBS must be assigned to such subject matter experts. These experts become the "activity managers" or "project leaders," who are responsible and accountable for planning and performance of those areas of work. In this way, the WBS represents not just an organizational chart of the work, but also an organizational chart of those responsible for the work.

■ THE OBS AND THE WBS

Figure 5.1 shows what is called an organizational breakdown structure (OBS). In common corporate terminology, how-

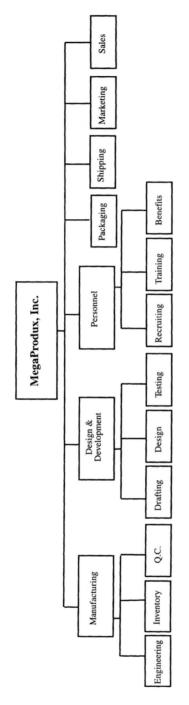

Figure 5.1 Organizational Breakdown Structure for MegaProdux, Inc.

ever, it would be called an "org chart." From the project view-point, the OBS lays out the hierarchical organization of the resources that are available for project work.

The WBS is similar, in that it is also a hierarchical format. However, the WBS organizes not the resources, but the *work* that has to be done on a project. Often I have seen WBSs that include entries such as programmers or landscapers. These are not activities and do not belong in a WBS. *Hire Programmers* or *Contract for Landscapers* would belong in a WBS; they represent work that has to be done, namely, obtaining resources. But the resources themselves do not belong in a WBS; they will be introduced to the project plan, and attached to the activities in the WBS at a later planning stage, when ABRAs are made.

Figure 5.2 shows the upper levels of the WBS for MegaProdux, Inc.'s MegaMan development project.[1]

These are the top or summary levels of the WBS. If the project manager can develop these levels and bring them to the initial WBS planning meeting, it can provide a good starting point. If not, the planning team will have to develop these levels.

Experience has shown that there are two good ways for a planning team to develop a WBS. One way is to start at the top, at the project name level, and work your way down by asking, "What are the components of which this level is comprised?" until the WBS is fleshed out in more and more detail. The other approach, which is often successful, is to simply have a brainstorming session: "What is all the work that we have to do on this project?" Each item is written on a sticky note and, after a reasonable number have been generated, the team starts grouping them together into the branches of a WBS. During this process, additional stickies will have to be filled out for the name of the group or summary level activity. Other work activities will be identified as it becomes clear that "stuff" is missing.

One thing must be understood about a WBS: There are really only two levels that are of prime importance, the top level and the bottom level. The top level is the project, its

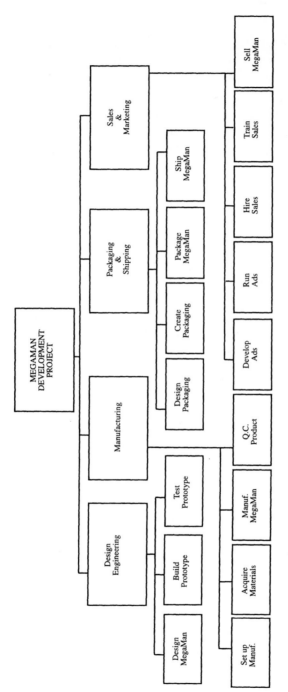

Figure 5.2 Work Breakdown Structure for the MegaMan Development Project

name, and its cost reference number, which signifies the project has been approved for funding. At the lowest level are the detail activities. These are the work items. It is where *all* of the project work gets done, where things get scheduled, and where resources get assigned. *No* work is performed at any level above the lowest level.

So what are the intermediate levels? They are the summary activities, and they serve three purposes:

1. They are a means of reaching the lower level, as each upper-level activity breaks into its components.

2. They are summaries of the lower-level activities, or "buckets" into which the information from the lower levels is poured. This means that summary reports can be prepared and printed based on the information at the summary levels. Thus how the summary activities of the WBS are designed should reflect the reporting needs of the project: what information must be reported on and which departments or individuals will need to see which reports. The coding structure of the WBS within a project management software package should be designed with this in mind.

3. They can be set up as cost accounts where the budgetary and cost accrual information from the activities below is captured and tracked. (Scheduling information needs to be controlled at a lower level than cost information. Thus resources, whose availability can greatly impact schedule, need to be injected at the detail activity level, even though the cost of those resources can be managed at a summary level.)

■ FUNCTIONAL VERSUS PRODUCT WBS

Traditionally, the upper levels of the WBS have reflected the org chart of the company. This means that the summary levels are designed to be the functional areas: engineering, manufacturing, marketing, and so forth. Increasingly, however, as companies have recognized the cross-functional needs of projects and have become more "projectized," the traditional WBS has adapted to these trends by also becoming more projectized, with the summary activities becoming components of the ultimate deliverable rather than functional departments. The differences are shown in Figures 5.3 and 5.4.

The advantage of the functional WBS is the ability to break it into chunks so that each functional department can isolate and focus on only those areas of its primary concern. The disadvantage is that each functional department *will* isolate and focus only on those areas of its primary concern. The functional WBS tends to support the throw-it-over-the-fence syndrome, where each of the departments overlooks both the need and the opportunity to coordinate work and schedules, with other areas of the project. This is one of the primary problems that TPC is intended to remedy.

The product WBS not only incorporates the advantage of presenting "the big picture" in terms of how the project will

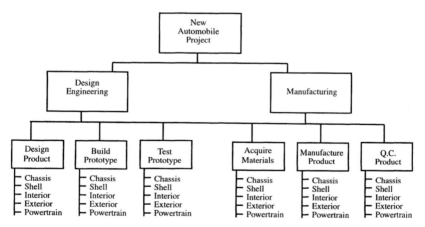

Figure 5.3 Sample Functional Work Breakdown Structure for an Automobile Development Project

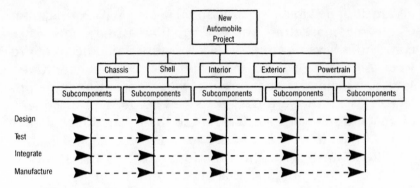

Figure 5.4 Sample Product Work Breakdown Structure for an
Automobile Project

be done, but also allows a better view of schedule and cost information by component. A customer, a project manager, and a portfolio manager all should have greater interest in seeing project data formatted through a product WBS than through a functional WBS. In a moment we will be discussing the VBS, and then we will see how the product WBS allows for clear comparison of value vs. cost.

Despite the fact that the product WBS provides the above advantages, this does not mean that a functional WBS is wrong, nor that a functional WBS is not infinitely preferred to no WBS at all.

Indeed, certain areas of a project probably should be summarized in functional format. Work that has been assigned to a vendor, for example, probably should be collected together and reported in a summary of all that vendor's work. It is a good idea to keep project management work on a project all under the same WBS summary activity. A WBS that contains elements of both product and functional types is sometimes referred to as a hybrid WBS.

➤ Breaking Down the WBS

A question that always arises with a WBS is: "How far down do we have to go? How much detail is enough?" The answer is of course, "It depends." A little later, I give some rules of thumb for how much granularity should exist at the lowest level of a WBS. But at this stage the planning team is dealing with the initial and upper levels of the WBS. The goal for now is simply to identify all the areas of work so that they can be assigned to subject matter experts who can provide further granularity and estimates. Individual members of the planning team can probably provide substantial further breakdown even at this point. But on a large or complex project, there will be areas where they will have to rely on input from others in their departments. For example, the planning team representative from the training department probably knows that training the sales staff will require some classroom instruction, some computer-based training, and a test to ensure that all the students are capable of doing the job. The representative therefore can provide the additional breakdown as shown in Figure 5.5.

But just how all this is to be done will likely require input from the individual instructional designers and CBT authors who will actually be responsible for the work. In addition all the other members of the planning team are doubtless faced with similar issues. This initial WBS planning meeting should therefore be adjourned as soon as each and every item in the WBS has been assigned as the responsibility of one individual. That individual is now an *activity manager,* responsible for managing that area of the project.

That responsibility starts with the need to get further input from people who may be more intimate with what will actually have to be done. Typically this means those

Figure 5.5 Additional Breakdown of Training Activities for the MegaMan Development Project

who will actually be doing the work. The activity manager may want to approach each of these workers individually, or may want to organize another WBS planning meeting, only this time to plan that particular branch for which that activity manager is responsible. Whatever approach is used, the activity manager should first review with the workers the planning done at the higher level meeting, including performing a brief sanity check of the input the activity manager has thus far given to the project manager. Then the activity manager should assist the workers in completing the breakdown of the WBS to the final level of work items or detail activities to be performed. The further breakdown on the MegaMan project for the training branch is shown in Figure 5.6.

The activity manager should also begin to prepare for the next step in the planning process by getting estimates of the durations and resource requirements for each detail activity. Additionally, he should collect predecessor/successor information for each detail activity, preferably by assembling a tentative CPM network logic diagram (see Chapter 6) on flip chart paper and sticky notes. All this information, about each activity at the lowest level of the WBS, should then be sent to the project manager, either through e-mail or entered directly into the project management software package on the Intranet. The project manager should then make sure that each member of the planning team receives a copy of the complete WBS and the preliminary scheduling information.

■ CODING THE WBS

Much is often made of the coding system of the WBS, because the software packages are dependent on the coding system for printing the correct information on the desired reports. However, from a management viewpoint, the coding of the WBS is of less importance than the fact that the WBS is comprehensive and contains correct information.

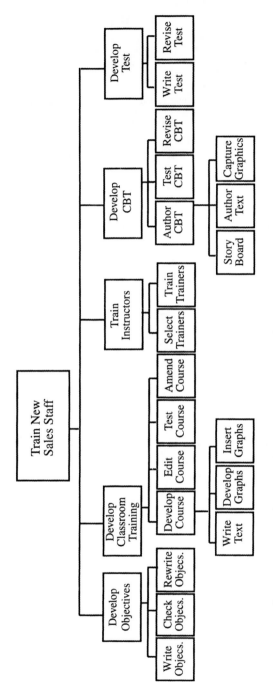

Figure 5.6 Complete Breakdown of Training Activities for the MegaMan Development Project

The primary purpose of WBS codes in most project management software packages is to denote the "parent/child" relationships, i.e., which lower activities belong to which higher, summary ones. Some software packages do handle this differently, usually by having an information field attached to each activity where the name or number of the parent is entered. Far more common is the method of giving each child of a given parent the same first names as the parent plus a unique identifier for the last name. Figure 5.7 shows a simple numerical coding system for the activity, *Train New Sales Staff*. Notice how easy it is to identify all the children of *Develop CBT* simply by the initial numbers of the code.

Some project managers like to put a period (.) between the numerals, as a place holder or designator of the level of detail. However, most software packages limit the user to a specific number of character spaces, and each period takes up one of these. Nevertheless, periods can be quite helpful, especially if some summary activities have 10 or more children. In this way, activity 1.4.1.13 will not be mistaken for activity 1.4.1.1.3.

Most software code fields also allow input of alpha characters. This can help describe the type of work occurring in a summary activity and its children; for example, GEN might designate all work to be done on the generator. In that case, all the child activities would also have to have the code designation GEN.

Codes can be used to designate other features of an activity: geographical location, vendor type, and even risk. For example, the fourteenth-character space could have a *1* entered for every high risk activity, a *2* for every medium risk activity, and a *3* for every low risk activity. In this way, a weekly report could be distributed on the progress of all activities with a 1 in the fourteenth-character space.

One more purpose that the code serves is to tie all the branches of the WBS into a single project. The coding system in Figure 5.7 represents only the WBS branch for the training activities. However, if it is loaded into the project management software package on the Intranet with a code consistent

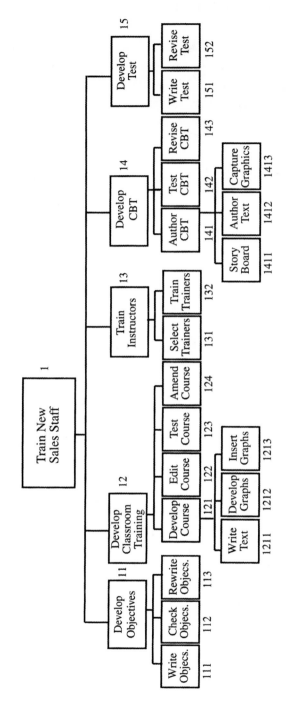

Figure 5.7 Coded Breakdown of Training Activities for the for the MegaMan Development Project

with that of the parent project, the complete WBS can be integrated through this code, as depicted in Figure 5.8.

Since most software packages provide more than one independent code field, it is usually possible to maintain one coding structure for the activity manager level and one for the project level.

Having the entire WBS integrated in the Intranet allows all the data to be summed up through the code, as well as the project manager or senior management to drill down to the level of detail they may need in order to assess and diagnose the cause of slippage or other project anomalies.

➤ The Detail-Level Activities

As mentioned earlier, all the project work takes place only in detail-level activities, or the level of the WBS where the breakdown ends. Therefore this is the level (usually called the activity level) at which all scheduling takes place and at which all activity-based resource assignments occur. At this level will be found two different types of activity: discrete activities and level-of-effort (LOE) activities.

1. A discrete activity is one that has a specific start and finish. The vast majority of activities in most projects are discrete activities. It is exclusively the discrete activities that comprise the critical path, and thereby determine the total project duration.

2. An LOE activity is one that is ongoing, usually on an on-and-off basis, throughout a portion of the project or throughout the project's entirety. Some examples of an LOE activity include oiling machinery 1 half-day every 2 weeks during manufacturing, performing Q.C. on a periodic basis, and filing periodic project progress reports. Typically, the start and finish of an LOE activity are triggered by another activity's start and finish, for example, oiling triggered by manufacturing. Therefore an LOE activity should never be on the critical path although its triggering activity often is.

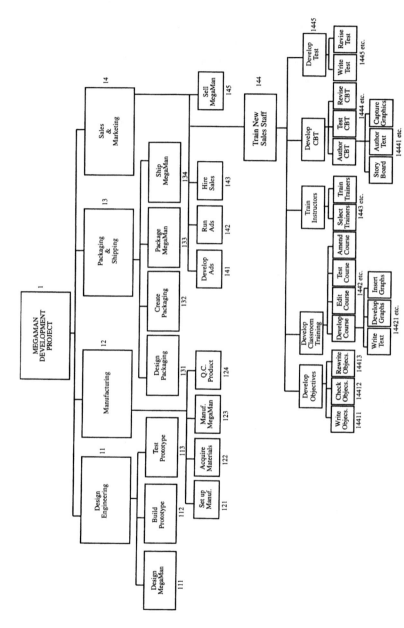

Figure 5.8 Coded WBS for the MegaMan Development Project, Allowing Integration of Training Activities with the Rest of the Project WBS

■ SIX GUIDELINES FOR DEVELOPING THE WBS

The following are six guidelines that are useful in developing a good WBS. I avoid using the word *rules* because it sounds too rigid. Nevertheless, these guidelines are more than mere suggestions—I have seen much confusion generated by WBSs that did not adhere to them.

1. Use activity names consisting of verb plus object (e.g., *Paint Superstructure*, or *Test Flexibility at Freezing Point*). First, this will make sure that the activity is really an activity. Second, this will allow the activity's name to identify the work taking place as clearly as possible.

2. Each activity should be product-oriented. In other words, its completion should be marked by some sort of component or deliverable, a tangible object that unmistakably denotes the completion of the activity. The goal is to make each activity's completion as binary as possible. An activity is either completed (product delivered) or still ongoing (product not yet delivered). There should be no argument as to what the completion criteria are.

3. The sum of an activity's children must equal the parent. When an activity is broken down into more detail, each work item planned in the summary activity must be specified in the detail-level activities. Remember, no work takes place above the detail level. Therefore to omit an item from the detail level that had been intended in the parent means not scheduling it and not doing it.

4. No parent should have an only child. This follows from guideline number 2 above. If the parent is the sum of its children, then a single child would mean a redundancy. Thus, eliminate one level or the other. (An exception is if working from a templated WBS where the upper levels are mandated by procedural requirements, e.g., a U.S. Department of Defense Contract WBS or project WBS. In such cases, single child parents are sometimes required in order to obey the mandated reporting requirements.)

5. Each activity must be assignable, as an integral unit, to a single department, vendor, or individual. This is the first answer to the question: "How far down should you break the WBS?" When more than one person is responsible for an activity, no one is responsible for it. This does *not* mean that one department cannot use resources from another organization in order to complete a given activity. However, if the work is sufficiently complex that two different departments really should be responsible, then break the single activity down to a lower level of granularity and assign each, integrally, to the different areas of responsibility. If each activity is assigned as a separate entity to a different department, then the stage is set for true activity-based costing. Each activity can be designated as a project-specific cost account within each department with its own deliverable, budget, and after scheduling, deadline. Performance of each department against budget and deadline can be tracked throughout the project, and eventually organization-wide budgeting can be driven by the resources that each department is expending on project activities.

6. The riskier the work, the greater the detail into which it should be broken down. This is the second answer to how far down you should decompose the WBS, which takes us back to the issues involved in the discussion of A-I-M F-I-R-E. Detail is one of the key methods of managing risk. The greater the granularity, the earlier it should be possible to identify and isolate a problem area, and to deal with it in an efficient manner.

➤ Two Rules of Thumb for the Level of Detail

The level of granularity desirable at the detail level depends on the nature of the project. On refueling outages in many nuclear power plants, activity durations are often measured in quarter-hour units, and schedule progress is reported at the end of every 8-hour shift. Manufacturing processes are sometimes analyzed using activity durations measured in seconds. In either of these cases, common sense says that most standard project rules regarding activity durations would not apply. However, for many typical projects, the two general rules listed below can be helpful.

➤ **Eighty Work Hours.** This guideline sets the upper limit of work effort for any activity at the detail level of not more than 80 work hours. If an activity is estimated to require more than 80 work hours, then it must be decomposed to a lower level. An organization-wide procedure enforcing this rule can be most helpful in pushing activity managers to provide the level of detail that both project and senior managers sometimes require.

➤ **One-and-a-Half Times the Progress Reporting Period.** If schedule progress is to be reported every 2 weeks, no activity should be longer than 3 weeks; once a month, then no longer than 6 weeks; and so on. The idea behind this rule is to make sure that no activity ever extends more than one reporting period without a status update, unless it has slipped.

Again, these are only guidelines. Experience, common sense, and a keen eye in detecting the riskiest areas of the project are the most reliable predictors of what level of detail is needed where.

■ THE WBS AS THE TOOL FOR MANAGING SCOPE CHANGE

The WBS is the work scope tool. It is astonishing that this blatantly obvious fact seems to escape experienced project managers and even project management consultants. I have often heard the WBS explained as: "It's the thing that allows you to get the reports you want out of your project management software." As if it were merely some contrivance developed by a software engineer.

The WBS takes the work scope and packages it into nice simple bundles, where the work can be easily visualized and even more easily modified. As soon as the WBS begins to take shape, it begins to help the project manager and planning team crystallize the work that has to be done. The "parent-is-the-sum-of-the-children" guideline allows all members of the planning team to be able to perceive items that have been omitted, often even where they have no personal expertise. For example, in Figure 5.9 it does not take either a genius or a programmer to figure out that if one is going to *Write Code* and *Debug Code*, then at some point one needs to *Test Code*.

In our earlier discussion of the A-I-M F-I-R-E approach, you may remember that the "I" in A-I-M stood for *Isolate*. Once the project manager becomes *Aware* of a variance from the plan, she must try to isolate those areas of the project that are not affected from those where the variance has occurred. The WBS allows her to do precisely that, because of the "firewalls" that exist between each work item in the WBS format. In the WBS for the MegaMan project (as shown in Figure 5.2), a schedule or cost variance in the training portion of the project can be isolated from prototyping, the Q.C., marketing, packaging, and so forth. (Of course, if there *is* spill over, that should be captured in the scheduling or costing processes.)

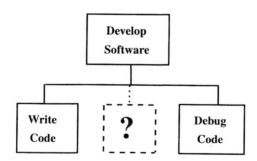

Figure 5.9 WBS Fragment for a Software Coding Project

Perhaps most important is the role of the WBS in managing scope change. Adding or subtracting work scope is as easy as inserting or deleting boxes in a WBS. For example, if we decide at some point to eliminate using new sales staff, prototyping, or Q.C., we simply remove those boxes from the WBS. If scheduling and resourcing have already been done, the schedule, resource, and cost impact of those boxes would also disappear. In other words, remove work items from the WBS and the effect of those work items will also be removed.

This is one of the reasons that greater granularity in the plan means less work to manage change during the project. It is easier to remove three or four small WBS items than to trim and adjust a large one.

It is also the reason that any project paradigm or template for repeatable projects (or fragments thereof) should be stored in the format of a WBS. Rarely is the work scope of one project identical with another. However, they may be very similar. It is relatively easy to take the WBS from a similar previous project, trim the items that are not needed, add new ones that are, and have a WBS for the new project which contains the actual data for schedule and cost collected from the previous project. This can represent an enormous benefit to companies that do repeatable projects. Several years ago I worked with a toy company that had a flagship product, a doll (call her Chrissie) that was supposed to be a fashion model and came with such accessories as handbags, mirrors, lighted ramps, and so on. The company developed a 1,200 activity WBS for the project, covering design and development, marketing, packaging, and distribution—everything but manufacturing. The WBS was further refined as the project was implemented, and the actual cost and schedule information for each activity was collected in the WBS.

By the following year, the market had changed. Desert Shield gave way to Desert Storm, and television was full of Stealth fighters and Patriot missiles and soldiers in desert fatigues, many of them women. Little girls no longer coveted fashion model dolls, but rather F-16 pilot dolls. And so

Chrissie changed. Her hair was cut, her skin tanned (Saudi Arabian sun), and her beautiful gowns exchanged for flight suits or fatigues. The handbag, mirrors, and lighted ramps were replaced by M-16, grenades, and helicopters.

But what about the WBS? The data related to the replaced accessories were now useless. New activities had to be developed for the tools of Chrissie's new trade. In addition, activities related to hair length or skin tone might have to be modified. But perhaps as many as 900 of the 1,200 activities from the original WBS were unchanged. Each of them now had actuals in terms of data, not the estimates that had to be relied upon the first year.

But what about unique projects? Surely no WBS template can help with such a project? Well, is there really such a project? I worked once with the aerospace research arm of a major university. They were interested in assembling an activity-based costing system. I pointed out the advantages to be gained by capturing and storing actual cost data in a WBS template, and reusing them when planning later projects. Initially, they dismissed the idea because "each satellite that is put up is different, so all our projects are unique." But what about the telemetry software? The hardware? The communications equipment and network? What about the testing activities? What about activities to transport the satellite to launch site? What about storage at the launch site? By the time we were finished, we had agreed that more than 60 percent of the activities they performed on every launch not only were not unique, but they had been performed again and again on launches in the past. No one had ever thought to capture and store the actuals in an easily accessible and reusable format like the WBS.

■ THE VALUE BREAKDOWN STRUCTURE (VBS)

VBS is a TPC concept that brings the scope/cost/schedule triangle of value analysis down to the microproject or activity level. It starts with the quantification, taken from the TPC Business Case, of the expected monetary value of the project. The purpose of the VBS is to push this quantification down to the level of the components and subcomponents of the project, where daily decisions are usually made without ever taking into account the relative value of the different types of work being done, or the impact of such work on the project duration.

In every project, there is work that is mandatory and work that is optional. Work may be mandatory for two different reasons:

1. The project may simply make no sense without a certain component or activity. For example, if our project is to build an airplane, we must have wings, landing gear, and a propulsion system. Now, precisely what the nature is of each of these components, and how they are designed, built, and tested, is optional. Wings may be longer or shorter, straight or swept back; landing gear may be wheels in a tricycle design, skis, or pontoons; propulsion might be by three jet engines, one nose propeller, or a bicycle contraption. But some component must be created, or our plane will be worthless, and have an EMV of approximately zero.

2. There may be a standard set by a governmental authority or senior management, that *no* project will be performed without the inclusion of certain work scope. Activities that are required by procedural standards are, by definition, mandatory.

A "product" WBS is much easier and more useful to adapt to a VBS. As we go down the branches of the VBS, we tend to get to smaller, optional, and less valuable subcomponents and work packages.

The first step is to determine which components are mandatory, and to assign such activities a value equal to that of the entire project. For the project cannot be performed without them. In the VBS in Figure 5.10, each such component has been given a value of $10 million, or 100 percent of the current project EMV.

We move next to the optional activities. For each optional activity, the question is: "What would be the value of this project if we performed all other activities but this one?"

Let us take our prototyping activities as an example. Obviously, it makes sense to group the activities for building and testing the prototype as one item since you can't test without building, and you build in order to test. What would happen if we were to go straight from design to manufacturing, without any prototyping? There may be some organizational information available, in the form of a historical database, of what has happened in the past when we designed and manufactured a product like MegaMan without a prototype.[2] If not, we should spend a few hours talking with the manufacturing engineer and/or marketing manager on our team. What *does* happen under such circumstances?

Well, when the team doesn't prototype a product like MegaMan, 50 percent of the time it makes no difference. A good manufacturing process is developed anyhow, and schedule, budget, and sales are unaffected. So 50 percent of the time, prototyping will add zero value to the project. The project would still have an EMV of $10 million without prototyping.

However, 30 percent of the time, there will be problems developing a good process. The result will be delays, scope pruning, and general chaos. From a combination of delays pushing out delivery dates into the actual holiday shopping season, and scope reduction "on the fly" making the product less attractive, our research shows that sales revenues are typically way off the original marketing estimates when prototyping of products like MegaMan is not performed. Overall, if we don't develop a prototype, 30 percent of the time there will be a 60 percent reduction in EMV. This means that, if we don't prototype, then 30 percent of the time the value of the project will only be 40 percent of $10 million, or $4 million.

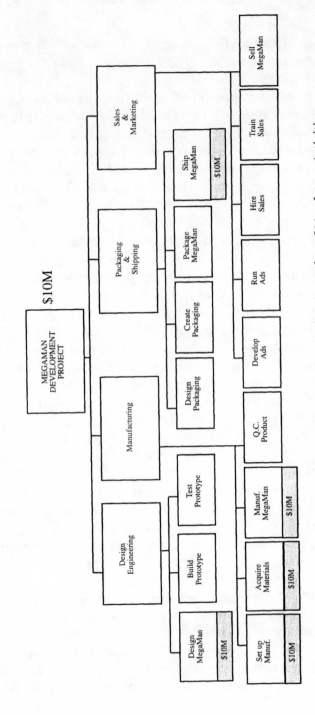

Figure 5.10 A Value Breakdown Structure Showing Value of Mandatory Activities

Now, the remaining 20 percent of the time, we are never able to manufacture a viable product. Rejects make the product worthless. The EMV is zero.

What is the EMV of the project if we *don't* prototype? It is the sum of the three possible outcomes multiplied by the percent chance of each outcome occurring. Figure 5.11 displays a "tree" diagram showing the value of each outcome.

As shown, a reasonable estimate of the value of the project if we don't prototype will be $5 million plus $1.2 million, or $6.2 million. Therefore the value that prototyping is *adding* to the project is the difference between $6.2 million and $10 million, or $3.8 million.

Let us look at one other activity, *Q.C. Product*. It certainly is optional. How much value is *it* adding? Once again the following question arises: *"What would be the value of this project if we performed all other activities but this one?"*

Again it is important to refer to whatever historical data exists, and to check with the quality control engineers. The gathered information thus shows that, 40 percent of the time,

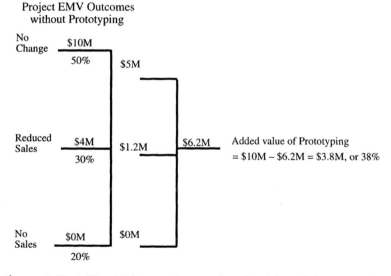

Figure 5.11 A "Tree" Diagram Computing the Value of the MegaMan Project without Prototyping

rejects will be within acceptable limits even without Q.C., and the project's EMV will not be impacted. However, a further 40 percent of the time, rejects will rise to a level where customer returns and customer dissatisfaction will lower sales by 50 percent, thus reducing the EMV to $5 million. The remaining 20 percent of the time, not only will the sales be lowered, but also injuries caused by our product will result in a class-action lawsuit that is likely to cost our company $100 million to settle, reducing EMV to negative $95 million.

What is the EMV of the project without performing Q.C.? It is the sum of the three possible outcomes multiplied by the percentage of chance of each outcome occurring. Figure 5.12 shows the calculation.

As shown, a reasonable estimate of the project's value without Q.C. will be –$19 million + $6 million, or $13 million. Therefore the value that prototyping is *adding* to the project is the difference between –$13 million and + $10 million, or $23 million. Except, of course, that the project is

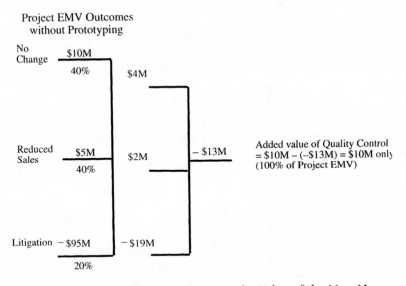

Figure 5.12 A "Tree" Diagram Computing the Value of the MegaMan Project without Quality Control

only worth $10 million in the first place. No activity in a project can be worth more than the project itself (or, indeed, more than the parent activity of which it is a part). Therefore the value of *Q.C. Product* is $10 million, since we should never perform this project without Q.C. If we don't perform Q.C., the value of the project should not be –$13 million, but zero.

This brings to us back to the issue of *Standards,* which we discussed earlier regarding the three attributes of each deliverable or component. At that time, we stated that *Standards* could be set by a governmental institution, or by the individual organization undertaking the project. Here we have a situation that cries out for a corporate standard. Q.C. may under certain circumstances have negative value for an individual project. For example, it might have to occur on the critical path, and schedule slippage might cause it to add 3 weeks to the project, worth $2 million each in irrecoverable revenues. Under such circumstances, the project manager might avail herself of the option of eliminating Q.C. The project could then finish on time, with perhaps a greater return-on-investment than if Q.C. had been retained. However, when the legal bills start draining the corporation dry, that cost will not be charged against the project budget. The corporation has a need to protect itself from such shortsighted (read "non-total systems") thinking. A standard should be adopted to make Q.C. a mandatory activity for all similar projects. As such, it would have a value-added equal to the entire project EMV, and would be as mandatory an activity as putting wings on an airplane.

As value-added is assigned to lower and lower levels of the VBS, it is good to bear certain things in mind.

➤ Although the value-added of a single child can never be greater than the value-added of its parent, the sum of the values-added of all a parent's children can be greater than that of the parent. (Indeed, a single mandatory parent could have several mandatory children.)

➤ In some cases, the values-added of children can be additive, summing to the total value-added of the parent. For example, if all sales of a product are to be made in one of two ways (e.g., telephone sales and door-to-door sales), then the value-added of these two activities should equal the value-added of selling the product.

➤ While it usually makes sense to compute activity value-added as a raw number, it should ultimately be translated into a percentage of the total project EMV. In that way, if the project EMV changes, due to market forces or schedule slippage or work scope pruning, the value-added would change accordingly, but remain a constant percentage of the project EMV, unless specifically altered.

Figure 5.13 shows what a VBS for all the activities at a certain level of the MegaMan project might look like. Notice that the packaging and advertising activities have been combined, just as the prototyping was. We will refer to this VBS during a later discussion of CPM scheduling.

➤ The Value of Computing Value

How accurate and useful is the estimating and assigning of value? Well, as the cliché goes, to some extent you get out of it what you put into it. Obviously, more analysis tends to generate more accurate numbers. But the fact is, project decisions are made all the time without any attempt whatsoever to quantify their impact.

Every day, projects are funded, expanded, delayed, and terminated. Resources are hired, reassigned, retrained, and fired. All this is usually done without any quantitative data being used for purposes of comparison between competing options. Work scope is designed and then trimmed; other activities are added, willynilly and on the fly; and, when the danger of a slipped deadline looms, resources are added or quality compromised without a scintilla of research to back

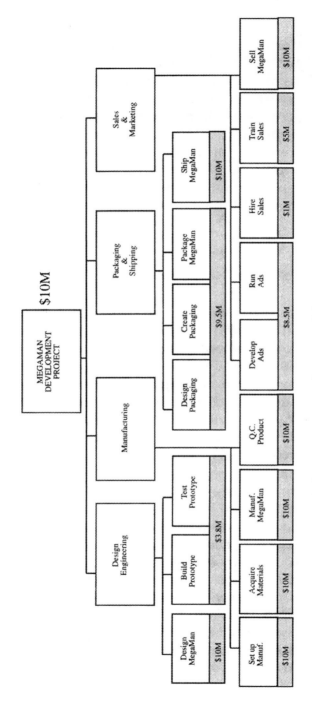

Figure 5.13 Complete VBS of the MegaMan Project

up the decision. The analogy it brings to mind is that of a poker player playing no-peek poker, where he must bet (read "invest his resources") without ever seeing any of the cards. Such games are known to minimize the impact of the skill levels of the various players, and to maximize luck. But no-peek poker prohibits all players from seeing the cards; no player in his right mind would volunteer to play no-peek while his rivals have a free view of the cards. But that is just what happens in the business world every day, and those players who take off the blindfolds have a huge edge.

■ THE WBS DATA DICTIONARY

The WBS data dictionary is the repository of the full activity-by-activity information about the project. It can be maintained in project management software, a relational database format, a three-ring binder, or on three-by-five cards in a shoebox. The important things are the order in which information is stored and the elements of the information.

The WBS data dictionary is intended for use during the project, and also as a historical database of reference for future projects. As such, the data must be stored in a way that will allow those who will refer to it in the future to find the information they need. They are likely to be looking for activities that contain work scope similar to that of the project they are currently working on. Therefore the data dictionary should be organized according to work scope, which means that its table of contents should be the coded WBS, which should be listed at the front of the data file.

Figure 5.14 displays a generic activity record for a WBS data dictionary. The information in all but the shaded areas should be assembled during the planning stage. For purposes of CPM scheduling (see Chapter 6), it is important that each activity have specified completion criteria, duration and work-hour estimates (work hours are used to measure what is

WBS __________
Activity ID __________

Activity Name __________ Other Codes __________

Parent Name __________ ID __________ Other Codes __________

Responsible Organization __________ Activity Mgr. __________

Estimates

Completion Criteria __________

Planned duration __________ Planned work __________

Actual duration __________ Actual work hours __________

Assigned individual(s) __________

Predecessors

Act. ID	Completion % required (explain if not 100%)	Relationship and lag

Successors

Act. ID	Completion % required (explain if not 100%)	Relationship and lag

Comments: __________

Estimator's Name __________ Signature __________ Date __________

Figure 5.14 Activity Record Form for a Generic WBS Data Dictionary

called *Effort*), and predecessor and successor data. Ultimately, the actuals can be checked to see how accurate the estimates were.

Typically, the estimator will be the individual responsible for planning, and perhaps performing, the specific activity. Sometimes it may be the manager of the functional department responsible for the activity. Or it may be the activity manager delegated by the functional manager to be part of the planning team. Either way, this person will have expertise in the specific type of work, will know how it should be performed, will know how much time and resources it should take, and will have the ability to commit those resources to the project. Later, after the activity has been scheduled for specific dates, if the resources are not available when needed, then this is an issue for both the project manager and the estimator, but particularly the latter, since this person has authority in the responsible department where the resources reside. If it turns out that the resources really cannot *be* available when needed, then the schedule will have to be adjusted. But the project manager cannot be held culpable for this; she is at the mercy of the subject matter experts, who estimate, and the resource managers, who control the resources.

■ ESTIMATING AND ACCURACY

Now is a good time to reflect on the issues surrounding estimating and accuracy. Scheduling project work is largely dependent on estimates. *Estimates*, by definition, are inexact. Efforts to increase the accuracy of project estimates are usually helpful, but also can sometimes backfire, resulting in precisely the opposite of the intended result, namely longer, more expensive projects.

➤ The person who is going to be responsible for the work should be the one who generates the estimates. This is probably the most important contributor to accurate estimates. The reasons for this are:

1. This person will be a subject matter expert, trained in the discipline necessary for the particular work.

2. This person is the only one who will know precisely how he or she plans to do the work.

3. He or she will usually have a vested interest in meeting his own commitment, and establishing the reliability of his or her own estimates.

➤ The work that is being estimated should be broken down to a sufficient level of granularity. This will both facilitate estimating, and provide sufficiently detailed milestones to provide early warning of inaccuracies.

➤ Estimates that turn out to be wrong should neither be allowed to pass unnoticed nor be treated as felonies. An estimate represents a commitment from the estimator to make every reasonable attempt to fulfill the prediction. Both individual team members and the entire organization depend on the accuracy of these estimates. Therefore an underestimated activity duration that results in schedule slippage should not be ignored. That said, however, we are all human. Sometimes things change, and sometimes we just underestimate what it's going to take to get the job done. There is no need to act as though this is a hanging offense. Consider instead the following approach:

You say you made a mistake in estimating, and your activity is going to take 4 weeks instead of 2? Fine, that's why there is a project plan on the computer. We will input this variance, adjust the schedule, and see what the impact will be on this and other projects, and on our DIPP and corporate bottom line. If the impact is serious, we will make other modifications to come up with the best possible solution. We can anticipate that, with practice, your estimating will become more accurate. Only next time please have enough detail in your plan to let us know about the slippage before the last minute!

➤ The *worst* thing that can be done is to punish, or even severely castigate, the individual responsible. Padded estimates are the death of good project management, and the surest way to acculturate padding across the entire organization is to crack down heavily on exceeded duration estimates. Haul just *one* activity manager "over the coals" for slipping a schedule, and from that day forward every duration estimate on every project in the organization is going to be padded, totally defeating the purpose of good scheduling: shorter project durations.

➤ Contingency planning at the activity level should be encouraged, with contingency time and cost being in the project plan as separate line items. Sometimes, depending on very specific circumstances, it is impossible to know precisely how long an activity is going to take. For example, it may be that a new computer-aided design software package has been purchased, which if it works as promised, will halve the normal amount of time that it has traditionally taken to do a specific activity, from 6 weeks to 3. The activity manager believes there is a 75 percent chance that the activity will take only 3 weeks. But there is also a 25 percent chance that the CAD system will not work as advertised, and the activity will take wind up taking the usual 6 weeks. *Both* duration estimates must be planned for, on a contingency basis, with a 25 percent risk factor for the longer duration, and a trigger mechanism, or fuse, built in 1 week into the design activity, by which time we will know which estimate is correct. But (and this is key) the 25 percent risk factor of a 3-week delay must be comprehended and accepted when estimating the project's EMV and DIPP for initial project funding.

➤ Finally, the most accurate predictor of the future is the past. A historical database reflecting the actual data for duration and cost from previous projects can be extremely valuable in the estimating process. Such databases can be purchased for some applications, for example, construction. However, databases that have been assembled from projects performed within the organization itself are likely to have greater accuracy and value. Ultimately, any imported database estimate must be checked against the reality of this specific project context. It's no use pretending you're riding Secretariat if what you've really got is a 30-year-old jackass!

Notes

1. This type of WBS is sometimes called a graphical WBS because of the graphic format. Some project management software packages assemble WBS data in a tabular format, where one tabs further in to depict each lower level of the hierarchical structure. Entering the data into the software in that fashion is fine, but it is important that the software be able to print out, preferably on a color plotter, a graphical WBS, since it is much easier to visualize and work with the data in graphical format.
2. If there is *not* such data, it may be very worthwhile to develop them, if necessary by hiring a consulting company that specializes in such studies.

Chapter

6

Scheduling I:
The Critical Path
Method (CPM)

Project management is about planning your project in a flexible format so that you can adjust to changes when they occur. Nowhere is that "flexible" format more in evidence than in CPM scheduling.

■ HISTORY OF THE CRITICAL PATH METHOD

Most project management literature puts the birth of modern project management as 1957 or 1958. These are the years in which CPM and PERT were developed in the construction and defense industries, respectively. Today the two terms are used more or less interchangeably. When the boss says: "Give me a PERT chart of this project!", chances are that he's asking for a CPM-derived network logic diagram of the activity schedule, even though PERT actually means something slightly different.

In 1964, IBM project managers developed an enhancement of the traditional network logic diagram, called Precedence Diagram Method (PDM). "Enhancement" is used here in quotes because it is arguable if it really represented a step forward. But the argument is somewhat mooted by the fact that the method has become commonplace, and is included under the name CPM in just about all project management software packages.

There are two different diagramming techniques used for displaying CPM work flow: activity-on-node (AON) and activity-on-arrow (AOA). In AON diagramming, the activity is represented by a box or node, while the predecessor/successor relationship is represented by an arrow pointing from the predecessor to the successor. Figure 6.1 shows an AON diagram, with activity A as a predecessor of both B and C, and both B and C being predecessors of D.

AON is by far the more intuitive and simpler method of diagramming CPM. With AOA, the arrow represents *both* the relationship *and* the activity, as an arrow running between the start of an activity and its finish. The arrow is therefore expected to serve two functions, and it cannot always serve both adequately. As a result, it is sometimes necessary to include "dummy" activities in an AOA diagram, that is, activities that don't really exist, and have zero duration, but which must be included in order to properly model the relationships. Figure 6.2 displays the same four-activity project as in Figure 6.1, but in order to show that both B and C are predecessors of D, we have to include a "dummy" activity to tie the finish of C as a predecessor to the start of D.

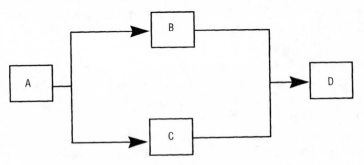

Figure 6.1 Example of an Activity-on-Node Diagram

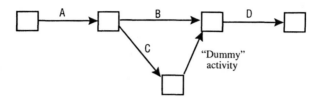

Figure 6.2 Example of an Activity-on-Arrow Diagram, Showing a "Dummy" Activity

AOA is an obsolete method that is rapidly disappearing as fewer and fewer software packages support it. It is still used in Europe and, to a lesser extent, Canada; but even there it is rapidly being replaced. Not wanting to support inferior methods, this book displays all logic diagrams exclusively in the AON format.

■ USING CPM

The fact that CPM is still so neglected and unknown in the corporate world, more than 40 years after its discovery, is a disgrace. Senior managers who balk about projects slipping, yet take no action to enforce good CPM practices, are providing a disservice to their companies.

In order to use CPM for scheduling, you need two items of information about each work activity: duration and precedence. This information should be supplied for each detail-level activity, as broken out at the bottom of each branch of the WBS by the activity manager, who is usually the subject matter expert (SME) responsible for the activity's work. With each chunk of the WBS delegated to a department, vendor, or individual, the hierarchy of delegation has been determined. Each delegate is responsible for supplying the information about the work package(s) that have been assigned to him or her.

Once duration and precedence information have been entered for every detail-level activity, the foundation will have been laid for implementing CPM.

➤ Duration Estimates

Duration estimates are the amount of elapsed time it will take to perform an activity. Depending on the type of work, the time may be measured in units ranging from seconds to months. On many projects with work planned to continue for months or years, estimating in days or weeks is satisfactory. On large maintenance projects, such as nuclear plant refueling or airliner maintenance cycles, durations may be estimated in 1-hour, or even quarter-hour units. In analyzing manufacturing processes, CPM is often implemented in units of seconds, in an attempt to identify delays and streamline the process.

Under any circumstances, it is important to remember that duration estimates are always *estimates*; they may be more or less accurate or grounded in historical data—but they always have the potential to be wrong. If they are wrong, the project manager needs to identify and measure the variance, and predict its impact, as soon as possible. Early variance identification is assisted by using short-horizon estimates. (If an activity is estimated for 10 days duration, it can take 10 days to detect a variance; if on the other hand, it is broken down into five 2-day activities, variance may show up at the start of day 3.)

If we know the amount of time it will take to perform each activity in a project, we are in a position to calculate the project's total work time. For example, suppose that we are planning to take an early morning airplane flight to another city. Table 6.1 identifies the activities that must be performed.

The sum of the durations of all the activities is 110 minutes. If our estimates are accurate, this project will take 110 minutes, since each activity must be completed before the next one can be started. Such activities, where each has to end before its successor may start, are said to be *serial activities*. One way to shorten the project would be to perform some of the activities simultaneously, or in parallel. It is then that the techniques of CPM come into play.

Table 6.1 Activities to Be Performed before Taking a Flight

Activity	Duration (min.)
Get Ready	45
Drive to Airport Shuttle	30
Ride Shuttle to Terminal	15
Purchase Ticket	15
Run Like Heck to Gate	5

Total project time = 110 min.

■ MANAGEMENT RESERVE, CONTINGENCY, AND PADDING

There is one more issue to address before leaving the airport project. Assume that each of the duration estimates is a median: 50 percent of the time the actual duration will be longer than the estimate, and 50 percent of the time it will be shorter. If we allow 110 minutes to catch our plane, what portion of the time would we expect to miss it? The answer is 50 percent. For most people, missing one's plane half the time is not acceptable. We should therefore add contingency time to the end of our project, a safety buffer which, if any of the five previous activities takes longer than expected, will still permit us to make our flight. The size of this safety buffer, sometimes called *management reserve,* can vary depending on such risk factors as time of day or urgency of the trip. A rush hour drive is likely to require more contingency; the next-to-last flight of the day may have the last flight as a back-up or contingency plan, and therefore we may feel safe allowing less contingency.

There is an important difference between management reserve and padding. Management reserve is always added either at the end of the project, or immediately before a major milestone. It belongs to the project manager and the entire project, and serves as a buffer in case any activity in the project slips. If it is not needed, it should not be used. On the other hand, padding is used for the buffer that the estimator builds in to each activity. It is the activity manager's slush fund of time or money that is usually added invisibly into the estimate and that almost invariably, by dint of Parkinson's Law (Work expands to fill time available.), winds up adding time, increasing cost, and reducing project EMV.

Notice the difference between padding of this sort and the contingency we discussed at the end of Chapter 5. That contingency was also included as part of the activity estimate, but as a separate and visible line item, for a specific reason, with a specific probability risk of being needed, and with a specific trigger date. If the contingency was not needed, it would disappear from the project plan and would not impact future activities. The chances of Parkinson's Law forcing a project delay through this type of contingency is much less.

➤ The Impact of Padding

Perhaps more than anything else, padded estimates are the spanners in the gearbox of project work. Estimators pad, that's a fact. The padding, combined with Parkinson's Law, turns 6-week projects into 5-month money pits, or worse.

Imagine that you are the activity manager responsible for *the Design the Packaging* activity on the MegaMan project. You are asked to develop a duration estimate. You talk to the individuals in the packaging department responsible for each subactivity: *Write the Text* that goes on the back of the package, *Typeset the Text*, and *Design the Graphics*. The text writer, Sam, knows from experience that his task will take about 8-dedicated hours. He might therefore be expected to estimate the task duration at 2 days. (Only the very naive would expect to be able to dedicate 8 hours of concentrated work into a single non-overtime business day.) Sam also knows that, far from dedicated work time, he will be required to switch off onto three other projects from time to time. Such multitasking is one of the great time wasters of corporate projects. Sam knows that writing speedily and well requires immersion in the subject matter and thought processes of the topic. Each time that Sam switches projects, he has to "re-tool" his brain, and this takes time. So Sam knows it is likely to take him about 12 work hours to do this job—say 16, to be on the safe side. He also knows that, with the other competing projects, he's not likely to get 16 hours in anything less than 2 weeks.

Sam also remembers. He remembers how, late last year, he had a project that he thought would take about 15 dedicated hours, and he'd submitted a formal estimate of a month. The writing, however, turned out to be more technical and complex then he'd anticipated. Then he'd been unexpectedly pulled off to work on a high priority project. (And, truth to tell, the hometown football team had been at a very interesting stage in its schedule, too!) Despite Sam's best efforts (including unpaid overtime), his 1-month estimate had turned out to be 2 weeks too short, and Sam had been chewed out by an irate project manager.

That's *not* going to happen again! If there is even a chance that this project is going to be more complex than it looks, Sam's going to be on the safe side this time. Thus, he gives you an estimate of 4 weeks.

The estimates you receive from the graphic designer and the typesetter are similarly inflated: 4 weeks for the graphics and 3 weeks for the typesetting. Now you have to provide your own estimate for the time it's going to take you to generate the overall design and coordinate and check the work of everyone else. Even though some of the work could occur in parallel, you too decide to be on the safe side. (Didn't you hear something late last year about someone in the department really getting reprimanded by a project manager?) Your estimate for *Design the Packaging* would be 2 months, except you know that the project manager is almost certain to arbitrarily shave your estimate by a third. (Well, not really "arbitrarily"; all the project managers in the company *know* that everyone pads, so . . .) So in the end you submit the formal estimate of 3 months.

You were right. The project manager trims your estimate to 2 months. Two months to do about 40 hours of work.

And it will take 2 months, too, because of Parkinson's Law. Even if it doesn't because a miracle happens—Parkinson's Law is repealed on this project, and the packaging design activity is completed in, say, 1 month—we'd like to be able to start the succeeding activity (making the packaging) a month earlier. Unfortunately, this means changing plans, often on a multi-project basis, and that is always disruptive and sometimes impossible. The project duration has been permanently swollen. There is still no guarantee that it will finish on schedule either. In fact, it's just the opposite: A corollary to Parkinson's Law is that a percentage of activities will always expand to take *even longer* than the available time. All the padding built into an estimate won't stop the human tendency to do everything at the last moment.

Anyone familiar with corporate project work will instantly recognize the syndrome described above. To summarize, projects take much longer than they need to because

➤ Duration estimates are padded.

➤ Parkinson's Law dictates that activities will almost always take at least their estimated durations.

➤ Critical path activities taking longer than their estimates always result in schedule slippage, whereas the rare instances of activities taking less time than their estimates seldom result in schedule acceleration.

Further, duration estimates are padded because the prime operative for project work is: *Finish on time! On time* is defined as the expected finish date of the baseline schedule. And therefore everyone goes to great lengths to guarantee that there is more time in the schedule that they need. The paradox is that the very emphasis on meeting schedules causes the project to take much longer than it otherwise would. (Of course, it can also cause disastrous scope reduction or quality compromises.)

➤ Eliminating Padding

The cost of such estimate padding, in terms of reduced EMV, is enormous. The pressures that cause padding must be eliminated from any company that is serious about its project work. But accomplishing this is much easier said than done.

First, all estimators must be instructed to provide estimates based on their median realistic expectations. The term realistic is intended to give pause to those wide-eyed optimists who believe that everything always goes smoothly, or that you really can spend each hour of an 8-hour day working. On the other hand, it is not intended to reflect what the duration will be if hurricane, tornado, flood, volcano, and plague of locusts all strike. However, if activity managers believe they will be crucified for not meeting their estimates, either through verbal castigation, negative performance review, or simply being required to work unwanted overtime, they will pad the estimate every time. The habit of padding, built up over years of being indoctrinated to meet duration estimates at all costs, can only be overcome through retraining. It must be stressed that the baseline plan is not intended to be a precise and accurate prediction of the future; instead, it is a flexible tool for identifying and adjusting to changes when they occur. If a duration estimate is wrong, so be it; we'll adjust. Whether under estimation or over estimation. It may not always be possible to draw in the schedule when an activity finishes early; but if you can, you do. It's a lot easier to do this when everyone understands the potential for change and the benefits of flexibility.

The cumulative padding from all the activities can then be saved and stored at the end of the project schedule, as management reserve, where it is available if any activity, or path of activities, slips. Figure 6.3 shows a project schedule in which each activity has a 20 percent padding factor built in as a margin of safety. Figure 6.4 shows the same project schedule, but with the 20 percent margins accumulated and stored at the end of the entire schedule.

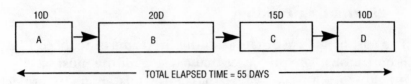

Figure 6.3 Example of an Activity-on-Node Diagram Schedule, with 20 Percent Padding Built into the Estimates

As the name suggests, management reserve belongs to the manager, that is, the project manager. There are two main advantages to scheduling the project shown in the second diagram:

1. The project team will be working to a schedule from which the padding has been factored out, thus removing the effects of Parkinson's Law.

2. If anything in the entire project schedule slips (even activities that are not on the critical path), the management reserve is there as a buffer.

It is important to remember, however, that there is usually a price to be paid for dipping into the management reserve. What would be the EMV of the project if it were completed 20 percent earlier, without resorting to any management reserve? In other words, what are the delay cost/acceleration premium values from the TPC Business Case? By managing the project at all times to maximum DIPP, both project manager and team members will utilize the management reserve only when it is unavoidable, or

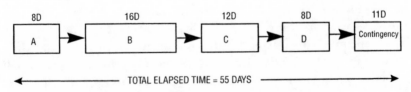

Figure 6.4 Example of the Same Project Schedule, with 20 Percent Reserve Management Instead

when the DIPP analysis shows that the delay is less costly than other remedies, such as additional resources or scope trimming.

■ WORKING TO THE DIPP

Indeed, the best lever for ridding the project of the padding mentality is a paradigm shift. One needs to shift away from the model that stresses deadline toward one that has the value of the project as its prime operating metric. If team members know that they are working on the critical path, and that every day of their activity's duration reduces the project value (as measured by the DIPP) by, say, $100,000, a new awareness comes into play. The data from the VBS will show the value that each activity is bringing to the project. TPC's DRAG and DRAG cost metrics will show how that value is being reduced by the activity's contribution to the project's overall duration. Right from the planning stage, team members will work together to optimize the project schedule, figuring out ways to reduce the duration of their critical path activities. Their goal will be to maximize that item on which they should be evaluated: the contribution of their work to the project EMV. Once implementation begins, the whole team will work to the DIPP-optimized schedule, like an orchestra playing a musical score.

■ THE IMPACT OF MULTITASKING

A second important factor that contributes to activity durations being needlessly long is multitasking of resources. Anyone who has ever worked in a corporation knows how wasteful this practice is. Yet its impact on project durations, and thus on EMV and profits, is studiously ignored because department managers want to make sure that their employees always have enough work to do. Otherwise they are likely to lose them the next time a cost-cutting fad hits the company. The one way to ensure that the graphics department keeps all its artists is to have each individual working on five different projects simultaneously. That way, graphics will be a bottleneck for every project, and it will be clear to senior management that head count cannot be reduced. Such situations are particularly common in organizations where critical path scheduling for projects is not standard operating procedure.

Of course, in situations like this, it becomes almost impossible to justify hiring additional resources, since the precise effect on the project schedules is impossible to measure. Such departments invariably become drastically understaffed. The individuals working in them labor long hours, hopping from project to project in order to keep everyone happy. ("See? Your project's coming along nicely. I'm planning to work some more on it tomorrow afternoon.") Project managers add more and more pressure to hurry up their critical path work, while the department manager, dealing with an impossible situation, reacts by creating a "black hole" department, in which there is so much pressure that not even information can escape. "I don't know when we'll be able to get to this. All my people are working on four different projects. I'll put someone on it as soon as I can, but don't expect it back in less than 3 weeks."

It is my observation, based on my years of consulting with a wide variety of industries, that every project-driven corporate organization is grossly under-resourced in critical functions on project after project. It is also observed that the situation remains unchanged year after year.

➤ Quantifying the Impact of Multitasking

All this leads to a strong recommendation: Estimators should be instructed to estimate activity durations based on a minimum assignment of at least one dedicated or full-time resource, unless doing so will make no difference to an activity's duration. For example, if a quality control person only needs to check the product coming off the assembly line for 1 hour a day, then there is no need to assume that such a resource is dedicated to the one project. But to assign a programmer, for example, to a specific software coding job for only 4 hours a day for 10 days is to double, at the very least, the length of that task. The estimator must assume that the programmer will be on the job full time, and estimate not more than 5 days. If it ultimately turns out that the programmer is only assigned half-time, then the activity's duration will have to be adjusted accordingly. It is crucial that such a lengthening of the activity be clearly attributable to the shortage of resources. This is the only way for an organization to start quantifying how much of the time being taken to do projects is a product of the way the work has to be done, and how much is due to insufficient or to multitasked resources. The first delay is more-or-less unavoidable, while the latter may be correctable through acquisition of more resources. But, in a project environment, such additional resources can only be cost-justified by quantifying the cumulative effects of their shortage on projects. Without the practice of assuming a dedicated resource for each activity, the inefficiencies of multitasking will remain invisible.

■ PRECEDENCE

A few years ago, while speaking on another subject to a management group at American Power Conversion in Rhode Island, I mentioned CPM in passing. I was asked to give a definition:

> *CPM is a technique for scheduling a project so that it takes the least possible amount of time, by doing all the activities at the same time, right up front . . . except the stuff you can't!*

The phrasing brought the intended laughs, but it also described exactly the way that CPM is intended to work. CPM allows you to determine the fastest way of doing the project, based on a given set of duration estimates, and assuming no resource bottlenecks. The aspect of CPM that tells you precisely what it is that you can't do at the same time, right up front, is *precedence* (sometimes called dependencies).

Precedence is the logical order in which the activities must occur. For example, in the airport project, we must drive to the airport shuttle before we can take the shuttle to the terminal. It is important to note that it is the nature of the work itself that determines the order of the activities in the CPM schedule. We must screw in the hinges before we can hang the door; we must erect all four walls before we can put on the roof. Resource bottlenecks or cost issues will be considered at a later planning stage, not during CPM scheduling.

Precedence determines an activity's place in a project schedule on the basis of two types of activity:

> ➤ A *predecessor activity* is one that must occur immediately before another activity. Driving to the shuttle is a predecessor of riding the shuttle bus to the terminal.

> ➤ A *successor activity* must occur immediately after its predecessor. Running to the gate is a successor of purchasing the ticket.

By arranging the five activities from the airport project into an AON diagram, the project resembles Figure 6.5.

In the definitions of *predecessor activity* and *successor activity*, note the use of the terms "immediately before" and "immediately after." In the airport project, for example, activity A is a predecessor of activity B, but not of C, D, and E. Similarly, activity E is a successor of activity D, but not of A, B, and C. The fact that an item of work must occur before a given activity does not necessarily make it a predecessor— for project management purposes, it is only the *immediately preceding*, and *immediately succeeding*, items that are relevant. When a project management software package asks

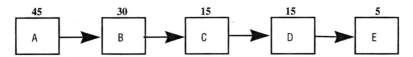

Figure 6.5 An Activity-on-Node Diagram of Airport Project

you to enter the predecessors of a certain activity, you are only required to enter the immediate predecessors.

■ ANCESTORS AND DESCENDANTS

The TPC methodology, however, requires us to define two new terms: *ancestor* and *descendant*.

> ➤ An *ancestor* is an activity that is on the same path as a given activity, and which must occur before it, but not *immediately* before it. In other words, an ancestor activity is a predecessor of a predecessor of a predecessor of a . . .

> ➤ A *descendant* is an activity that is on the same path as a given activity, and which must occur after it, but not *immediately* after it. In other words, a descendant activity is a successor of a successor of a successor of a . . .

By these definitions, in the airport project, activities C, D, and E are descendants of activity A, and activities A, B, and C are ancestors of activity E.

The terms ancestor and descendant help to denote which activities share the same path, and will therefore be indispensable in helping to define and quantify TPC's new CPM metric, DRAG.

■ CPM LOGIC DIAGRAMS WITH PARALLEL ACTIVITIES

While projects with serial activities do occur all the time in our personal lives (laundry, spring cleaning, etc.), they are a rarity in business, where there are usually a variety of resources available to be utilized. In such cases, we can shorten the total project time by performing two or more activities at once, or in parallel. It is for such projects that the CPM process becomes invaluable, since it is precedence that determines which activities have to wait for the conclusion of which other activities. Given the logical precedence constraints, CPM helps to determine the shortest possible time the project will take, and what the schedule is for each activity.

In order to explain all the nuts and bolts of the CPM methodology, I will create a project that consists of just five activities. That will be sufficient to show how everything is designed to work, without needlessly complicating the picture with other activities. The five activities, presented in Table 6.2, are as follows.

It is easy to see that the sum of the durations of the five activities is 105 days. (For purposes of this example, we shall deal in days. However, in general, we can simply regard the durations as being in generic units of time: hours, 5-day weeks, 7-day weeks, months, etc. Whatever is true for days will also be true for any other time unit.) But the project does not necessarily have to take 105 days. If, for example, we could start all five activities immediately and perform them simultaneously, the project would take only as long as the longest activity, that is, 40 days. To determine which activities can be started immediately, and which must wait for

Table 6.2 Activity Durations in 5 Activity Projects

ID	Activity	Duration
A	Design Product	20D
B	Manufacture Product	40D
C	Design Packaging	10D
D	Create Packaging	20D
E	Package and Ship Product	15D

other work to be completed first, we must determine our precedence relationships.

It is reasonable to assume that we can neither manufacture the product nor design the packaging until completing activity A, *Design Product*. Thus A is a predecessor of both B and C, both of which can start as soon as A is finished, but not a second earlier. Similarly, we must *Design Packaging*, activity C, before we can *Create Packaging*, activity D. And we must both *Manufacture Product*, activity B, and *Create Packaging*, activity D, before we can *Package and Ship Product*, activity E.

Based on this information, we can denote the predecessors and successors as shown in Table 6.3.

From this table one can see the following:

➤ Activity A has no predecessors. Such an activity is sometimes called a *source* activity.

➤ Activity E has no successors. Such an activity is sometimes called a *sink* activity.

With this information, we can chart the workflow of the project. Duration estimates allow us to turn such a flow chart into an AON diagram (Figure 6.6).

This diagram shows two separate paths through the project: ABE and ACDE. Both paths must be completed in order to finish the project, therefore the project will take as long to complete as whichever is the longer path.

Table 6.3 Predecessors and Successors

ID	Activity	Duration	Predecessors	Successors
A	Design Product	20D	—	B,C
B	Manufacture Product	40D	A	E
C	Design Packaging	10D	A	D
D	Create Packaging	20D	C	E
E	Package and Ship Product	15D	B,D	—

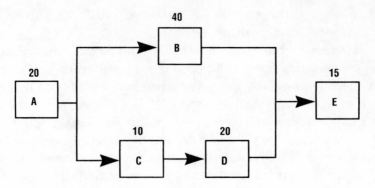

Figure 6.6 An Activity-on-Node Diagram with Durations

Thus comes the definition *critical path*. It is the longest path of activities through the project, and it is critical for three reasons:

➤ The longest path determines the length of the project.

➤ Any delays on the longest path makes the project even longer.

➤ If we want to shorten the project, we must do so by shortening the longest path.

Let's add the durations of the activities on each path:

Path ABE = 20D + 40D + 15D   = 75D
Path ACDE = 20D + 10D + 20D + 15D = 65D

If this is our schedule, the project will take 75 days and path ABE is the critical path.

■ THE FORWARD AND BACKWARD PASSES

All this seems very simple when dealing with just five activities and two paths. But what if the project were even a medium-sized one—say, 400 activities and 150 paths—how would we figure out the schedule and critical path?

When I ask this question in my seminars, the answer I invariably get it is: "Use a computer!" But using a tool when you have no idea how it works is a dangerous route to travel. You will have no idea if the answers you get are the right ones. Especially since in this case the term *right* is relative. To get the best results from CPM software, you have to understand what this software is programmed to do.

Project management software packages contain an algorithm designed to calculate what are called the *forward and backward passes*. The output of this algorithm is the traditional CPM schedule, with the total project duration. In addition, the algorithm provides crucial scheduling information about each activity.

➤ The forward pass traces the precedence logic from the first activity to the last, and calculates the early start (ES) and early finish (EF) of each activity. These are the earliest dates that any activity can start or finish, based on the logic and durations.

➤ The backward pass traces the precedence logic from the last activity to the first, and calculates the late start (LS) and late finish (LF) of each activity. These are the latest dates that any activity can start or finish, without delaying the end of the project.

By convention, this information is displayed in each activity box in the manner shown in Figure 6.7.

DURATION

ES		EF
	ID	
LS		LF

Figure 6.7 An Activity Box with Durations and Schedule Data

➤ Formula for the Forward Pass

The forward pass consists of five steps:

Step 1: Assume that each activity will start first thing in the morning and finish at the end of its final day. (Or, for 5-day weeks, 8 A.M. Monday and 5 P.M. Friday. Or, for hours, 00:01 and 59:59.)

Step 2: Set the early start for the first activity to Day 1 (Figure 6.8).

Step 3: Compute the early finish for the first activity by adding its duration to its early start, and then subtracting 1 (Figure 6.9).

$$EF = ES + Duration - 1$$

You would subtract because, by convention, in step 1 we set the first day of the project (really day 0) as day 1. Try the formula on an activity that starts on Monday and has a 3-day duration. When will it finish? On Wednesday, day 3, not Thursday, day 4, as would be the case if we simply added the duration (3) to the early start (1).

Step 4: A successor activity can start the morning after its predecessor ends. Therefore:

$$ES = Predecessors' \ latest \ EF + 1$$

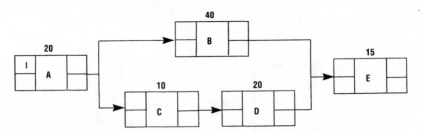

Figure 6.8 Activity-on-Node Diagram of the Product Development Project after STEP 2 of the Forward Process

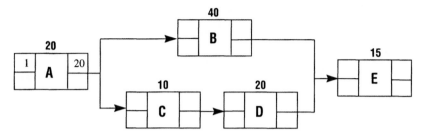

Figure 6.9 Activity-on-Node Diagram of the Product Development
Project after STEP 3 of the Forward Process

In other words, if an activity has more than one predecessor, use the latest early finish among its predecessors. Both B and C have only a single predecessor, A, and so can start the morning after A finishes. However, the specific phrasing of step 4 will have relevance when we get to activity E, which has both B and D as predecessors. Both will have to finish before E can start. On the forward pass, it is the latest finish date of the predecessor that pushes the schedule out (Figure 6.10).

Step 5: Calculate the early starts and finishes for the remaining activities, as shown in Figure 6.11, by successively applying steps 3 and 4 of the formula:

$$EF = ES + Duration - 1$$

$$ES = Predecessors'\ latest\ EF + 1$$

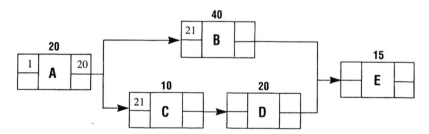

Figure 6.10 Activity-on-Node Diagram of the Product Development
Project after STEP 4 of the Forward Process

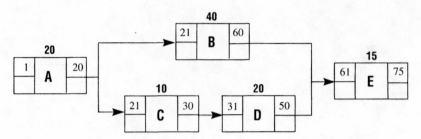

Figure 6.11 Completed Forward Pass of the Product Development Project

The forward pass gives the project duration of 75 days, just as we had computed by adding up the durations on each path. But the forward pass can be quickly calculated, even manually, for much larger and more complex networks than one could ever do by adding up each path. Even more important, the forward pass also provides other vital information: the earliest dates that each activity can start and finish. This tells us the earliest moment that we'll need the resources for each activity. There is no point whatever in reserving the resources for activity D for day 20; we can't use them until, at the earliest, day 31.

Now we'd like to know what is the latest that each activity can start or finish while still allowing us to finish the project in 75 days. This is the output of the backward pass.

➤ **Formula for the Backward Pass**

The backward pass also consists of four steps:

Step 1: Since we don't want to delay the completion of the project, set the late finish of the final activity equal to its early finish (Figure 6.12).

Step 2: Calculate the late start for the last activity by subtracting its duration from its late finish and then adding 1 (Figure 6.13).

$$LS = LF - Duration + 1$$

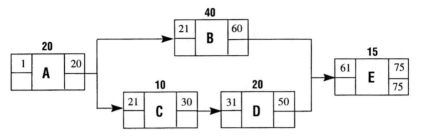

Figure 6.12 Activity-on-Node Diagram of the Product Development Project after STEP 1 of the Backward Process

Step 3: Each activity must finish the day before its successor can start. Therefore to calculate the late finish for each activity, subtract 1 from the earliest late start of its successors.

$$LF = \text{Successors' earliest LS} - 1$$

Step 4: Go backward through the network, repeating steps 2 and 3 (Figure 6.14).

Each of D, C, and B has only a single successor, and so must finish the afternoon before the morning that the successor must start. Activity A, however, has both B and C as successors. A must finish before either can start. C can start as late as day 31 without delaying the end of the project. But B *must* start no later than day 21 if it is to finish by day 60 so that E can start no later than day 61,

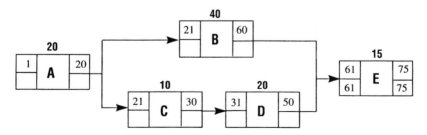

Figure 6.13 Activity-on-Node Diagram of the Product Development Project after STEP 2 of the Backward Process

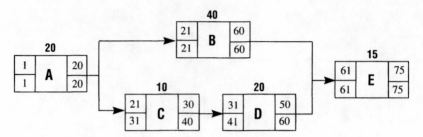

Figure 6.14 Complete Activity-on-Node Diagram of the Product Development Project

and the project finish no later than day 75. On the backward pass, it is the earlier alternative that constrains the late finish dates.

With the backward pass completed, we now know the latest that any activity can occur without delaying the projected 75-day duration. This allows for three additional important items of information:

1. We know the latest dates that we will need the resources for each activity.

2. If this were the final schedule, we'd know that if any activity either started or finished after its late date, we would be running late, and remedies would have to be sought in order to get back on schedule. In other words, an early warning system would be in place: as early as day 21, if activity A is still ongoing, we would know that, unless something changes, the project is going to be late.

3. We have also identified our critical path. It is:

   ➤ The longest path through the project.

   ➤ The path where no slippage can occur without delaying the project, because the early and late dates are identical.

➤ The path where, if we want to shorten the project, we need to change something.

■ TOTAL FLOAT

Total float (TF), also sometimes called total slack (TS), is the quantification of how much an activity can slip without delaying the end of the project. It is calculated using the formula:

$$TF = LF - EF$$

Based on this formula, total float for each activity in the product development project would be as shown in Figure 6.15.

Activities A,B, and E all have total float of 0, with identical early and late finish dates. This makes sense, since this is the critical path. Activities C and D each have total float of 10 days. That means that each can slip up to 10 days without delaying the end of the project. This is useful information to have when assigning resources; unlike the critical path activities, C and D are somewhat flexible in terms of when they need their resources. They can use them as early as their early starts, but can also wait until their late starts 10 days later without delaying the end of the project. In this way, the total float metric is used by project management software during the resource leveling process, discussed in Chapter 9.

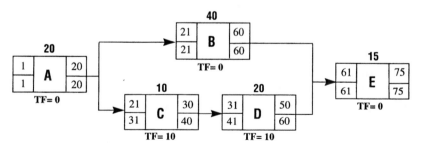

Figure 6.15 Complete Activity-on-Node Diagram of the Product Development Project Showing Total Float for Each Activity

It is important to note that total float is not additive along a path. The fact that both C and D have 10 days total float does not mean that each can be delayed for 10 days, up to a total of 20 days. Whatever total float gets used up by activity C is deducted from the total float available to activity D. The total float of the path CD is only 10 days.

■ FREE FLOAT

Both activity C and activity D have 10 days of total float. But is there any difference between the type of total float in activity C and that in activity D? In other words, is there any difference in the implications of allowing activity C to slip versus allowing activity D to slip?

If activity D starts on day 31, its early start date, but takes an extra 10 days, so that it does not finish until the end of day 60, does it delay the end of the project? The answer is no; the 10 days are total float and therefore, by definition, the end of the project is not delayed. Does such a delay in activity D impact the schedule of anything else in the project? Again the answer is no; activity E is not scheduled to start until day 61 anyway. The project is completely unaffected by D's 10-day slippage.

Now imagine that it's activity C that starts on time, day 21, but takes an extra 10 days and does not finish until day 40. Does this slippage delay the end of the project? Again no—it's total float. But does it impact this schedule or anything else in the project? This time the answer is yes. The effect of activity C slipping is that activity D can no longer start and finish on its early dates; the 10-day slippage pushes D to its late start and finish. If this were the working schedule, the resources for activity D might be assigned for days 31 through 40. On day 41, those resources might go away, assigned perhaps to a different project. Thus activity D might wind up slipping even more, delaying the end of the project. So even though activity C has total float, its slippage could indirectly impact the end of the project.

The difference between activity D and activity C is that D's total float is of a type called *free float* (FF). Whereas total float is defined as the amount of time an activity can slip without delaying the end of the project, free float (or free slack), is defined as the amount of time an activity can slip without delaying the early start of any other activity.

It is calculated for each activity by the following formula:

FF {Activity X} = Successors' earliest ES – EF {Activity X} – 1

Using this formula, we can compare the free float for activity C with that of activity D:

FF {Activity C} = 31 (Successors' earliest ES)
  – 30 (EF {Activity C}) – 1 = 0

FF {Activity D} = 61 (Successors' earliest ES)
  – 50 (EF {Activity D}) – 1 = 10

So activity D has 10 days free float, whereas activity C has none.

■ SCHEDULING CONSTRAINTS

Will the critical path activities always have total float of zero? The answer is no. For example, at the start of the project, we may get ahead of schedule. In that case, the critical path will have positive total float. Or we may fall behind schedule. In such an event, our critical path will have negative total float (sometimes described as being supercritical). In fact, we may have three or four paths with negative total float. In that case, which would be our critical path? There are two correct answers:

1. The path whose total float is the most negative would be the longest path to the end of the project, and therefore would be the critical path.

2. All the paths that have negative total float will delay the project beyond its planned duration unless we do something about them, and therefore all can be regarded as critical.

Both interpretations are valid and useful.

But what about before the project starts, at this initial stage of the planning process? When we complete our first forward and backward passes, will the total float on the critical path always be zero? Not necessarily.

The reason is that sometimes calendar-based considerations take priority over precedence logic. For example, a new union contract, climactic changes, or a global meeting, may make it desirable that a certain activity occur, or not occur, on certain dates. Most project management software contains the functionality for the project manager to enter schedule constraints that override precedence relationships in CPM scheduling.

There are three types of schedule constraint:

1. **NET or no earlier than.** This prevents an activity from being scheduled to start (or finish) before a specific calendar date. For example, if your project might require you to sail through the Caribbean in September, you might want to put an NET constraint to delay the trip until October 15, after the hurricane season.

2. **NLT or no later than.** A union contract may expire on June 30, with potential for a strike. In that case, you may want to make sure certain work gets performed before then.

3. **ON.** This one means what it says. The global marketing meeting for this project has been planned for the

week of September 15. Flights have been booked, hotel rooms reserved, and so on. This activity must occur that week, even if the product isn't ready.

What effect could the use of one of these constraints have on the critical path? It could put total float onto the critical path prior to the point of an ON or NET constraint. If our sailing activity could start in September, but we aren't going to start until October 16, every activity on the path prior to that point will have total float added to it. Would it still be the critical path, even if it has total float? I think so! Some software packages, which define the critical path as the path without positive float, will say that, in the above case, the critical path suddenly appears on October 16. But that path has always been the longest one (with the constraint, it's even longer), and therefore is the critical path throughout the project.

Of course, an ON or NLT constraint can also cause a path to have negative total float.

■ USING CPM TO OPTIMIZE THE SCHEDULE

The above calculations of the forward and backward passes are exactly what a software package does when it is commanded to compute a CPM schedule. And, all too often, the project manager accepts this first version as *the* schedule, and the next step becomes to assign resources. This is because she has forgotten that the "M" in CPM stands for method. The reality is that the first network is only the tentative schedule, giving just the data to implement the method fully. Once the initial CPM schedule has been computed and a logic diagram produced, the project manager is in a position to use CPM and the logic diagram, to save time and money. If, for instance, we want to shorten the project duration, we now know where to start: the critical path.

Thus there are two ways of trying to shorten a project:

1. **Remove an activity from the critical path.** We can do this by finding a way to make it no longer dependent on its predecessor. For example, if in the product development project we could find a way of making activity E no longer a successor of B, we could remove it from the path and thus shorten the project.

2. **Shorten the duration of an activity on the critical path.** There are three different ways of doing this:

   ➤ Use more resources (or make them work more hours).

   ➤ Use different resources (a backhoe instead of 10 laborers with shovels, or a CAD system instead of a draftsperson).

   ➤ Cut scope. (This is often done, but invisibly, and with no computation of what effect it will have on the project's EMV.)

But the question is: Where should we add these resources? Where should we cut scope? What will the effect be of such actions on the schedule, cost, and EMV of the project? For this we need TPC metrics.

■ DRAG

If one is using traditional project management software, the data that it will compute for you are those described above: It will give the project duration, and the early and late starts and finishes of each activity. It will also show you the critical path.

If an activity is not on the critical path, the software will quantify the amount by which it is removed from the critical path by calculating total float. Most software packages will also calculate the much less important, but still useful, free float measurement.

But what if an activity is on the critical path? What will the software tell you about it? What kind of quantification will it give you? It will tell you that its total float is zero, which is tantamount to repeating that it's on the critical path. That's all that it will tell you!

Now here is the question: Which is more important, activities that are ON the critical path or those that are OFF?

The answer, of course, is those that are on the critical path. Yet, when an activity is off the critical path, the software gives you all kinds of quantifications. For the really important activities, the software tells you ZERO!

Other than quantifying the total duration of the project and identifying the critical path, the *most* important item of scheduling information that the project manager needs is: How much time is each activity adding to the project duration? But about this, all commercially available project management software is silent.

Devaux's Removed Activity Gauge (DRAG), is the quantification of the amount of time each activity is adding to the project. It is the opposite of total float, in that total float is always located off the critical path, and is the amount of time an activity can be delayed before it becomes part of the critical path (with total float of 0). DRAG is

➤ Only on critical path activities, and

➤ The amount of time an activity can be shortened before it has a DRAG of zero (and another path becomes critical).

It is a quantification of the amount of time that an activity is adding to a project's duration. Alternatively, it is the amount of time that potentially can be saved by removing an activity from the project, or by reducing an activity's duration to zero.[1]

➤ Computing DRAG

Take the network diagram from the product development project (Figure 6.16). Which critical path activities are adding how much time? Alternatively, how much time could be saved by eliminating each activity, or reducing its duration to zero?

Immediately we can see that activities C and D are adding absolutely no time to the project—they are off the critical path and each has 10 days of total float. We would save no time by either shortening or eliminating C or D.

On the other hand, we can save time by shortening any of the critical path activities. How much? Well, if we shorten activity A, we will shorten both paths, and thus the entire project. The same is true of activity E. However much time we reduce either of these activities by, we will shorten the project by that much. The maximum amount that we can shorten an activity is limited by its duration—you can't shorten an activity by 3 weeks if it's only 2 weeks long. Thus the DRAG of activities A and E are their durations:

$$A = 20 \text{ and } E = 15$$

Activity B is also on the critical path, and has a duration of 40 days—longer than A and E put together. On the surface, it would seem that such an activity would be adding a lot of time to the project, and offer a good opportunity to reduce

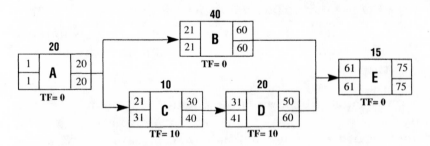

Figure 6.16 Diagram of the Product Development Project

the total duration. But activity B is actually adding less time to the project than either A or E—it's only adding 10 days. Why? Because, as the network diagram clearly shows, once the duration of B is reduced by 10, to 30 days, the project will be 65 days long, and the path through C and D will also become critical. If you keep reducing B, all the way down to 0 days, you will gain no additional time—the project will remain 65 days long, with ACDE as the critical path, and activity B will merely accumulate total float.

What is it that limits the DRAG, or the amount of time that can be gained, on activity B? Not its duration of 40 days, but the total float of the parallel path. The 10 days of total float on activities C and D represents the amount of time that can be gained on the critical path activities in parallel with C and D before that critical path changes.

The formula for computing DRAG on a simple critical path network schedule is as follows:

1. If an activity is off the critical path, its DRAG = 0.

2. If an activity is on the critical path *and* has nothing else in parallel, its DRAG = its duration.

3. If an activity is on the critical path *and* has other activities in parallel, its DRAG = *either* its duration *or* the total float of the parallel activity with the *least* total float, *whichever is less.*

To illustrate part 3 of this formula, look at an example of a network diagram in which there are not one, but two, paths parallel to the critical path, as shown in Figure 6.17.

The addition of activity F, with a duration of 35 days and 5 days of total float, means that if the duration of activity B were reduced by 10 days, to 30 days, before ACDE can become critical, AFE will; ACDE would wind up with 5 days of total float. This is what is meant by a saying that the DRAG of a critical path activity is limited to the total float of the parallel activity with the least total float.

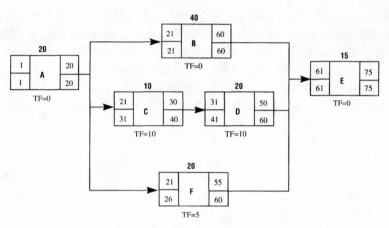

Figure 6.17 Network Diagram of a Project with Two Non-Critical
Parallel Paths

Now look at Figure 6.18. Activity B has been divided into
two activities: B and B'. The sum of these two activities is still
40 days, so the total project duration and the total float of
activities C and D remains 10 days. But this time the duration of activity B is 38 days and the duration of activity B is
2 days. Now what will be the DRAG of the critical path activities B and B'?

The DRAG of activity B will remain at 10 days, equal to
the total float of the parallel activity with the least total. But
the DRAG of activity B' cannot be 10 days because its entire

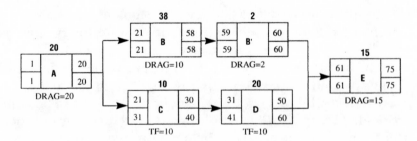

Figure 6.18 Network Diagram of the Product Development Project with
Activity B Divided into activities B and B'

duration is only 2 days. Therefore, since its duration is less than the total float of the parallel activity with the least total float, its DRAG is limited by its duration to 2 days. An activity cannot have more DRAG than its duration.

The ability to look at a network logic diagram and calculate the DRAG on the critical path activities is vital because

➤ The activities with DRAG are the ones that are pushing out your project duration, so in order to shorten your project you need to focus on the activities with the most DRAG. There is where you can expect to get the most "bang for your buck" by adding resources or pruning scope.

➤ Once a project schedule has been adopted and implemented, the DRAG will be the time that each activity is actually adding to the project duration. And, as we discussed earlier, *time* on a project is money, reducing the EMV of the project. Therefore the DRAG of an activity has a cost: the amount that that project's EMV is reduced as a result of taking longer to complete. (This, you may recall, was one of the items of information required in the TPC Business Case.) If an activity, like activity B, has 10 days of DRAG, and the TPC Business Case indicates that the project's EMV would be increased by $200,000 if it finished 10 days earlier, then activity B has a DRAG cost of $200,000. Whatever the budget for activity B's resources, its total cost is $200,000 more.

➤ Project management software packages do not calculate DRAG. At the current time there is no alternative for the project manager but to learn to compute it by eyeballing the network logic diagram.

Let us now try to compute the DRAG of the critical path activities in a slightly more complicated network, with 10 activities and several paths, as shown in Figure 6.19.

The critical path is ACFIJ, marked by the dark arrows. The other activities all have total float, which can be computed by

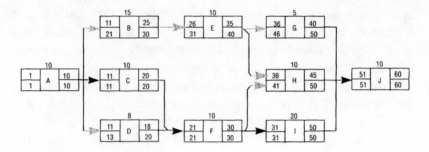

Figure 6.19 Network Diagram of the Ten Activities

subtracting the early finish date from the late finish date. This yields the results as shown in Table 6.3.

In computing an activity's DRAG, the first stipulation is that only the critical path activities have DRAG; so only A, C, F, I, and J have DRAG. The second stipulation is that, if an activity has nothing else in parallel, then its DRAG is equal to its duration. Activities A and J have nothing else in parallel, and therefore their respective DRAGs are both 10 days. The third stipulation is that, if an activity does have other activities in parallel, its DRAG is equal to the lowest total float of the parallel activities or its own duration, whichever is lowest.

This means that, in order to calculate the DRAG of activities F, I, and J, we have to determine precisely which activities are in parallel with each. This is not as simple as it sounds, it requires the utilization of two newly defined terms, ancestor and descendant. You may recall that ancestor was defined as a predecessor, or a predecessor of a predecessor,

Table 6.3 Total Float Calculations

Activity	Early Finish	Late Finish	Total Float
B	25	30	5
D	18	20	2
E	35	40	5
G	40	50	10
H	45	50	5

Table 6.4 Ancestors and Descendants

Activity	Ancestors	Descendants	Parallel
C	A	F,I,H,J	B = 5
			D = 2
			E = 5
			G = 10
F	A,C,D	I,H,J	B = 5
			E = 5
			G = 10
I	A,C,D,F	J	B = 5
			E = 5
			G = 10
			H = 5

and so on, and descendant was defined as a successor, or a successor of a successor, and so on. We can now define parallel activities by their negative, as those activities that are not either a successor or a descendant of the given activity.

Using this definition, let us determine the ancestors and descendants of the activities F,I, and J (Table 6.4). The other activities, by definition, will be in parallel.

Thus the DRAG of all the critical path activities (Table 6.5) is, in descending order:

Up to 10 days can be gained by shortening or eliminating A or J, whereas only 5 days can be gained on F or I (despite I's 20-day duration), and only 2 days on C (because of the total float of the parallel activity D). Therefore if the project

Table 6.5 DRAG of Critical Path

Activity	DRAG
A	10D
J	10D
F	5D
I	5D
C	2D

manager wants to shorten the project by adding resources or cutting scope, A and J offer five times as much potential as C.

Of course, none of this takes into account just what the nature of the work is in any of these activities, or whether that work is of a sort that can either be trimmed or shortened by the addition of resources. Some activities are more resource elastic than others. (Later, we will introduce a metric for the resource elasticity of an activity: DRED.) But remember, the project network that we have been looking at is only 10 activities long; if this were a real project, we might be dealing with 1,000 or 10,000 activities. The critical path itself might be 500 activities long. It would therefore be most helpful to have some simple method of determining where we should look to try to reduce the project's duration. DRAG totals listed in descending order would provide a starting point. Armed with that information, the project manager can contact the individual activity managers, the subject matter experts, of the activities with high DRAG. They should be able to answer whether or not their activity's duration could be shortened, and what the impact on cost or schedule might be. Through negotiation, compromise, and careful analysis of the impact of the delay cost on the project's EMV, a profit-optimized project schedule, as measured by the DIPP, can be generated.

Note

1. In a schedule derived through CPM, DRAG is found only on activities located on the critical path. But later, when we get to the resource-leveled or resource-limited schedule, delays due to resource unavailability can add time to non-critical activities. Then it is possible for resource DRAG to appear off the critical path, or even to cause a different path to become critical. For purposes of CPM scheduling, DRAG will be found only on critical path activities.

Chapter

7

Scheduling II: The Precedence Diagram Method (PDM)

Around 1964, an enhancement of the traditional critical path method (CPM) was developed. This enhancement has become so standard today that it has been totally incorporated under the term CPM while the term PDM has all but disappeared. Today, when a project management software package says that it does CPM scheduling, it really means PDM scheduling.

■ FS, SS, FF, AND SF

One problem with the original CPM was that all predecessor/successor relationships had to be finish-to-start; that is, a successor activity would start immediately after the finish of its predecessor. To get around this, project managers would sometimes have to break individual activities into three subactivities: beginning, middle, and end. By offering new ways of linking activities, PDM seemed to make this process simpler. However, in the adoption of the new scheduling technique, some of the more profound aspects of scheduling may have been lost.

PDM recognizes that it is not always the finish of the predecessor and the start of the successor that should be linked. That type of link called finish-to-start, (or FS, in PDM) remains the most common, and is usually the default relationship in scheduling software. But PDM introduced the possibility of other types of links.

➤ **Start-to-Start (SS).** Sometimes it is the start, and not the finish, of the predecessor that allows the successor to start. The classic example of this is a public works project to lay a new sewer pipe through town. There are two activities: activity L, *Digging the Trench* beside the road, and activity M, *Laying the Pipe*. You don't have to finish digging the entire trench all the way through town before you begin to lay the pipe. However, you can't start laying the pipe until you have started digging the trench. The SS relationship would be diagramed as illustrated in Figure 7.1, with the arrow going from the start of the predecessor to the start of the successor.

➤ If the earliest that activity L can start is the morning of day 11, then that is also the early start date for activity M. Having determined the two early start dates, we compute the early finish dates in the normal way, by adding the duration of each activity and subtracting 1.

➤ On the backward pass, we would move backward along the arrows (Figure 7.2). Let us assume that the backward

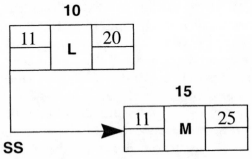

Figure 7.1 Forward Pass in a Start-to-Start Relationship

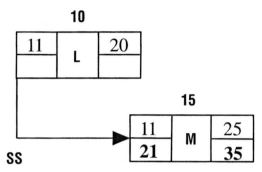

Figure 7.2 Start of the Backward Pass in a Start-to-Start Relationship

pass calculations on the rest of the network provide a late finish date for activity M of day 35. We would then compute M's late start date as day 21.

➤ Moving backward along the arrow, we go from M's late start back to L's late start and then derive L's late finish (Figure 7.3). If the latest that M can start is the morning of day 21, then with an SS relationship, that moment is also the latest that L can start. If the latest it can start is day 21, then the latest it can finish is 21 + 10 – 1, or day 30.

➤ **Finish-to-Finish (FF).** Sometimes it's not the starts of the predecessor and successor activities that are related at all; it's the finishes. One activity has to finish before another activity can finish.

For example, suppose that we are going into the citrus fruit business. We are going to truck oranges up from Florida

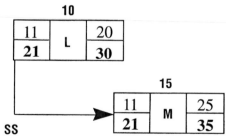

Figure 7.3 Completed Backward Pass in a Start-to-Start Relationship

to sell them in Manhattan. We are also building a warehouse in Manhattan to store our oranges. We cannot have our orange trucks arrive in New York until we have completed the warehouse. Therefore we will make activity N, *Build the Warehouse*, an FF predecessor of activity O, *Deliver the Oranges*. The FF relationship would be diagramed as shown in Figure 7.4, with the arrow going from the finish of the predecessor to the finish of the successor.

If activity N starts day 11, the earliest it can finish is the evening of day 20. The FF relationship means that day 20 is also the early finish date for activity O. Having determined activity O's early finish date, we compute its early start date as we would on a backward pass, by subtracting its duration and adding 1.

On the backward pass, we would again move backward along the arrows. Let us assume that the backward pass calculations on the rest of the network provide a late start date for activity O of day 26. We would then compute O's late finish date as day 30 (Figure 7.5).

Moving backward along the arrow, we go from O's late finish back to N's late finish and then compute B's late start. If the latest that O can finish is the evening of day 30, then, with an FF relationship, that moment is also the latest that N can finish. If the latest the oranges can arrive is the end of day 30, then the warehouse has to be completed by the end of day 30.

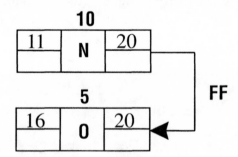

Figure 7.4 Forward Pass in a Finish-to-Finish Relationship

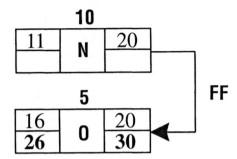

Figure 7.5 Start of the Backward Pass in a Finish-to-Finish Relationship

And if the latest it can finish is day 30, then the latest it can start is 30 – 10 + 1, or day 21 (Figure 7.6).

➤ **Start-to-Finish (SF).** This is the most unusual precedence relationship—instead of the successor's start being dependent on the predecessor's finish, the successor's finish is dependent on the predecessor's start.

We organize many aspects of our personal lives according to this type of logical dependency (e.g., we don't quit our old job until we have a new one; many people don't end the old romance until they find someone new). But there are actually at least two types of important business situations, which also should be modeled by using an SF relationship. These are "just-in-time" inventory controls in manufacturing, and

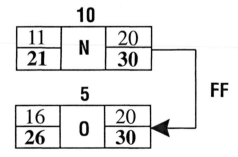

Figure 7.6 Completed Backward Pass in a Finish-to-Finish Relationship

replacement of "legacy" computer systems. Let's see how each of these should be modeled in scheduling a project.

Using the old finish-to-start relationship, in each case the predecessor activity is the one that must occur first chronologically (Figure 7.7). The inventory must be delivered before the goods can be manufactured; the legacy system must be closed out before the new computer system is started.

The trouble with this modeling method, however, is that we really want the predecessors, *Deliver Inventory* and *Close Out Legacy System*, to be scheduled based on the timing of their successors. The whole purpose of just-in-time inventory is to deliver the inventory only when manufacturing is ready to use it; we don't want to close out the legacy system until the new system is ready to go on line. So what would happen if, because of delays in other predecessors of *Manufacture Goods* and *Install New Computer System*, those activities were to wind up slipping 10 days? As shown in Figure 7.8, because *Deliver Inventory* and *Close Out Legacy System* are predecessors, their schedules would not be affected; the inventory would rot on the loading dock for ten days, and for 10 days there would be no computers.

Such relationships should be modeled with SF relationships (Figure 7.9). In such relationships, the driving event (i.e., the start of manufacturing, or the new computer system) can be made the predecessor of the activity that really is dependent in terms of scheduling. If manufacturing is

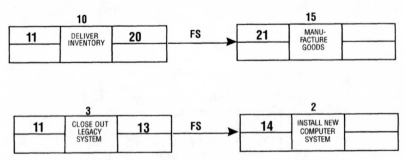

Figure 7.7 Two Projects Modeled with a Finish-to-Start Relationship

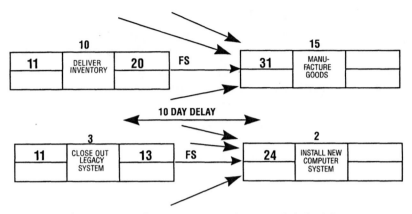

Figure 7.8 Delays on Two Projects Modeled with a
Finish-to-Start Relationship

scheduled to start the morning of day 21, then we need to
have the inventory delivered by the end of day 20. If the new
computer system is scheduled to go on line the morning of
day 14, then the old system should be scheduled to be phased
out by the end of day 13.[1]

Now let us see what happens if the same 10-day delays
occur, forcing manufacturing out to an early start of day 31 and
the new computer system to an early start of day 24. Because
the other two activities are now SF successors instead of finish-
to-start predecessors, they cannot be scheduled to finish until

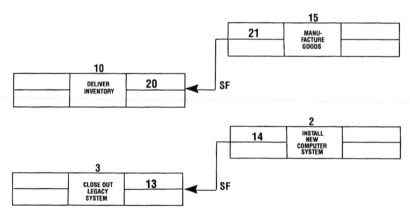

Figure 7.9 Two Projects Modeled with a Start-to-Finish Relationship

their predecessor is ready to start. Thus they slip out the same 10 days as their predecessors; the just-in-time principal is maintained, and we keep using the old computer system until the new one is ready (Figure 7.10).

On the backward pass of an SF relationship, the calculation would go backward along the arrow, from successor to predecessor. If the latest that the successor can finish is Thursday evening, then the latest that the predecessor could start would be Friday morning. This seems like the next day, but actually it is the first second of the nearest morning to the finish date of Thursday evening. Such backward passes are shown in Figure 7.11.

In most projects, 70 percent or more of the relationships can be expected to be finish-to-start. About 25 percent are usually SS, and almost all of the rest FF. Start-to-Finish relationships tend to occur less than 1 percent of the time.

Sometimes, two activities need to be tied together by more than one relationship. For example, an SS relationship such as the one between *Digging the Trench* and *Laying the Pipe* also requires a tie between their finishes: We can't finish laying the pipe until we finish digging the trench. Therefore we would also need to make digging the trench an FF predecessor of laying the pipe.

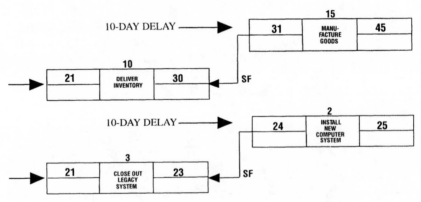

Figure 7.10 Delays on Two Projects Modeled with a Start-to-Finish Relationship

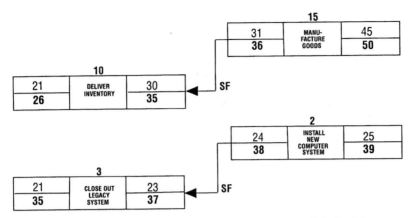

Figure 7.11 Backward Pass on Two Projects Modeled with a
Start-to-Finish Relationship

■ LAG

The precedence diagram method also introduced lag. Lag is a delay factor injected as part of the relationship between a predecessor and successor.

For example, we may have two activities, with *Build Deck* as a finish-to-start predecessor of *Paint Deck*. But, as everyone who has ever built a wooden deck knows, you shouldn't start painting as soon as you are finished building; you should wait 2 weeks for the lumber to dry. Therefore we should inject a delay, or lag, of 14 days between the scheduled finish of building the deck and the scheduled start of painting it. Such a relationship would be called an FS14 relationship, and it would be diagramed and scheduled as shown in Figure 7.12.

Such lags can be built into any type of relationship (Figure 7.13). For example, we can't really start laying the pipe at the same instant that we start digging the trench; it probably makes sense to spend 2 days digging the trench before we start the pipe-laying. This would be an SS2 relationship. Similarly, an FF2 relationship would assure that the successor did not finish until at least 2 days after the predecessor finished. An SF2 relationship would mean that the successor did not finish until 2 days after the predecessor starts.

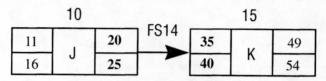

Figure 7.12 Forward and Backward Passes in a Finish-to-Start Relationship with Lag

Note that in the SF2 relationship, the effect of the 2-day lag is to cause the two activities to overlap for 2 full days.

Lag may be input as either positive or negative. Rather than being a delay factor, negative lag has the effect of subtracting time on the forward pass.

In project management software, the default is lag of zero. If the network diagram does not indicate a lag value in a relationship, the lag is understood to be zero.

➤ Two More Ways to Shorten a Project

Earlier, we discussed two techniques for shortening a project:

1. Remove an activity from the critical path.
2. Shorten the duration of an activity on the critical path.

Precedence and lag now give two additional ways to shorten a project, for a total of four:

1. Change the relationship between a critical path predecessor and successor (e.g., from FS to SS plus lag).
2. Decrease one or more lag values on the critical path.

Adding resources to shorten an activity's duration is sometimes referred to as "crashing the critical path." Techniques 3 and 4 are sometimes referred to as "fast tracking."

Obviously, not all of the above methods can work on any given project, path, or activity. A 30-day test is a 30-day test,

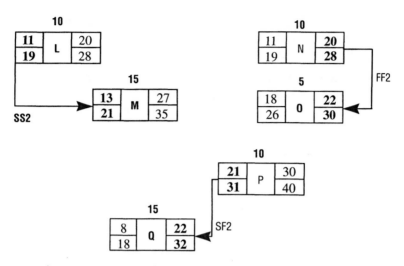

Figure 7.13 Forward and Backward Passes in Precedence Relationships with Lag

no matter how many resources are assigned. You can't package a product until you have finished making it.

Where these tools are applicable, however, CPM readily reveals the optimal ways of shortening the project. And if a TPC Business Case has been developed, the monetary benefit to be derived from such shortening techniques is measurable.

➤ The New Product Project with PDM

With precedence capability, we can shorten our product development project's planned duration.

➤ **Change 1:** We don't have to wait until the new product is completely designed before starting to set up our manufacturing lines as part of our manufacturing process. Twelve days into the design process, we should be able to start setting up for manufacturing. This will make *Design Product* an SS12 predecessor of *Manufacture Product*.

➤ **Change 2:** We don't have to have the entire output of manufacturing before we start packaging. After 35 days of manufacturing, we will have enough product to start getting it ready to ship. This will make *Manufacture Product* an SS35 predecessor *Package and Ship Product*.

➤ **Change 3:** Due to problems with packaging in the past, senior management has mandated that all packaging must be approved by the vice president of marketing. This will cause a 1-week delay after the packaging has been designed. This will make *Design Packaging* an FS5 predecessor of *Create Packaging*.

➤ **Change 4:** We don't need to wait until all the packaging has been created before we start the packaging and shipping process. After 15 days of creating the packaging, we would have enough to start the process on any product that has been manufactured. This will make *Create Packaging* an SS15 predecessor of *Package and Ship Product*.

The effect of these changes will be to produce the following table of relationships (Table 7.1). The new relationships can be diagramed as shown in Figure 7.14.

With the logic diagramed, we can compute the forward and backward passes of the CPM schedule (Figure 7.15).

The schedule data that are shown in Figure 7.15 are what almost all project management software packages would give us. As we look at the CPM computations, we can see that the project duration is 65 days, and the critical path (with the dark arrows) is ACDE. Activity B, we are told, has total float of 3 days.

Table 7.1 PDM Data for the New Product Project

ID	Activity	Duration	Predecessor/ Precedence	Successor
A	Design Product	20D	—	B/C
B	Manufacture Product	40D	A/SS12	E
C	Design Packaging	10D	A	D
D	Create Packaging	20D	C/FS5	E
E	Package and Ship Product	15D	B/SS35	—
			D/SS15	—

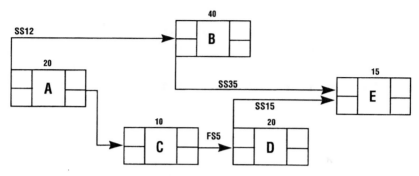

Figure 7.14 Diagram of New Product with Precedence Relationships and Lags

But this raises certain questions about the algorithm that is being used. For instance, total float is defined as the amount of time an activity can slip without delaying the end of the project. What would happen if B slipped out another 5 days? If B does not finish until day 65, it still will not delay the end of the project, at least the way it is currently diagramed.

What about activity D? It is on the critical path, and reflects this with its identical early finish/late finish dates for zero total float. But what, in fact, would happen if it slipped? Could its finish also not slip out by 10 days, to day 65, without delaying the project's completion?

Clearly, the answer to both these questions, based on the diagramed precedences, is yes. The question we must therefore

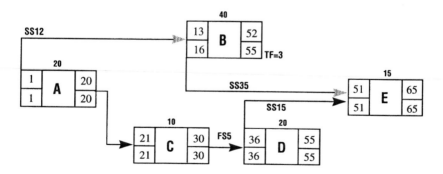

Figure 7.15 Forward and Backward Passes of the New Product Project with Precedence Relationships and Lags

ask is, do these relationships adequately model the logic of the situation? Is it in fact possible for either activity B or activity D to extend until the end of day 65, and for the project still to finish on that same day? To answer this we have to look at the actual nature of the work: Can we manufacture, or create the packaging, up until the last day of packaging and shipping?

The answer, it seems, is no. But for the moment, assume that the answer is yes. In that case, the late dates for activities B and D should be the last dates on which they can start or finish without delaying the end of the project beyond day 65. In that case, both B and D would have late finishes of day 65. Activity B would still have to start by day 16, because of its SS35 relationship with E, which means that B must start no later than 35 days before E starts, and E must start no later than day 51. So the work that needs to be completed in the first 35 days of B can only slip by 3 days. But B's finish could go out to day 65, which means that the last 10 days of B's duration could take an additional 10 days, or 13 days total.

In a somewhat similar manner, the start of activity D is on the critical path, and it has to start on day 36. Its SS15 relationship with E means that the work to be performed in D's first 15 days has to be completed no later than the end of day 50, so that E can start on the morning of day 51. However, if the last 5 days of work in D really *can* slip out all the way to day 65, then its late finish is actually day 65 and it should have 10 days of total float on its finish, even though its start is on the critical path.

In a situation like this, however, almost all currently available project management software would compute the data as previously discussed. That is because it is programmed to calculate the late finish of any activity whose finish is not constrained by simply adding its duration to its late start date. The very first project management software package I ever worked with was a mainframe number-cruncher that allowed the user the flexibility to decide which algorithm to use in doing the backward pass. That software package offered what it called the slip option. This meant that, if an activity's late finish was not otherwise constrained, it could slip out as far as it would go without delaying the end of the project. The slip option algorithm would have given day 65 as the late finish for both B and D, as shown in Figure 7.16. However, most of today's microprocessor-based packages do not include the slip option.

In our specific example, I would suggest that we need to complete both the manufacturing and the creation of the packaging material at least 3 days before completing the packaging and shipping. We therefore need to add two FF relationships, between B and E and between D and E, with lag of three days on each. The inclusion of these constraints on the activities' finishes will normally be enough to trigger the algorithms of today's inexpensive software packages to re-calculate the backward pass and to give us the correct finish dates for B and D, as shown in Figure 7.17.

Unfortunately, some of the most popular current software packages do not allow more than one relationship between the same two activities. In such cases, we may have to "fool" the software by "gerryrigging" a final milestone, called *Project Completion*, to which B and D are FF predecessors and E is an FS predecessor. There is no good reason why we should have to do it this way, nor why there shouldn't be more than one relationship between the same two activities; this is just another case of software that is produced by designers who don't really understand the purpose of their product.

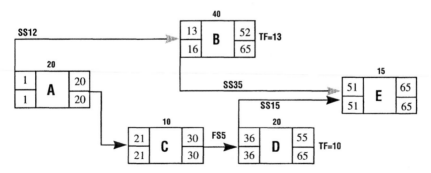

Figure 7.16 Backward Pass of the New Product Project Using the "Slip Option"

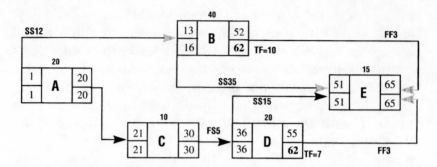

Figure 7.17 Backward Pass of the New Product Project Including FF
Relationships to the Sink Activity

■ COMPUTING DRAG TO A PDM NETWORK DIAGRAM

And now to get back to functionality that none of the currently available software has—the ability to compute DRAG. This is an even more important deficiency, because the complexities of SS, FF and SF relationships, not to mention lag values, make it very difficult to compute DRAG manually.

Refer to the PDM network diagram in Figure 7.17, with the FF3 relationships at the end. The critical path is ACDE, but how much time is each of those activities actually adding to the project? How much time could we save on any one of those activities by adding resources or otherwise compressing the activity's duration?

First think about this for a moment. Here you have a network that's just about as simple as it's possible to get: five activities and four paths. Yet it is almost impossible to figure out something as basic as how much time each activity is adding to the project duration. Imagine how difficult it is to figure out when you're dealing with even a medium-sized project; say, 500 activities and 400 paths. And the software gives you no help with this crucial information.

Since you're not going to be able to rely on your computer for DRAG data, let's see if we can learn how to compute DRAG by looking at the network diagram, which fortunately the software will give you. The formula we learned earlier for calculating DRAG was as follows:

1. If an activity is off the critical path, its DRAG = 0. So the DRAG of activity B = 0.

2. If an activity is on the critical path *and* has nothing else in parallel, its DRAG = its duration. It's pretty easy to see that activity C has nothing else in parallel; but what about D? A? E? Partially in parallel? What does that mean?

3. If an activity is on the critical path *and* has other activities in parallel, its DRAG = *either* its duration *or* the total float of the parallel activity with the *least* total float, *whichever is less.*

So what's in parallel with A? Is C's DRAG equal to B's total float of 10 days? Perhaps surprisingly, the DRAG totals of each of the four critical path activities, shown in Table 7.2.

■ WAS PDM REALLY AN ADVANCEMENT?

Computing these numbers based simply on the above PDM network is tricky for anyone but the most experienced schedulers. The reason is that the PDM relationships make the process of determining parallelism difficult. And the truth is that PDM designations are not indispensable for

Table 7.2 DRAG Totals of Each of the Four Critical Path Activities

ID	Activity	DRAG
A	Design Product	15D
C	Design Packaging	3D
D	Create Packaging	3D
E	Package and Ship Product	7D

modeling such relationships. Long before the PDM relationships were conceived in 1964, project managers understood only too well that relationships other than simple finish-to-starts existed. But they modeled such relationships in the finish-to-start format by decomposing activities to a finer level of detail and by incorporating more milestones, representing the start and finish of activities.

It is not as though from 1957, when CPM was developed, to 1964, that construction project managers dug trenches for miles along the highway before going back and laying the first length of pipe. Managers understood that the relationship between these activities would allow them to proceed in parallel. They just modeled it differently—by breaking the trench-digging into two different activities: *Dig First 20 Yards of Trench* and *Dig Rest of Trench*. In that case, *Dig First 20 Yards of Trench* became an FS predecessor of both *Dig Rest of Trench* and *Lay the Pipe* (Figure 7.18).

In PDM modeling of the new product project, activity A looks like one activity. But the same schedule could be accomplished using only FS relationships by decomposing activity A into two activities (Table 7.3).

In this case, A would become an FS predecessor of both activity A' and activity B, while A' would be the FS predecessor of activity C. SS and SS + lag relationships can be modeled in a purely FS schedule in this way.

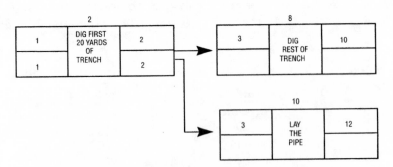

Figure 7.18 A Typical Start-to-Start Relationship Modeled Using Exclusively FS Logic

Table 7.3 FS Relationships by Decomposing Activity A into Two Activities

ID	Activity	Duration
A	Design Product Sufficiently to Start Manufacturing	12D
A'	Finish Designing Product	8D

The effect of an FS + lag relationship, such as between activity C and activity D can be modeled by changing the lag value to what it really is: An activity, whether that activity is *Watch the Lumber Dry*, as was the case following the deck-building activity, or, in the new product project, *Marketing V.P. Checks Packaging*.

FF relationships can be modeled by creating a milestone (basically, an activity with duration of 0) as an FS successor of both the FF related activities. The lag with an FF relationship would be modeled as with an FS relationship, as an activity.

By these means, the entire project can be modeled to produce the same schedule that we produced in the PDM network, but, in this case using only FS relationships. The chart below shows the relationships and new activities, and the diagram thus produced is shown in Figure 7.19.

Then, with our project relationships all finish-to-start, our formula should work as shown in Table 7.4.

ID	Activity	Duration	FS Predecessor	Successor
A	Design Product Sufficently	12D	—	A'/B
A'	Finish Designing Product	8D	A	C
B	Begin Manufacturing Product	35D	A	B'/E
B'	Finish Manufacturing Product	5D	B	LAG2
LAG2	Delay after Final Manufacture	3D	B'	M
C	Design Packaging	10D	A'	LAG1
LAG1	V.P. Checks Packaging	5D	C	D
D	Start Create Packaging	15D	LAG1	D'/E
D'	Finish Create Packaging	5D	D	LAG3
LAG3	Delay after Final Packaging	3D	D'	M
E	Package and Ship Product	15D	B,D	M
M	Project Complete Milestone	0D	E/LAGS 2,3	—

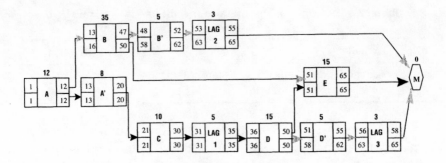

Figure 7.19 New Product Project with All Relationships
Modeled with FS Logic

Table 7.4 Calculating DRAG Through Decomposing Activities

ID	Critical Path?	Duration	Parallel Activity/Total Float	DRAG
A	Y	12D	None	**12D**
A'	Y	8D	**B = 3D**, B' = 10D, LAG2 = 10D	**3D**
DRAG of activity A = 15 days total				
B	N	35D	—	0D
B'	N	5D	—	0D
LAG2	N	3D	—	0D
C	Y	10D	**B = 3D**, B' = 10D, LAG2 = 10D	**3D**
DRAG of activity C = 3 days total				
LAG1	Y	5D	**B = 3D**, B' = 10D, LAG2 = 10D	3D
DRAG of LAG1 (really an activity) = 3 days total				
D	Y	15D	**B = 3D**, B' = 10D, LAG2 = 10D	**3D**
D	N	5D	—	0D
DRAG of activity D = 3 days total				
LAG3	N	3D	—	0D
E	Y	15D	B' = 10D, LAG2 = 10D, **D' = 7D, LAG3 = 7D**	7D
DRAG of activity E = 7 days total				
M	Y	0D	None	0D
DRAG of milestone M = 0 days total				

The first 12 days of activity A are on the critical path and have nothing else in parallel. The remaining 8 days of A are also critical, but have three activities in parallel (i.e., that aren't either ancestors or descendants): B, B', and LAG2. Of these, the one with the least total float is B with 3 days. Thus the DRAG of A' is 3 days, and the DRAG of the entire activity A = 12D + 3D = 15 days.

With the decomposed activities, the DRAG calculations for the other activities are a little simpler. C and LAG1 have the same three activities in parallel as A', and so their DRAG totals are the same: 3 days. D has been split into D and D', but D' is not on the critical path. Therefore D's DRAG is all located in its first 15 days, and is equal again to the total float of the parallel activity with the least total float: B = 3 days. Finally, we can now see that E is parallel with B', D, LAG2, and LAG3. Of these, D' and LAG3 have the least total float at 7 days, and so that is E's DRAG.

Activity DRAG totals should be listed in descending order, so that the ones with the most DRAG appear at the top of the list. Additionally, the DRAG should be related to the DRAG cost. Based on the amount that, according to the TPC Business Case, the EMV of the project would increase if that activity were eliminated so that the project would finish that much sooner. Thus if our project has delay costs of $50,000 per day, we should generate the following table (Table 7.5).

Can we spend $50,000 to shorten A by 5 days? It sounds like it would certainly be worth it!

Table 7.5 Activity DRAG Cost with Delay Costs of $50,000/Day

ID	Duration	DRAG	DRAG Cost ($)
A	20D	15D	750,000
E	15D	7D	350,000
C	10D	3D	150,000
LAG	5D	3D	150,000
D	20D	3D	150,000

➤ Generating the CPM Schedule for the MegaMan Project

In the previous chapter, we produced a WBS and then a VBS for the MegaMan project. That VBS is reproduced in Figure 7.20.

The next step in planning this project would be to assemble an initial CPM schedule for the project. In order to do this, we first need duration estimates for each detail-level activity. So suppose that we have spoken to the activity managers/subject matter experts for each activity, and assembled the duration estimates listed in Table 7.6.

The next task is to arrange these activities in the order in which they can be performed. This is a task that can often be done best by meeting with the planning team. We would write the name of each detail-level activity on a sticky note, and then arrange them all from left to right on flip chart paper with the earlier activities preceding later ones.

Table 7.6 Duration Estimates for the MegaMan Project

Activity	Duration
Design MegaMan	8W
Build Prototype	5W
Test Prototype	2W
Design Packaging	3W
Create Packaging	6W
Package MegaMan	6W
Ship MegaMan	2W
Set Up Manufacturing	3W
Acquire Materials	3W
Manufacture MegaMan	14W
Q.C. Product	14W
Develop Ads	6W
Run Ads	8W
Hire Sales	6W
Train Sales	5W
Sell MegaMan	16W

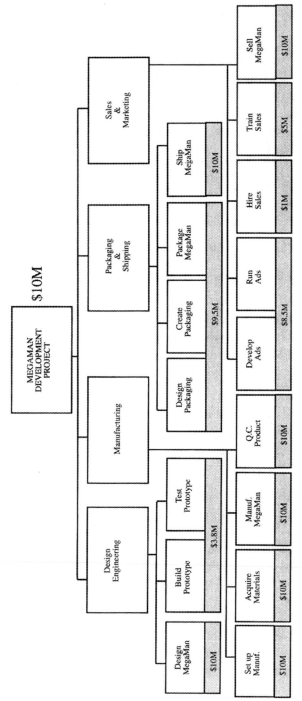

Figure 7.20 The Complete VBS for the MegaMan Project

Relationship arrows can then be drawn in pencil, and the forward and backward passes computed either by entering the data into a software package, or by doing the mental computations on the sticky notes.

At this point, some fast tracking (i.e., SS relationships) is helpful, but we don't need to obsess over it too much at this point—the schedule is going to change anyway as we optimize it.

Figure 7.21 shows a tentative CPM schedule for the MegaMan project.

Some of the logic decisions made in putting this schedule together include:

➤ Complete the design of MegaMan before starting the prototype.

➤ Have a completed prototype before the start of both designing the packaging or acquiring the materials to manufacture.

➤ Include the packaging in the advertising, and so do not develop the advertising until after the design of the packaging is finished.

➤ Hire and train sales staff. Be prepared to start selling MegaMan as soon as we start running the ads and for at least 1 week after we finish running the ads.

➤ Q.C., selling, and packaging will all be completed before shipping begins.

The resulting CPM schedule shows a duration of 40 weeks. But this is only the first pass at a schedule. Is this our best CPM schedule? And what does the word "best" mean in this context?

According to the TPC approach, *best* means of greatest benefit, or most profitable. To determine what our most beneficial schedule is, we must refer to our TPC Business Case.

You may recall that our MegaMan project needed to be completed so that the toy could be in the stores for the start

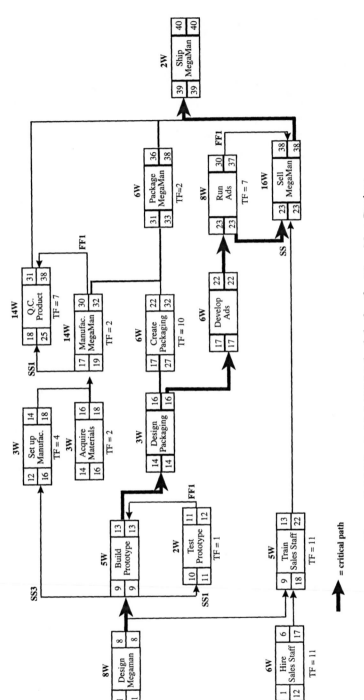

Figure 7.21 The Initial CPM Schedule for the MegaMan Project

of the holiday shopping season, 30 weeks hence. If completed by that date, the project was estimated to be worth $10 million. For every week later, the value will drop by $2 million. This means that after 35 weeks, the shopping season will have passed and the project will be worthless. For every week earlier than week 30 that the project finishes, the value would increase by $400,000. Obviously, the current 40-week schedule is unacceptable. We must find some way to shorten the project. This means examining the critical path, particularly those activities on the critical path that have the most DRAG.

Figure 7.22 shows the DRAG totals of the critical path activities.

In looking at the diagram, we can see the following:

➤ *Design MegaMan* and *Ship MegaMan* have nothing else in parallel and so have DRAG equal to their durations: 8 weeks and 2 weeks, respectively.

➤ *Build Prototype* is parallel to the *Train Sales Staff* activity with total float of 11 weeks; *Set Up Manufacturing* with total float of 4 weeks; and *Test Prototype*. *Test Prototype* has total float of only 1 week. But since *Build Prototype* is an SS1 predecessor, the first week of *Build Prototype* is *not* in parallel with *Test Prototype*. So, if we decompose *Build Prototype* into a 1-week activity and a 4-week activity, the first week, when compared to *Test Prototype*, will have DRAG of 1 week, and the 4 weeks will have DRAG equal to *Test Prototype*'s 1 week of total float. Thus *Build Prototype*'s DRAG is 2 weeks.

➤ *Design Packaging* and *Develop Advertising* are both parallel with *Acquire Materials* and *Manufacture. MegaMan*, which each have total float of two weeks; therefore *Design Packaging* and *Develop Advertising* each have DRAG of 2W.

➤ *Sell MegaMan* is parallel with *Package MegaMan* and its 2 weeks of total float; so its DRAG is 2W.

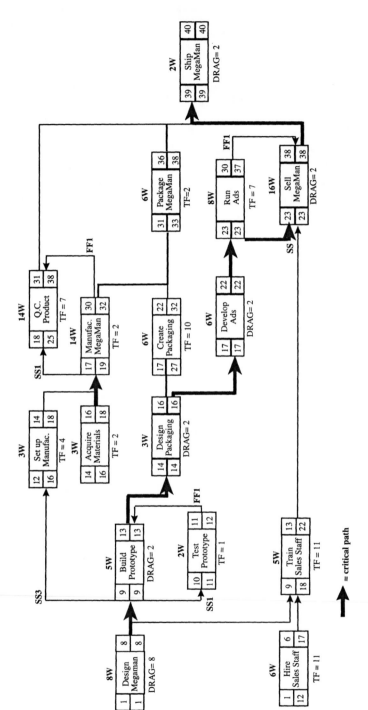

Figure 7.22 The CPM Schedule for the MegaMan Project, Showing DRAG Totals

173

Table 7.7 Critical Path Activities in Descending Order of Their DRAG Cost

ID	Duration	DRAG	DRAG Cost ($)
Design MegaMan	8W	8W	6,000,000
Build Prototype	5W	2W	0
Design Packaging	3W	2W	0
Develop Advertising	6W	2W	0
Sell MegaMan	16W	2W	0
Ship MegaMan	2W	2W	0

MegaMan project current estimated duration = 40 weeks
MegaMan project current estimated EMV = $0

The TPC critical path report should list critical path activities in descending order of their DRAG, along with their durations and DRAG cost (Table 7.7).

Notice the totals in the DRAG Cost column. The last five activities listed all have 2 weeks of DRAG. Therefore if any one of them was eliminated, the project would have a duration of 2 weeks less, or 38 weeks. According to the TPC Business Case, the project will have zero value at either 38 or 40 weeks. Therefore 2 weeks of DRAG has no DRAG cost.

However, *Design MegaMan* has DRAG of 8 weeks. If it were eliminated from the project (or its duration reduced to 0), the project would be 32 weeks long. The TPC Business Case indicates that the 32-week project would have an EMV $6 million. That is $6 million more than the 40-week project. Therefore *Design MegaMan* is costing $6 million because of its DRAG. We would save $6 million by eliminating its total duration. (Compare this to the value of shrinking the *Sell MegaMan* activity from 16 weeks to 0; absolutely no change in the value of the project because only 2 of the 16 weeks are DRAG, so that its DRAG cost is 0.)

■ USING DRAG TO OPTIMIZE THE PDM SCHEDULE

Obviously, this information is of great value in determining how to target additional resources. But for the moment, we are trying to shorten the CPM schedule exclusively by fast-tracking, or changing precedence relationships to do more work in parallel. The DRAG data is useful for this, also.

1. Start with *Design MegaMan* and its 8 weeks of DRAG. If we start building the prototype before the design is completely finished, we can change its relationship with *Build Prototype* from FS to SS + lag. Of course, we would also have to make sure that the design is completed before we finish building the prototype, so we would need an FF + lag relationship also. The time saved will be the difference between the current 8 weeks before *Build Prototype* is able to start and the lag value attached to the SS. An SS5 relationship would save 3 weeks.

2. Currently, we are planning to finish building the prototype before we start designing the packaging. This is a conservative approach. By designing the packaging based on the design specs for MegaMan, we would slightly increase the risk of a problem occurring in the prototyping process, which would force us to change our design. But *Design Packaging* has 2 weeks of DRAG that we could save if we succeeded in removing it from the critical path. By making it an SS7 successor of *Design MegaMan*, we should shorten the project by another 2 weeks.

3. The last activity, *Ship MegaMan*, has DRAG of 2 weeks. But if we change its relationships with predecessors *Package MegaMan* and *Sell MegaMan* from FS to SS + lag, so that we can start shipping before we finish packaging and selling every last unit, we can save still more time. However, we need at least 1 week after the last unit has been sold and packaged before we can finish shipping. By drawing FF1 relationships between packaging and selling MegaMan and *Ship MegaMan*, we reduce *Ship MegaMan*'s DRAG to 1 week and thereby gain 1 more week.

The overall gain is 6 weeks, reducing the project duration to 34 weeks as shown in Figure 7.23.

The critical path has changed, and so the DRAG totals have changed (Table 7.8).

Eliminating any of the activities with DRAG of 1 week would shorten the project duration to 33 weeks and thus increase the EMV by $2 million to $4 million. Eliminating *Design MegaMan* would shorten the project duration to 29 weeks and this increase the EMV by $8.4 million (2 million each for the first 4 weeks, $400,000 for the fifth week) to $10.4 million.

But an EMV of $2 million is not very attractive when one considers that

➤ A 400 percent increase in profit seems almost within grasp, just 4 weeks away.

➤ The current schedule allows for no slippage, with zero management reserve. With a tight schedule (and the number of activities with just 1 week of total float shows how tight it is), the probability of slipping beyond 34 weeks seems too dangerous to embark on such a project.

➤ We have not yet factored in resources, and the impact that bottlenecks and shortages could have on our CPM schedule.

Table 7.8 DRAG and DRAG Cost for the MegaMan Project's Critical Path

ID	Duration	DRAG	DRAG Cost ($)
Design MegaMan	8W	5W	8,400,000
Build Prototype	5W	1W	2,000,000
Acquire Materials	3W	1W	2,000,000
Manufacture MegaMan	14W	1W	2,000,000
Package MegaMan	6W	1W	2,000,000
Ship MegaMan	2W	1W	2,000,000

MegaMan Project Current Estimated Duration = 34 WEEKS.
MegaMan Project Current Estimated EMV = $2,000,000.

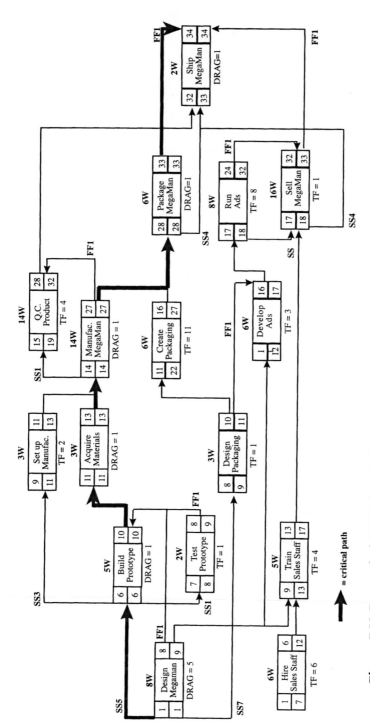

Figure 7.23 Fast-tracked CPM Schedule for the MegaMan Project, Showing New Critical Path and DRAG Totals

177

To undertake this project, we are going to have to find a way of knocking several more weeks off the schedule. That means that we need to do some more fast-tracking even off the critical path. If we can increase the total float on all the activities that currently have just 1 week, it will have two beneficial effects:

1. We will decrease the risk of those activities slipping (due either to resource shortages or to slower performance) and becoming the critical path, thus delaying us during project implementation.

2. We will also increase the DRAG on some of the critical path activities, and thus create the opportunity for further optimization.

So we continue to analyze the network, and find a fourth method of optimizing the schedule, this time on the second longest path:

3. Even though by moving *Design Packaging, Develop Advertising* was taken off the critical path, it still has only 1 week of total float. This will limit the DRAG on many of the critical path activities to 1 week, and thus constrain our future efforts to shorten the project. But even though we want to incorporate the packaging design in our ads, there is really no reason why we cannot start *Develop Advertising* until the packaging is completely designed. Instead of an FS relationship, an FF1 would allow us to develop most of the advertising, requiring just 1 week after the packaging design has been finalized to incorporate the precise packaging into the ads.

The result of this third enhancement is shown in the network diagram illustrated in Figure 7.24.

This time, although the critical path has remained the same, several of the DRAG totals have changed because of the shortening of the second longest path (Table 7.9).

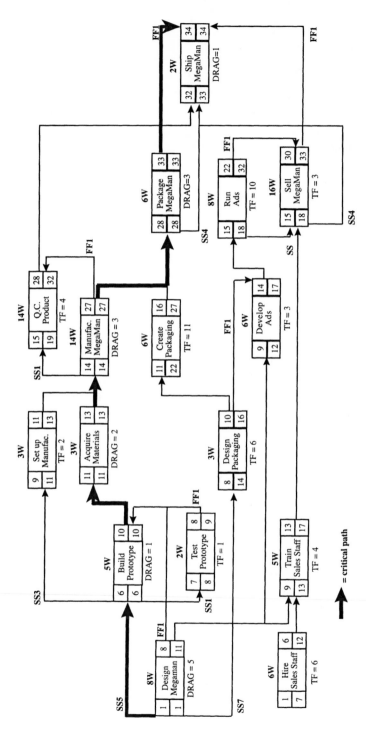

Figure 7.24 Fast-tracked CPM Schedule for the MegaMan Project, Showing Further Optimization Off the Critical Path, and thus New DRAG Totals

Table 7.9 DRAG Totals as a Result of Shortening the
Second Longest Path

ID	Duration	DRAG	DRAG Cost ($)
Design MegaMan	8W	5W	8,400,000
Build Prototype	5W	1W	2,000,000
Acquire Materials	3W	2W	4,000,000
Manufacture MegaMan	14W	3W	6,000,000
Package MegaMan	6W	3W	6,000,000
Ship MegaMan	2W	1W	2,000,000

MegaMan project current estimated duration = 34 weeks
MegaMan project current estimated EMV = $2,000,000

Now we have a systematic way to go about trying to shorten the project. We know where the critical path is, and the increased DRAG values on the critical path give us some room for further shortening. The next step is to involve the activity managers and subject matter experts. The first 5 weeks of *Design MegaMan* are costing us $8.4 million. What can be done to reduce these 5 weeks and make the project profitable? Can the individuals performing this activity somehow do the work faster to allow the *Build Prototype* activity to start sooner? If we can cut the lag relationship to SS3, we'll save 2 weeks, and $4 million.

Another big opportunity lies in the *Package MegaMan* activity. Its 6-week duration includes 3 weeks of DRAG at a cost of $6 million. Are we using two shifts for this activity? Three shifts? Do we need to hire more packaging labor? Buy more machines? We've got up to $6 million to spend, if we can shorten the activity by 3 weeks.

The two changes above offer the potential to shorten the project by a total of 6 weeks, worth $8.8 million. The first 4 weeks, which would take the project duration to 30 weeks, are worth a total of $8 million. Thereafter, we would be delivering our product to the retail outlets before the prime holiday-buying season, and the TPC Business Case tells us that weeks gained before week 30 are worth "only" $400,000 each.

This step down in the weekly cost of DRAG can make things a bit tricky. Let us take a look at the *Build Prototype* activity. It has DRAG of 1 week based on the 1 week total float of its parallel activity *Test Prototype*. This is where we must avoid the tunnel vision sometimes inherent in concentrating on each activity, one by one. In fact, the two prototyping activities, if regarded as one activity, would have DRAG of 2 weeks, based on the total float of parallel activity *Set Up Manufacturing*.

Now let us look back to the VBS that we developed in Chapter 6 (Figure 7.25).

It is evident that the prototyping activities are *not* mandatory, but they *are* valuable, to the tune of $3.8 million. But that is $200,000 less than the cost of 2 weeks of DRAG if those weeks push the project out to between week 32 and week 35. If we can do prototyping and still finish the project by week 30, then those two weeks of DRAG would cost only $800,000, or about $3 million less than prototyping is worth. If the two weeks straddle week 30 (in other words, weeks 30 and 31), then the DRAG cost of prototyping would be $1 million + $400,000, or $1.4 million.

So whether we should include prototyping depends on what our project duration is projected to be. If we are headed for a completion date of week 31 or earlier, the prototyping activities will have greater value-added than their DRAG cost, and should be performed. If, however, we are headed for a completion date beyond week 31, the time consumed may be more valuable than the activity of prototyping, and we should carefully analyze the possible impact of going straight to manufacturing without the intermediate steps of creating a working prototype and testing it.

These decisions should all be made before we ever start actually doing the project. Perhaps discussion with the activity managers will allow us to shorten the *Design MegaMan* and *Package MegaMan* activities by a total of 6

182

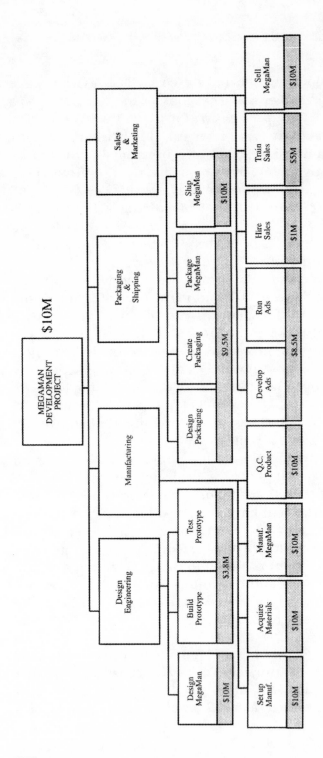

Figure 7.25 Complete VBS of the MegaMan Project

weeks, giving us a 28-week schedule without deleting the prototyping. But 2 weeks is not much of a safety net on a 7-month project. In our particular case, we don't have much time to decide—*Build Prototype* will be scheduled to start at the beginning of week 4, and, being a 5-week activity, it will start adding time to the project if *Acquire Materials* is delayed from starting beyond Monday morning of week 7. If we believe that there is a substantial risk of a schedule slippage of 3 additional weeks, we should seriously consider either deleting the prototyping and its 2 weeks of DRAG before we ever start, or abandoning it after 3 weeks, at the end of Week 6.

■ DRED

In our MegaMan project, with only 16 activities, it is relatively easy to identify the options for shortening DRAG-heavy activities by adding resources. With only a couple of activities to worry about, we can meet with the activity managers and discuss our options. But if we were dealing with a project of 1,600 activities, the process would be much more complex. It would be nice, in such a situation, to have readily available data informing us as to where such resource additions might provide the most impact. DRAG hopes to do this by quantifying how much each activity is delaying the project. But once we identify an activity as having a certain amount of DRAG, we still have no way of knowing whether adding resources to that activity will have any impact on its duration. Some activities are very resource elastic: If you double the number of resources, you will halve the duration. Other activities are impervious to resource increases: A 20-day test is a 20-day test, no matter how many people are being tested or how many testers are conducting the test.

What we need is some simple way of quantifying this quality of resource elasticity. To this end TPC has developed the Doubled Resource Estimated Duration (DRED). As the name suggests, the DRED of an activity is an estimate of how long it would take if the rate of resource usage anticipated in estimating its duration were to be doubled. For example, digging a trench 100-meters long might be estimated to take 4 days with a single backhoe. But if we rented a second backhoe (and driver) each day, how long would it take? Two days? Three days? Whichever we determine to be the correct answer would be the DRED of that activity. Another type of activity (e.g., growing a crop of produce) might occur no more rapidly no matter how many resources you assign.[2]

Note that the DRED does not necessarily mean that the number of assigned resources has to change. It may just be that the same resources are utilized for more hours. For instance, adding a programmer to an activity could result in confusion, overlap, bugs, and resultant delay; but one could also assume that just the one programmer will work longer days and weekends to provide the resourcing level of the DRED. (Obviously, one would also have to take into account the exhaustion factor on the resources working the extra hours.)

The DRED does not have to be adopted in its entirety. It is merely an index of resource elasticity. If the activity's manager estimates that an activity's duration could be halved by going to the DRED resourcing level, the project manager can usually (not always) interpret that to mean that a 50 percent, or 33 percent, increase in resources will have a lesser, but still significant, effect. There should be no need to take on more resources than are required to eliminate an activity's DRAG.

Nor can the DRED be resorted to blindly by the project manager. What the DRED does is allow the project manager, when looking over a network diagram of 1,500 or more activities, to see those places where additional resources might be added productively. Then the project manager must check with the activity manager that a certain number of additional resources will have the desired impact on the activity duration.

The project manager must also ensure that the additional resources are in fact obtainable. NASA might be able to do a lot more with two Hubble telescopes, but, unfortunately, there's only one.

Table 7.10 shows the DREDs we may have gotten on the activities in the MegaMan project.

A glance by the project manager should suggest that meetings with the activity managers for the *Design MegaMan*, *Manufacture MegaMan*, and *Package MegaMan* activities are indicated. Whether those meetings will result in further shortening of the project duration depends on the specific resource issues in each department. We will cover this in detail in Chapter 8.

Table 7.10 DREDs for MegaMan Project Activities

Activity	Duration	DRED	DRAG
Design MegaMan	8W	6W	5W
Manufacture MegaMan	14W	12W	3W
Package MegaMan	6W	3W	3W
Acquire Materials	3W	3W	2W
Build Prototype	5W	3W	1W
Ship MegaMan	2W	1W	1W
Test Prototype	2W	2W	
Design Packaging	3W	2W	
Create Packaging	6W	3W	
Set Up Manufacturing	3W	2W	
Q.C. Product	14W	9W	
Develop Advertising	6W	5W	
Run Ads	8W	8W	
Hire Sales	6W	5W	
Train Sales	5W	4W	
Sell MegaMan	16W	16W	

■ SUMMARY OF THE BENEFITS OF CPM

Let's summarize the benefits that this wonderful yet woefully underused technique called CPM offers.

1. **It allows accurate calculation of the project duration, based on the activity duration estimates.** The project may take longer, but will almost never take less time than the CPM estimate. If the project is on a tight deadline, you can't know that you'll make it unless you can put together a CPM schedule that meets that deadline.

2. **It provides data for optimization of the schedule.** Not by guesswork and wishful thinking, but by logic and decision making.

3. **It determines the schedule for each activity.** This is extremely important. If we know when each activity must occur, we are in a position to start lining up resources, seeing if they will be available, in the required amounts, when they are needed. If they aren't, we can do something about it now. Perhaps workers can be hired and trained in advance. Or perhaps they can't, so that we will have to delay the activity in question until the resources become available. Maybe that delay will cause the project to lose so much value that it will no longer be worthwhile; in which case we can cancel the project now, instead of wasting resources and money on it for 3 months before realizing that the effort is fruitless.

4. **It provides a "musical score" for the project manager, each activity manager, and each individual worker, showing when and how quickly each must perform.** In addition to the scheduling of resources, this can save valuable time on handoffs between activities. While this may seem a commonplace benefit, studies have estimated that delays on handoffs are

responsible for wasting huge amounts of time on complex projects and processes. In organizations where resources are multitasked, handoffs are particularly inefficient. Project durations can easily be doubled due to the time wasted on handoffs. I strongly recommend that the project schedule always be maintained in hard copy, as a network diagram chart on the wall, with each individual responsible for

➤ Initialing and dating the activity box at the time of starting.

➤ Informing all successor activity managers immediately upon finishing (or reaching an SS handoff point).

➤ Initialing and dating the activity box at the time of finishing.

5. **It shows opportunities for savings on resources and/or cost, by cutting resources on non-critical path activities (i.e., trading total float for resources).** This, of course, is exactly how the process of resource leveling works, which we will discuss in Chapter 9. In scheduling resources, priority is given to critical path activities, and non-critical path activities are delayed within their float.

6. **It provides an early warning system once the work has begun on the project.** If the first activity in a 6-month project takes 4 weeks rather than the scheduled 3, the precedence relationships will immediately show that, under the current plan, each successive critical path activity will be delayed, and the project will finish a week later (at the minimum). Without CPM precedences, one activity slipping has no explicit impact on the rest of the project. This can lead to what Bill Moch, who used to run the program office for the F-16 program at General Dynamics, called the "T & T syndrome."

We have a program team meeting at the end of February. We're told everything is on a schedule and within budget. End of March, we're told the same thing. End of April, same thing. Then, at the end of May, we're told that we are 10 months behind schedule and $50 million over budget. How can this happen? How is it possible?" (Here Bill sighs, and shuffles some papers. He is a big man, who looks and sounds exactly like the actor George Kennedy.) "Steve, there's only two ways this can happen. I call 'em the 'T & T Factor': 'Tornadoes and Termites.' 'Tornadoes' is that, after everything was going smoothly through April, sometime in May a tornado came through Fort Worth, hit the hangar where we were building the plane, killed all the engineers, destroyed all the work, and we had to start over. But, Steve, I live in Fort Worth, and I know that no tornado came through there in May. No, Steve, it was termites. Termites that were there in the hangar in February and March and April, but no one could detect them. And then in May they ate through a beam, and the whole building collapsed, killing all the engineers and destroying all the work. And that's what it was, Steve, it was termites. . . ." and here Bill leans forward confidentially, ". . . Only it wasn't termites in the building; it was termites in the schedule. And because they weren't working to the critical path schedule, no one could tell they were there until it was too late.

7. **When slippage is detected, CPM provides a tool for seeing how to get back on schedule by "crashing the critical path," that is, increasing resources to shorten critical path activities.** There may be no clear reason to target one activity or path instead of another for "workarounds" that will bring the project back on schedule, without TPC. The TPC concept of DRAG, of course, helps to make this targeting process much more precise.

8. **With a computer, CPM allows analysis of the project plan through "what-if" scenarios.** Because of the

precedence relationships, changes can be input to the plan as "trial balloons," and their impacts assessed. When slippage or other unforeseen occurrences threaten the plan, a variety of remedies can be tested through CPM modeling, and the best remedy selected. Without CPM, the impact of such what-ifs is virtually non-existent, since there are no precedences to show the schedule interdependence of activities.

9. **Developing the CPM schedule allows for distinction between project delays that are due either to the nature of the work or the logical order in which it must be performed, versus delays that are caused by the lack of sufficient resources.** This is a benefit that is never attributed to using CPM; yet it's the only way to achieve anything like right-sized staffing levels in a project-driven organization. Resource delays are something that the organization can do something about. If the lack of sufficient programmers, jack-hammers, or stainless steel, is costing the organization millions of dollars through project delays, that is something that can be addressed—but only if those delays can be separated out from other, unavoidable delays and their impact quantified. This process is greatly facilitated by adopting a standard operating procedure that all activity estimates be based on the underlying assumption of at least one dedicated unit of each resource throughout its duration whenever it would be advantageous.

There may be some corporate projects that would not benefit from CPM scheduling. Small, simple projects with little corporate investment may be scheduled and performed adequately without CPM techniques. But without a doubt, any corporate project requiring more than 500 person hours, or of more than 2 months' duration, must utilize CPM techniques if it is not to fritter away a large quantity of dollars through avoidable inefficiencies.

Yet corporations continue to shut their eyes to this fundamental and decades-old project management technique. Business schools don't teach it adequately; project managers don't use it competently; and senior managers neither mandate it nor provide the necessary supporting infrastructure of procedures and software. Corporations don't use it because they understand neither its functioning nor its value. Those project-driven companies that *do* come to understand it and use it as standard practice will sooner or later drive their competition into obsolescence.

■ OTHER METHODS OF SCHEDULING PROJECTS

So corporations and government agencies don't often use CPM to schedule their projects. Yet thousands, if not millions, of projects are performed every day. Although many of them seem to be performed willynilly, with nothing planned or scheduled in advance, some projects certainly start out with a schedule in place. So presumably, some scheduling method is being used. What is it?

The first method of scheduling projects is probably the one that is most commonly used: none. That is to say, nothing so formal and systematic as to deserve the term *method*. Typically, the project manager, either in isolation or during a tour through the involved departments, determines that the programming will be done in June and July, the documentation and testing in July and August, training and advertising in September, and the release on the first Friday in October. This random selection of dates is then often displayed and distributed on a Gantt chart, perhaps to give the whole thing the right "project management odor."

➤ The Gantt Chart

The Gantt chart is a perfectly respectable project management tool—in fact, it is one of the most venerable project management techniques still incorporated in project management software. First developed by Henry Lawrence Gantt at the Philadelphia Naval Shipyard in 1908, it was used to display transatlantic shipping schedules, and later it was used for work on any sort of project. It still does this well. The date ribbon at the top of the chart shows the timing of the work; the activity bars allow the viewer to see work that is occurring simultaneously; the bars are proportional to the length of the activity, so that one can get a sense of which activities are longer and which shorter; and, by using different colors and shadings, two schedules, such as plan versus actual or resource use versus resource availability, can be requirements compared on the same chart.

But the Gantt chart is a display tool—it is not intended for schedule calculation. The schedule is much more easily calculated on a network logic diagram, such as the ones shown in this chapter, and then translated into the Gantt format. However the data are displayed, they should be based in the techniques of the CPM method.

Figure 7.26 shows the PDM diagram from Figure 7.15 and then a Gantt chart displaying the early (forward pass) versus late (backward pass) schedule.

➤ Backward Scheduling

There is a scheduling methodology that is by far the most common technique for scheduling projects. It's called backward scheduling, and we've all been involved in projects in which this technique was used. Here is the way it works.

Imagine that we have an idea for a new product: a remote-controlled lawn mower. This lawn mower will allow the user to mow the entire yard while lounging in a chaise on the deck. The control panel for the mower is a four-way remote that also runs the television, VCR, and cable box. Every Saturday afternoon, you'll be able to mow the lawn while clicking back and forth between the sports events on television.

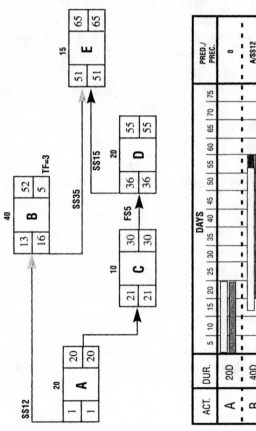

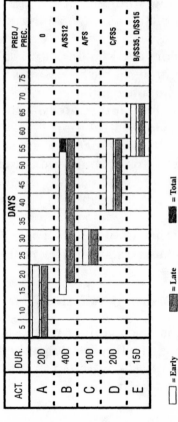

Figure 7.26 Early and Late Schedules of the New Product Project in Both Network Diagram and Gantt Chart Formats

But there are schedule constraints. Today is October 1, and our TPC Business Case tells us that if we're going to realize the $50 million in sales we're anticipating, we need to have our mowers in the stores by no later than May 1. Every week later will reduce our sales by $25 million, down to zero after May 15. How do we schedule our project so that we meet our deadline?

We have two all-important bits of information: Today is October 1, and we don't want to go beyond May 1. Thus, the project manager wants to make sure we don't go beyond May 1. All the mowers have to be in the stores May 1, which means they have to be shipped out of our manufacturing plant no later than April 24. All this means they have to be packaged no later than April 20, which means we have to finish manufacturing no later than April 10.

If we're going to sell these lawn mowers, we have to advertise them. We should probably start running the television ads April 15, which means we have to have them produced no later than April 1, which means we have got to have the scripts ready, and so on.

We'll also need to train the salespeople in the stores on how to demo the mowers, program the remote control, and so forth. So that training will have to be completed by no later than April 20, which means we have to have the training materials ready no later than April 12. What we wind up with is a project schedule that looks like the one shown in Figure 7.27.

There is one absolutely astounding aspect to this method of scheduling: It is simply amazing how often, when all the work that needs to be done is scheduled, and all the "must be done bys" have been accounted for, the schedule brings us right back to—yes, you guessed it!—October 1.

Let us consider just how we have developed this schedule. Ignoring for the moment the fact that each duration estimate was generated on the basis of meeting this schedule, in each case we have scheduled the work on the basis of when it has to be done. Throughout this chapter we have periodically

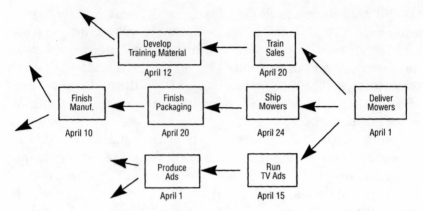

Figure 7.27 Backward Scheduling for the Lawn Mower Project

scheduled activities on precisely that basis—on the backward pass of the critical path method.

Here is the $64,000 question: What is the difference between the forward pass and the backward pass? Difference, remember, is represented arithmetically by the minus sign (–). The backward pass computes, among other things, the late finish (LF) of each activity; the forward pass computes the early finish (EF) of each activity. The difference (–) between the late finish and the early finish (LF-EF) equals . . . total float! Thus everything is on the critical path.

What this means is that the schedule for the lawn mower project is one from which every last iota of float has been factored. If one thing slips, no matter how trivial, either we will be late, or we will devastate our resources on exhausting and expensive workarounds, trying to get back on schedule. Or, most likely of all, both.

When, in one of my senior management seminars, I point out the aforementioned problems with the backward scheduling method, someone (usually a manager who has put together just such as schedule within the previous week) is sure to say: "But you don't understand! It's probably not going to take all the way up to April 20 to do the packaging! It'll probably finish by April 16. The rest of the time is just in there as 'bank time.'"

Or safety time, or contingency time. Its real name, however, is padding. The problem with padding is the following:

➤ When padding is built into activity estimates, profitable projects are vetoed, bids are inflated, contracts are lost, unnecessary resources are hired, competing projects are delayed, and businesses are bankrupted.

➤ There is also Parkinson's Law to remember. If the deadline for packaging is April 20, do you really think it's going to get done by April 16, even if it could?

➤ Assume that a miracle happens: For our lawn mower project, Parkinson's Law is repealed! Manufacturing, scheduled to finish on April 10, actually finishes April 1. Whenever an activity on the critical path (and usually elsewhere in the project) finishes early, we'd like to start its successors immediately after. But that never happens in a backward scheduled project. It's hard enough to make it happen in a CPM-schedule project, where activity managers are usually more aware of the issues of float and the potential uncertainties of the schedule. But in a backward scheduled project, the dates are in concrete; it's easier to blow up the deliverable then to move a date forward.

So how should the lawn mower project be scheduled? Remember, we want to finish by May 1, no matter what.

For the moment, let's forget the impending due date. The last thing we need is wishful thinking interfering with our business judgment. If we can't get this project finished by the deadline, we need to know that now, not after we've spent a couple of million dollars in a futile effort to reach an unattainable goal. We need to know what work we have to do and how long it's going to take to do each item. Once we've determined that, then we can start to think about the schedule.

In order to determine what all the work is that needs to be completed, we must do several things. First, we develop a work scope document listing the specific deliverables, along with appearance and performance standards. Then, we construct a

WBS detailing all the work items that have to be completed in order to produce and market those deliverables. All this should be done without any consideration of scheduling issues.

Finally, duration estimates for each of the activities should be obtained, and they should be arranged into a critical path network. Then the forward pass dates should be calculated. Suppose that when we do this, we get a project completion date of May 29. Now what? This is just what we'd feared, right? If we miss the May 1st deadline, the project will be worthless. Shall we scrap it now?

Not at all. We don't even have a critical path as of yet. We have to do the backward pass. Now we have a critical path and now we have activities that have float. Additionally, with TPC, we can tell how much time each critical path activity is adding to the project. We can now optimize our project schedule by fast-tracking, by targeting our resources to the critical path activities and by trimming scope.

If, at the end of that systematic and methodical process, the duration is still such that the TPC Business Case tells us that the project would be unprofitable, then we cancel it. But much of the time the above techniques do work to bring the completion date back. Not just to May 1, but to early enough in April that we can build some contingency in at the end of the project. Not the padding we talked about earlier, built invisibly into each activity estimate, but a true safety net at the end of the project where it's available if anything slips. Because activities are going to start slipping, as soon we try to assign resources and discover they aren't there when we need them.

➤ The Program Evaluation and Review Technique (PERT)

Backward scheduling is not an acceptable technique for scheduling projects, and would not be recommended by anyone who is knowledgeable in project management theory.

On the other hand, PERT most definitely is recommended by many knowledgeable individuals.

PERT was developed in 1958 by consultants from Booz Allen Hamilton working on the U.S. Navy's Polaris missile project. This was 1 year after CPM was developed in the construction industry. Today the terms CPM and PERT are used interchangeably. But originally there was a difference, based in types of projects for which they were used: construction and guided missile development.

What is the difference between constructing a building and developing a missile that could be fired from a submerged submarine and hit a target a thousand miles away? The answer is that the construction industry had been putting up buildings for many generations. But no one had ever built a Polaris-type missile system before. So whereas a project manager could get a fairly reliable estimate of how long it would take to build a foundation, erect a wall, or install a window, it was extremely difficult to get a similar estimate of how long it would take to develop the Polaris guidance system, the firing mechanism, or the trigger for arming the warhead.

As a result, the scheduling people on the Polaris project developed a formula for predicting the length of an activity. This formula is based on the normal distribution curve of eighteenth-century French mathematician Abraham de Moivre. In a nutshell, de Moivre's work demonstrated that the results of a set of random trials will distribute themselves around their average value in a bell-shaped curve. The Polaris schedulers decided to ask estimators for not one but three estimates of duration: What is the average amount of time the activity in question should take; what is the most optimistic estimate, and what is the most pessimistic estimate? Then, working backwards, they sought to normalize the estimates into de Moivre's distribution curve by using the formula:

Duration = optimistic estimate + 4 (most likely estimate)
+ pessimistic estimate ÷ 6

Let us take an example from the MegaMan development project. Suppose that we ask for the three duration estimates for the *Design MegaMan* activity. The estimates we are given are:

Pessimistic = 13W

Optimistic = 6W

Most likely = 8W

According to the PERT formula, the duration for the *design MegaMan* activity would be:

13W + 4 (8W) + 6W ÷ 6 = 51W ÷ 6 8. = 5 weeks

The standard deviation of the six data points (6, 13, and four 8s) is 2.14. If this were truly a normal distribution curve, based on random events, 68 percent of the time an activity's duration should be within one standard deviation of the mean, and 95 percent of the time, within two standard deviations. On the basis of this, 68 percent of the time the activity should take between 6.36 weeks and 10.64 weeks. 95 percent of the time, it should be between 4.22 weeks and 12.78 weeks. Therefore if we want to make sure that we allow enough time for the activity, by allowing 12.78 weeks, we should slip only 5 percent of the time.

There are at least half a dozen things wrong with these figures, however. What exactly is meant by the terms optimistic, pessimistic and most likely? The difference between the glass being half-full and half-empty isn't just a semantic one—it's a real difference in the way that individuals react in judging the identical element of information. Even if you try to quantify these terms by defining, for example, pessimistic as the duration that will suffice 90 percent of the time, you are still dealing with a subjective estimate. Trying to "scientize" the process by introducing a mathematical model (especially one that is unrelated both in origin and application) is to risk losing sight of the fact that you will always be dealing with, and adjusting to, estimates that are fraught with human fallibility.

Probably the most glaring flaw is that trying to make duration estimates fit into a curve derived from naturally occurring events is a particularly Procrustean distortion. A project is not the result of a set of random trials. Once a set of estimates is given, there are reasons, vested interests, in one or more of those numbers being justified by the ultimate result. Yes, baseball and cricket averages, shot put distances, or sprinting times may fit the de Moivre curve, and, yes, they too are the results of human effort. Let's say that we asked all the students of a high school to throw a ball, with the one who throws farthest to receive a $100 prize. You would expect the distances registered by the participants to distribute themselves around the median in a bell-shaped curve. Now suppose that you also offer a $50 prize for the student whose throw is closest to precisely 30 meters. And another $25 prize to the one whose throw is closest to precisely 20 meters. You would certainly expect these secondary incentives to completely distort the results, and in a very predictable way: bulges of throws around the 20- and 30-meter marks. The same thing has been shown to happen on projects scheduled using the PERT formula. With the sixth week, eighth week and thirteenth week estimates for the design MegaMan activity, I would expect the real probabilities to be distributed as shown in Figure 7.28, with a small cluster at 8 weeks and a much larger one around 13 weeks (and out!).

The terms self-fulfilling prophecy and, once again, Parkinson's Law are the core of the problem. In fact, some studies have shown that the pessimistic estimate tends to be by far the most accurate. The reason for this is simple: If you ask someone for an optimistic and pessimistic estimate, you might regard their deadline to be the most likely date, but they will consider it to be the pessimistic estimate. It's not that they deliberately waste time; it's just that it is human nature to work faster and more efficiently (not to mention longer hours) when a deadline and their own personal commitment is on the line.

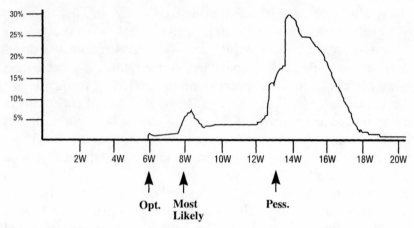

Figure 7.28 Clusters of Duration Probabilities for PERT-Estimated Design MegaMan Activity

Meeting a duration estimate is primarily a function of the effort made to fulfill that estimate!

Not of the amount of data, nor the time spent in analysis prior to the estimate. Of course, both these items can help improve estimates. A historical database of how long similar activities have taken in the past can be a very helpful tool. It can, for instance, tell you when either estimates or work performance by a specific individual or team deviates significantly from the norm of actual past events. But, that said, the work we are estimating is going to be performed on this project by these individuals under this specific set of circumstances, and for that there is no database because that has not occurred before.

■ THE TPC DURATION ESTIMATING PROCEDURE

The TPC procedure for duration estimating is as follows:

1. The individual responsible for the work should generate the estimate (basing it, if possible, in historical data).

2. The estimate should assume a minimum availability of one unit of each assigned resource throughout the activity's duration (to isolate those delays which are generated by insufficiency of resources).

3. The estimate should be the median expected duration, with an equal chance of being shorter or longer.[3]

4. Activities that are foreseen to have a specific identified risk factor that may increase their duration should also be scheduled, as a contingency plan, with the additional duration. This contingency should be included in the activity's and project's plans as a separate line item, enumerating the specific reason, the additional time, the percentage probability of it being needed, and a fuse date by which, if the contingency is not triggered, it may be deleted from the schedule.

5. Activity durations being estimated should be no longer than 50 percent of the project's reporting period, or contain more than 2 work weeks of resource effort. If an activity's estimate is greater than either of these limits, it should be decomposed into its subactivities and new estimates generated.

6. The activity estimate should also include a DRED estimate, or how long the activity might be expected to take if the level of assigned resources were doubled.

■ THE TPC DIFFERENCE IN PROJECT SCHEDULING

Traditional project management, for all its contributions, has placed altogether too much emphasis on the reliability of scheduling techniques. Although it may not have started out that way, 40-odd years ago, it has come to conceive of the main purpose of activity scheduling as being to generate a schedule which will meet an artificially imposed deadline without causing organizational disruptions or volatility of staffing levels.

As valuable as such benefits are, a much more important benefit in today's market economy is the ability to complete projects in less time, which is the motive force behind the TPC approach to project scheduling. The purpose of TPC is not so much to come up with an accurate schedule as a valuable schedule. Valuable in the sense that the EMV of the project's deliverable is maximized. And, in most cases, a valuable project schedule is a short project schedule!

Thus the need to

1. Identify the activity (and the type of resource) that is causing the project delay.
2. Quantify the amount of delay it is causing.
3. Translate that delay into the unit that allows profit-driven decisions to be made: Dollars.

Thus we can understand the importance of DRAG and of DRAG cost. When we look at the PERT duration estimates for an activity, each of the three different estimates may come with a dollar figure attached if the activity could migrate to the critical path. In the *Design MegaMan* example, you may recall that the activity had a duration estimate of 8 weeks and DRAG of 5 weeks. When we used the estimates from the PERT formula, we had an optimistic estimate of 6W, a most likely estimate of 8W, and a pessimistic estimate of 13W. At $2 million per week, the DRAG cost of ending up at the most likely estimate would be $4 million more than the optimistic estimate, and the DRAG cost of the pessimistic estimate would be $14 million more. That's not pessimism, that's stupidity! Add resources, cut scope, do whatever it takes, but find some way to not be at 13W.

In many cases, an activity may be off the critical path if it is completed within its optimistic or most likely duration, but be critical, with lots of DRAG and DRAG cost, if it slips out to its pessimistic duration. All of which makes the task of quantifying DRAG and DRAG cost, and using them to optimize a schedule, even more problematic. But this is a reason for abandoning the PERT formula, with its dubious benefit, rather than for not using DRAG and DRAG cost.

Keep in mind that PERT also has a value. There are two purposes it serves, both involving the generation of "quick and dirty" scheduling information. They are: (1) A sanity check on an activity duration estimate. If an estimate seems to have lost touch with reality, ask the estimator for the three PERT estimates. This process might cause him or her to rethink his original estimate; or it might provide conclusive evidence of its inaccuracy. (2) A thumbnail computation of the project duration. While still in the initial planning stages, a PERT-based schedule calculation at the summary activity level might indicate how attainable or otherwise the deadline goal is. It is important to remember that: The ultimate project schedule should be based on single duration estimates, adjusted only after modifications of work scope or assigned resources.

■ SUMMARY

Scheduling projects through CPM is one of the most valuable techniques that traditional project management has developed. Yet this decades' old technique is rarely used when it should be, because of ignorance and inertia.

➤ CPM provides the means of shortening projects, determining the dates when specific resources are needed, identifying slippage as soon as it starts to occur, gauging the effect of such slippage, and determining the best course of action.

➤ When CPM is implemented as part of the TPC approach, the TPC metrics DRAG and DRAG cost demonstrate how to get the most value from the project, cutting scope or adding resources when the benefit to be gained, in terms of EMV, is greater than the cost.

➤ The DRAG cost metric is particularly valuable, since the value of project deliverables is greatly decreased by project completion delay.

➤ In order to get value from implementing this metric, both the TPC Business Case, quantifying the project's value and the impact on that value of acceleration or delay, and the VBS, which drives the EMV of the TPC Business Case down through the WBS to the activities, must be developed and tracked.

➤ The mechanics of the CPM scheduling technique rely heavily on duration estimates. Unfortunately, the principal virtue of the technique itself has been misunderstood. It has been interpreted as a tool for getting accurate schedules, rather than shorter schedules and more valuable projects. As a result, activity and project managers have developed the habit of injecting safety nets, or padding, into activity duration estimates. This, when combined with the effects of multitasked resources and Parkinson's Law, result in projects that are much longer than they need to be. Rather than padding each activity's duration estimate, a much better approach to ensure that project deadlines are met is to extract the padding from each activity and include it instead at the end of the project, as a management reserve that is available if anything in the project slips. Activity managers and workers should aim (and be incentivized) to complete critical path activities in the shortest possible amount of time, with the understanding that if the schedule varies, either positively or negatively, the plan will simply be adjusted accordingly.

➤ Multitasking of resources is a particularly problematic issue for project scheduling. Not only does it add large amounts of time to every project utilizing the particular resource, but it does so *invisibly* by hiding within the activity duration estimates. This means that it's usually very difficult to see precisely how much projects are being delayed by the insufficiency of a particular resource, not to mention how much those delays are costing.

➤ It is crucial that organizations be able to quantify project delay that is caused by CPM and work logic versus that which is caused by insufficient resources. To accomplish this, duration estimates for CPM scheduling should always assume a minimum of one dedicated resource throughout an activity's duration, whenever advantageous, even though the current organizational structure may make such a dedicated resource an impossibility. In this way, when resource delays are factored into the activity durations, the negative impact of multitasking and other resource insufficiencies will not only be evident, but quantified. And, over time, they should provide both the evidence and the motive for addressing the problem.

Notes

1. Notice when the two letters, and the times of day represented, are the same (as in SS and FF relationships), both activities will start or finish at the same time and on the same day (respectively). However, if the two letters are different (as in FS and SF relationships), starts and finishes will be connected. These *always* occur at different times of the day (or week or . . .), so the dates will be different—the finish (F) will always be the day before the start (S).
2. In some cases, an activity can actually be delayed by increasing the resources. There can be an optimal "team" size for a job, and getting more people involved can simply cause them to get in one another's way. Imagine moving a sofa: four people, one at each corner, is ideal. Any other number could potentially delay things.
3. During a seminar at a medical device development company in Pittsburgh, one project manager took great exception to the idea that estimates should be based on the median expected duration. He pulled out a calculator and said: "Based on that, a

20-activity project would have only a 2 percent chance of finishing on time!" It was immediately obvious that he was making a major error in the way he was scheduling his projects. Fifty percent of estimates should, perhaps not surprisingly, result in finishing the project by the estimated duration 50 percent of the time—unless you never take advantage of activities finishing in less than the median time. Clearly, this project manager was used to invoking safe estimates of 70 percent or more reliability, and never taking the opportunity to tighten up the schedule when an activity finished early. The cost of this to his organization was undoubtedly millions of dollars a year.

Everyone working in project-driven organizations has to be educated to the fact that scheduling a project is an inexact science; that project schedules can slip out or be tightened; and that the reason to use a project management methodology, including CPM, is because it allows quick and relatively painless adjustments to the vagaries of project work.

Activity-Based
Resource Assignments

At the end of the CPM scheduling process, we have a schedule for the MegaMan development project that will last 34 weeks. We know from the TPC Business Case that with such a delivery date, we can expect sales of only $2 million, or 20 percent of what they would be if we could finish 4 weeks earlier.

We also know that our current CPM schedule assumes no slippage. But how realistic is that? Right now, we have no idea if the resources that we need to meet this schedule will be available when they are needed. Without that information, we are still stumbling around in the dark. Even our current 34-week duration is probably unattainable.

We know the DRAG totals of each critical path activity, and have DRED estimates of each activity, which might save us a considerable amount of time. But can we implement those estimates? Are these additional resources available? Again, we have to do what so many project-driven companies make no attempt to do: systematically determine how the availability of resources might impact our project schedule.

Without having put together the CPM schedule, we would have no way of assessing the impact of resource availability, because we would have only the vaguest idea of when the resources would be needed for each activity. But with those data available from the CPM schedule, we should not only be able to determine where we don't have sufficient resources, but also the impact that such shortages will have in delaying the schedule.

Even if we have put together a CPM schedule, however, we still may not have sufficient information to identify our resource shortages. For that, we also need to have information about resource availability. In all my years of project consulting, no deficiency has been more striking than the lack of such information. Organizations whose revenues are 100 percent project-driven, and in which every employee is working on four and five projects a week, nevertheless make no attempt to either forecast or track their resource availability and usage. Of course, that means that they can never measure the impact of resource shortages on their project durations, so they can never justify additional resources. This means greater resource insufficiency, more bottlenecks, more multitasking, and longer projects. What we have here is the paradigm of a vicious cycle.

Let me state that it is an absolute requirement for any organization doing multiple projects that it must assemble and maintain an up-to-date resource availability database (usually called a resource library). This is mandatory even for those organizations that assemble dedicated project teams. However, for that vast number of companies that operate within a loose matrix structure, it is even more important—it just has to be done.

It is precisely in such organizations, with shared resources, multitasking, and strong lines of functional management, that maintaining a resource library, reflecting assignments and availability across time, is the most difficult. It is here that the vast inefficiencies and waste are generated. The greatest need for such data lies with the project and project manager; but the means to maintain such a database lies with the functional manager. All too often, this individual sees no personal, or departmental, benefit in assembling such a database.

One of the most important practical benefits of the TPC approach is to show how assigning resources to project activities can benefit not only the organization and the project manager, but also the functional manager. It does so by justifying, in the clearest possible terms, the additional resources that the functional manager knows are needed, and has probably been screaming about for months.

This whole issue raises what I believe is often the case in the project management process: Whenever there appears to be a conflict between the interests of the project and the interests of an individual within the project, the conflict is not real, but rather is caused by process disintegration and/or a lack of understanding of the overall process. If the organization's life blood flows from projects, then all the individuals within it should also benefit by determining how best to do their part in the project management process.

■ ABRA AND ABC

The first step in resource scheduling is to determine what resources will be needed for each activity. This is called activity-based resource assignments (ABRA). It is the foundation for an important technique in cost accounting that has received much attention in recent years: activity-based costing (ABC). The fundamental concept behind ABC is that the cost for doing work must be assembled and tracked at the level of each activity. Although this has tended to become the bailiwick of the much-maligned "beancounters," ABC is a project management technique. The data for ABC are generated by assigning resources activity by activity, which is ABRA without the cadabra of cost. When the dollar rate of the resource usage is included, and computed for each activity, then we have the cadabra, or ABC.

But even without ABC, ABRA provides indispensable benefits. Resources are the essential items that fuel each activity. Each activity requires its own unique profile of resources. To try to manage a project and its resources at the overall project level is to risk muddying and blurring the work effort. Resources are not interchangeable among activities; programmers need to work on the programming activities and carpenters on the carpentry activities. Therefore resources need to be planned and tracked at the activity level. Yet even where a resource database is maintained, it is almost always done at the overall project level, far too high for useful clarity.

In performing ABRA, there are three items of information regarding resource requirements that need to be determined for each activity.

1. What resources are needed?

2. How much of each resource is needed in order to complete it within its estimated duration?

3. When will each resource be needed?

In order to keep the size and complexity of our sample project at a manageable level for this book, we have been operating at a fairly high summary level—the 16 activities of the MegaMan development project, which we identified and scheduled in earlier chapters. We will now assign and schedule our human resource needs (which tend to be the most problematic type of resource) at this level. On a real project, however, resource assignments should be made at a much lower level of detail, preferably the lowest level of the WBS, and all resources—not just human resources—should be assigned and managed in this manner.

In Table 8.1, we have also determined how much of these resources would be needed to complete each of these activities in the estimated amount of time. As mentioned earlier, the operating assumption for each activity is dedicated resources throughout the activity's duration except where it would not be advantageous to do so. For example, *Acquire Materials* is a 3-week activity, but most of that time will be spent waiting for delivery. To have the material acquisition clerk and the inventory controller dedicated to this activity

Table 8.1 Resource Assignments for the MegaMan Development Project

Activity	Duration	Assigned Resource	Work Days (WD)
Design MegaMan	8W	1 Prod Mgr	40
		2 Prod Designers	80
		1 Dsgn Engr	40
		1 Drafter	10
Build Prototype	5W	2 Dsgn Engrs	50
		1 Mfg Engr	10
Test Prototype	2W	2 Dsgn Engrs	20
		1 Test Engr	10
Design Packaging	3W	1 Pkging Dsnr	15
		1 Pkging Engr	15
		1 Mfg Engr	5
Create Packaging	6W	1 Mfg Engr	30
		1 Mfg Spvr	30
		5 Mfg Workers	150
Package MegaMan	6W	1 Pkg Mgr	30
		1 Pkg Spvr	30
		10 Packagers	300
Ship MegaMan	2W	1 Shipping Clerk	4
		1 Shipping Spvr	10
		2 Shippers	20
Set Up Manufacturing	3W	2 Mfg Engr	30
		1 Mfg Spvr	6
		4 Mfg Workers	60
Acquire Materials	3W	1 Mat'l Acquis Clerk	3
		1 Inventory Controller	5
Manufacture MegaMan	14W	2 Mfg Engr	140
		1 Mfg Spvr	70
		20 Mfg Workers	1400
Q.C. Product	14W	1 Quality Engr	28
		1 Q.C. Worker	28
Develop Ads	6W	1 Mkting Mgr	12
		1 Ad Writer	30
		1 Graphics Spec	15
Run Ads	8W	1 Mkting Mgr	10
Hire Sales	6W	1 Recruiter	30
		1 Sales Mgr	15

(continued)

Table 8.1 (Continued)

Activity	Duration	Assigned Resource	Work Days (WD)
Train Sales	5W	1 Instruc Dsnr	25
		1 CBT Dsnr	25
		1 Trainer	10
		5 Telemarketers	25
		5 Field Sales	25
Sell MegaMan	16W	1 Sales Manager	80
		5 Telemarketers	400
		5 Field Salespeople	400
Total Workdays: 3,691			

for 3 weeks would be absurd, and affect the duration not a whit. The project plan is therefore adjusted so that the clerk works just the first 3 days of the activity, ordering the materials, and the inventory controller works just the last week, checking the materials in. (Of course, this would probably be a non-issue if we were assigning resources at a lower level of detail, where the ordering and checking in activities would be scheduled as separate activities.)

The required resources having been assigned, the next step is to match them against the resources within the organization. Resources with an organization are located in the departments that comprise the hierarchical structure of the company. This is also called the OBS. You may recall that we displayed the OBS of MegaProdux, Inc., in Figure 5.1. We now show it again in Figure 8.1, but this time with the resources available in each department.

In addition to showing the internal resources of each department in MegaProdux, Inc., the OBS should also contain cost information about each resource. This is where the "C" in ABC comes from. For human resources, these cost data should be based on salary standards, not on the actual salaries of the individuals. This keeps individual salary information confidential while providing a project manager and team with approximate numbers for planning cost without the necessity of knowing exactly which individuals will

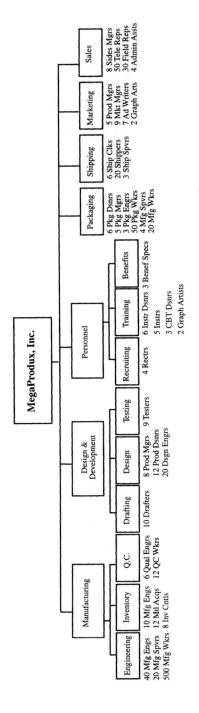

Figure 8.1 OBS of MegaProdux, Inc. Showing Internal Resources

be assigned. For example, it is sufficient to know that the standard cost for a shipping clerk is $500 per week; we don't need to know whether it will be Jean Smith at $550 per week or Angus Patel at $475 per week.

Activity-based costing is a much more complex subject then we can adequately cover here; readers who are interested in exploring it in depth should read the several fine books on activity-based management by James A. Brimson and John Antos. For our purposes, we need three things:

1. A fairly accurate budget for each resource being used, for each activity, and for the whole project. To this end, standard salaries, burdened by overhead costs (health and dental insurance, clerical support, equipment, energy, and physical plant costs such as rent, etc.), are adequate. These will allow comparisons and decision making both within a project and across projects.

2. A schedule that shows how the cost of a resource changes over time. For example, each shipper may be available 60 hours per week; but while the first 40 hours may be at a rate of $6, the other 20 hours may be at the overtime rate of $9. This information needs to be taken into account both when planning a project and when determining what staffing level to maintain in the shipping department.

3. A schedule that shows the availability of a resource changes over time. It is this calendar information that transforms the OBS into a resource library, the implication of the term library being that it allows us to see what resources are available, and which have been checked out, and when they are expected back, so that we can schedule the resources for our project over time, as we need to do.

If MegaProdux's OBS contains the necessary costing information, we can get our labor budget for:

➤ Each activity.

➤ Each summary-level activity.

➤ Each supporting MegaProdux department, specifically for the MegaMan project.

➤ The entire project. In fact, this is precisely how a project budget should be generated, and the only way in which one should be generated.

■ RESOURCE LIBRARY

Almost all the project management software packages that are currently available incorporate the functionality of a resource database. Some do this better than others; some allow for the work hours of a resource to change in both cost and availability several times a day; others are less flexible. There may be desired ways of "slicing and dicing" resource usage that are not available in less expensive packages. But almost all provide the ability to do at least some rudimentary ABRA and ABC. Like all the other project management techniques we have examined, this functionality is, for the most part, ignored in most organizations, because it takes time and effort to keep such a database maintained and up-to-date. Organizations just can't be bothered. After all, they've got projects to do, right? And they're under-resourced as it is.

They will remain under-resourced, too, because the only way to justify additional resources in a project-driven organization is to contrast the costs of those resources versus the impact of resource shortages on project schedules and EMV. Without a resource library, this is all but impossible.

■ PROJECT BUDGETS

So now let us load the MegaMan project resource requirements into our software and assign the necessary resources from the organizational OBS. As the resources are assigned, the cost data come with them. In Table 8.2, we have the labor budget for each activity.

Table 8.2 Labor Budget for Each MegaMan Project Activity

Activity	Duration	Resource @ $/D	Work Days (WD)	Cost ($)
Design MegaMan	8W	1 Prod Mgr @ $600/D	40	24,000
		2 Prod Dsgners @ $500/D	80	40,000
		1 Dsgn Engr @ $350/D	40	14,000
		1 Drafter @ $250/D	10	2,500
		Total labor Budget:		**80,500**
Build Prototype	5W	2 Dsgn Engrs @ $350/D	50	17,500
		1 Mfg Engr @ $400/D	10	4,000
		Total Labor Budget:		**21,500**
Test Prototype	2W	2 Dsgn Engrs @ $350/D	20	7,000
		1 Test Engr @ $300/D	10	3,000
		Total labor budget:		**10,000**
Design Packaging	3W	1 Pkg Dsnr @ $400/D	15	6,000
		1 Pkg Engr @ $350/D	15	5,250
		1 Mfg Engr @ $400/D	5	2,000
		Total Labor Budget:		**13,250**
Create packaging	6W	1 Mfg Engr @ $400/D	30	12,000
		1 Mfg Spvr @ $300/D	30	9,000
		5 Mfg Workers @ $200/D	150	30,000
		Total Labor Budget:		**51,000**
Package MegaMan	6W	1 Pkg Mgr @ $350/D	30	10,500
		1 Pkg Spvr @ $250/D	30	7,500
		10 Packagers @ $150/D	300	45,000
		Total Labor Budget:		**63,000**
Ship MegaMan	2W	1 Shipping Clerk @ $150/D	4	600
		1 Shipping Spvr @ $250/D	10	2,500
		2 Shippers @ $150/D	20	3,000
		Total Labor Budget:		**6,100**

(continued)

Table 8.2 *(Continued)*

Activity	Duration	Resource @ $/D	Work Days (WD)	Cost ($)
Set Up Manufacturing	3W	2 Mfg Engr @ $400/D	30	12,000
		1 Mfg Spvr @ $300/D	6	1,800
		4 Mfg Workers @ $200/D	60	12,000
		Total labor Budget:		**25,800**
Acquire Materials	3W	1 Mat'l Acqis Clk @ $200/D	3	600
		1 Invntry Cntrller @ $200/D	5	1,000
		Total labor Budget:		**1,600**
Manufacture MegaMan	14W	2 Mfg Engr @ $400/D	140	56,000
		1 Mfg Spvr @ $300/D	70	21,000
		20 Mfg Workers @ $200/D	1,400	280,000
		Total labor Budget:		**357,000**
Q.C. Product	14W	1 Quality Engr @ $300/D	28	8,400
		1 Q.C. Worker @ $150/D	28	4,200
		Total labor Budget:		**12,600**
Develop Ads	6W	1 Mkting Mgr @ $500/D	12	6,000
		1 Ad Writer @ $350/D	30	10,500
		1 Graphics Spec @ $250/D	15	3,750
		Total labor Budget:		**20,250**
Run Ads	8W	1 Mkting Mgr @ $500/D	10	5,000
		Total labor Budget:		**5,000**
Hire Sales	6W	1 Recruiter @ $350/D	30	10,500
		1 Sales Mgr @ $400/D	15	6,000
		Total labor Budget:		**16,500**
Train Sales	5W	1 Instruc Dsnr @ $350/D	25	8,750
		1 Cbt Dsnr @ $350/D	25	8,750
		1 Trainer @ $300/D	10	3,000
		5 Telemarketers @ $250/D	25	6,250
		5 Field Sales @ $350/D	25	8,750
		Total labor Budget:		**35,500**
Sell MegaMan	16W	1 Sales Mgr @ $400/D	80	32,000
		5 Telemarketers @ $250/D	400	100,000
		5 Field Sales @ $350/D	400	140,000
		Total labor Budget:		**272,000**

Again, these are just the labor budgets. Accurate costing requires that all types of resources be assigned to activities, in order to determine the budget for each activity. To save time on our MegaMan project example, we are simply going to estimate the total costs by assuming the labor budget is a variable percentage, depending on the type of activity (Figure 8.3). Each type of activity is a different type of work and can be expected to be more or less labor intensive. Manufacturing, for instance, will require more equipment and materials than designing, while advertising will require paying for placing the ads. For each of the four summary-level activities, we will estimate what percentage of the total budget the labor budget represents. The one exception will be *Run Ads*, where a major expense is incurred in the placement of the advertisements. An additional $400,000 will be added for this.

Table 8.3 Total Budget for the MegaMan Development Project

Summary Activity	Budget Percent	Activity Name	Labor Budget ($)	Total Budget ($)
Design	75	Design MegaMan	80,500	107,333
and		Build Prototype	21,500	28,667
Prototyping		Test Prototype	10,000	13,333
		Design Packaging	13,250	17,667
		Total:	**125,250**	**167,000**
Packaging	50	Create Packaging	51,000	102,000
and		Package MegaMan	63,000	126,000
Shipping		Ship MegaMan	6,100	12,200
		Total:	**120,100**	**240,200**
Manufacturing	30	Set Up Manufacturing	25,800	86,000
and		Acquire Materials	1,600	5,333
Q.C.		Manufacture MegaMan	357,000	1,190,000
		Q.C. Product	12,600	42,000
		Total:	**397,000**	**1,323,333**

(continued)

Table 8.3 (Continued)

Summary Activity	Budget Percent	Activity Name	Labor Budget ($)	Total Budget ($)
Sales	20	Develop Advertising	20,250	101,250
and		Run Ads	5,000	425,000
Marketing		Hire Sales	16,500	82,500
		Train Sales	35,500	177,500
		Sell MegaMan	272,000	1,360,000
		Total:	**349,250**	**2,146,250**

And so we can summarize the budget numbers all the way to the top for the entire project:

Project	Labor Budget	Total Budget
MegaMan Development Project	$991,600	$3,876,783

■ CALCULATING THE PROJECT DIPP

The result of our cost analysis is a project with a budget of $3,876,783 which, if it's completed in 30 weeks, has an EMV of $10 million. This would give us the following DIPP:

$$\text{DIPP} = \text{EMV} \div \text{ETC}$$
$$= \$10,000,000 \div \$3,876,783$$
$$= 2.58$$

But the current schedule calls for it to take 34 weeks. At 34 weeks, the EMV is only $2 million. Thus the current DIPP is much less than 1:

$$\text{DIPP} = \$2,000,000 \div \$3,876,783 = 0.52$$

We have four alternatives:

1. Cut costs drastically
2. Reduce the duration
3. Increase scope to increase expected value (with probable increases in cost as well)
4. Cancel the project

■ ANALYZING AND IMPLEMENTING THE DRED

With our activity budgets computed, we can now calculate the estimated DRED cost of the critical path activities, or what the cost might be of adding resources in order to reduce the DRAG. This can then be compared to the dollar value of the DRAG time that would be saved on that activity.

I use the term "might be" rather than "would be" because adding resources would probably not result in a straight-line increasing of the cost of the activity for two reasons:

1. When the resources per time unit are increased, the amount of time over which they are used decreases. This is the whole point of utilizing the DRED duration, to shorten the activity. If the activity's duration is halved when the resources per week are doubled, then we have a 1:1 ratio, which would leave the resource usage unchanged from the original duration. If the cost rate of that usage also remains the same, the cost would stay the same.

2. It is very possible that we may have to go to time-and-a-half labor rates, or pay some other premium, in order to get the additional resources. This would have to be determined during the resource scheduling and leveling processes.

But if the resources are readily available, we can compute the cost of the DRED level of resources. We will then have some numbers which, while not necessarily and absolutely accurate, are ballpark figures that we can analyze and, ultimately, check for accuracy when we do resource scheduling against the resource availability database. These will allow us to compare the DRED cost with the DRAG cost and try to arrive at the most profitable schedule. Notice how analyzing resources on this basis starts us moving toward resource levels that are "right-sized" in terms of their value to the project and to the organization.

The DRED is an indication of resource elasticity, and the duration estimate based on the assumption of doubled resources is a valid presumption, in that the activity manager and/or subject matter expert has said: "Yes, given twice the resources per day, we could probably finish this activity in X number of days." However, it would be dangerous to assume that the DRED represents some sort of precise metric or constant, based on "straight-lined" logic that if doubling the resources cuts the project duration by 20 percent, then tripling the resources should cut it by 40 percent, 30 percent, or any other number. Such an inference would always be dependent on the precise nature of the work. The Law of Diminishing Returns may determine that, on a given activity, there is zero additional impact, or even a negative impact, from tripling resources.

Rather, what the DRED does is give the project manager a sense of what might be the effect of adding resources to an activity. For instance, if an activity has a duration estimate of 12 weeks and a DRED of 10 weeks, it may be that adding just 50 percent more resources, rather than doubling, might result in an 11-week duration. It may be that tripling the resources would reduce the duration to 8 weeks, but the project manager cannot assume that. Such an inference must always be run past the original estimator: "Okay, Joe, you said that if you had twice the resources, you could shave the time needed for this work by 2 weeks. But this activity is on the critical path with DRAG of 3 weeks. What would it take to cut it by 3 weeks? Is it possible? Would putting six people on it, instead of the current two, be enough? Would five do the trick?" If Joe says that even if you get the entire U.S. Marine Corps working on it, you're not going to be able to cut it by 3 weeks, then that is the reality with which the project plan must be reconciled.

Ultimately, we would have to find out whether such resources (and, remember, the assumption is that they are identical to the original resource estimates: equal skills, equal training, etc.) would be available. The cost of the additional resources would have to be computed and weighed. But, for the moment, we just want to know whether or not, if the additional resources were applied, it would have a beneficial impact. To just assume that they are unavailable, and therefore ignore what impact they could have, is to turn a blind eye to the fact that

➤ Resources that may be completely unavailable at current market prices might become quite plentiful when the cost of not having those resources (i.e., DRAG cost) is quantified.

➤ If the potential beneficial impact of increased resource levels is ignored in project after project throughout the organization, there will never be justification for those additional resources.

The DRED comes with a cost component: What is the additional cost, without overtime or other premium, when we double the resources? It's not as simple as doubling the budget, because the amount of time during which we use all the resources, or the work hours, will be cut by the difference between the duration estimate and the DRED—that, after all, is why we'd be implementing the DRED. The tentative DRED budget (prior to adjustments for availability premiums) would be computed as follows:

DRED budget = 2 (activity budget) × (DRED ÷ by duration)

Let us take the activity *Develop Advertising*:

Activity	Duration	DRED	Budget
Develop Advertising	6W	5W	$101,250

Based on this, *Develop Advertising*'s DRED budget would be:

$$2 (\$101,250) \times (5 \div 6)$$
$$= \$202,500 \times 0.83$$
$$= \$168,075$$

This in turn leads to DRED cost, or the cost of implementing the DRED duration, as being equal to:

$$\text{DRED Budget} - \text{Activity Budget}$$
$$= \$168,075 - \$101,250$$
$$= \$66,825$$

In other words, doubling the resources on *Develop Advertising*, will cost us $66,825, before taking into account overtime or other availability premiums.

In this case, *Develop Advertising* is off the critical path and therefore has no associated DRAG cost. But if it were on the critical path, the 1 week saved, at $2 million, would be easily worth the cost. In fact, the premium would have to be very large (or the DRAG cost small) for it *not* to be worthwhile to implement the DRED.

Table 8.4 shows the results of this analysis for the critical path of the MegaMan development project. It shows the cost of implementing each DRED duration, and then it shows the results, in both schedule and net profit. Notice that the activities are arranged in descending order of the benefit of utilizing the DRED.

Table 8.4 Results of the Critical Path of the MegaMan Development Project

Activity	Duration	Budget ($)	DRAG	DRAG Cost ($)	DRED	DRED Cost	Time Saved	Net $ Gain
Package MegaMan	6W	126,000	3W	6.00M	3W	0	3W	6.00M
Design MegaMan	8W	107,333	5W	8.40M	6W	53,662	2W	3.95M
Manufacture MegaMan	14W	1,190,000	3W	6.00M	12W	850,000	2W	3.15M
Build Prototype	5W	28,667	1W	2.00M	3W	5,733	1W	2.00M
Ship MegaMan	2W	12,200	1W	2.00M	1W	0	1W	2.00M
Acquire Materials	3W	5,333	2W	4.00M	3W	—	0W	0

The numbers in the chart above are based on a hypothetical case study, yet they are fairly typical in terms of the economic situation they portray: The cost, without availability premiums of the resources needed to shorten a project, is almost invariably less by large amounts than the cost, in EMV reduction, of not shortening the project. This suggests that the availability premiums that are justifiable are also large. For example, the net gain of $6 million on the *Package MegaMan* activity suggests that we could pay out a bonus of $100,000 for each of 20 packagers working on the activity at its DRED level of resourcing, along with a cool $250,000 for the two supervisors and two managers, and still make $3 million more in profit than if we just sit and say: "Gee, we don't have any more packaging personnel!" Think we could find 10 more packagers for a $100,000 bonus for 3-weeks work? I bet we could get them for a $2,000 bonus, and increase our profit by almost the full $6 million!

Such premiums are not routinely implemented on projects, because the vast majority of business organizations aren't even using the rudiments of traditional project management, far less these new TPC metrics. They aren't even using CPM, so how can they ever determine where they need more resources? The biggest difficulties are in determining where the additional resources will do (1) *any* good, and, (2) the *most* good.

This is precisely the analysis that the TPC metrics DRAG, DRAG Cost, DRED, and DRED cost are designed to facilitate. Without that analysis, paying out availability premiums is usually just throwing money away, so you're probably better off not paying them at all. (Of course, this doesn't stop some organizations from paying such premiums anyway. How often do companies pay early or on-time delivery incentives to suppliers, and then have the new parts sit around for weeks until the rest of the project team is ready to use them?)

➤ Making the Scheduling Decisions

Many people find it easier to make decisions when there are no data available. This is because, without data, you can never be shown to be wrong, but you can still be wrong, even if the data don't immediately show it. Unfortunately, when the data do eventually come to light, it may be under the heading "Corporate Bankruptcies."

The TPC methodology does not make the decisions for the project manager. It simply provides data on which project decisions can be based. Many decisions, which previously might have been seen as close issues and where the wrong call may well have been made, should now become no-brainers. But for other decisions, the data may merely highlight the evenness of the competing solutions.

The data from Table 8.4 relating the DRED to potential gain now needs to be applied to the actual details of the project schedule. We must return to the network logic diagram of our MegaMan development project to make each decision and change sequentially, assess the impact of each, and move to the next decision (Figure 8.2).

From Table 8.4, we could see that *design MegaMan*, with a budget of $107,333, is costing us $8.4 million in DRAG. Going

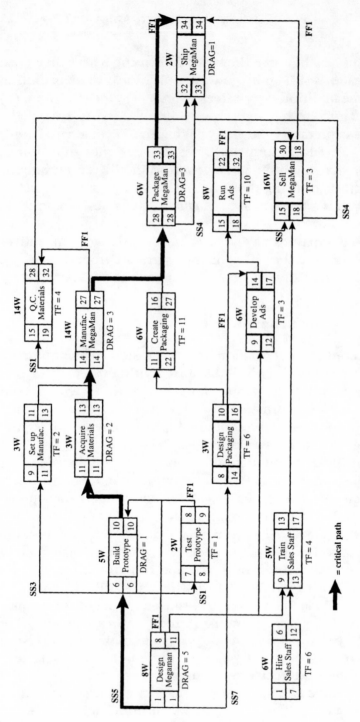

Figure 8.2 Current CPM Schedule for the MegaMan Project, Showing DRAG Totals

to the DRED would cut the DRAG by 2 weeks (and the project duration to 32 weeks), saving $4 million in DRAG cost for an additional $53,662 in resources, a net gain of $3.95 million. Clearly, the DRED should be implemented if at all possible. But why not keep adding resources, if possible? At what point should we stop? We know that the activity is quite resource elastic, because doubling the resources is expected to reduce the duration by 2 weeks, or 25 percent.

In addition, *Manufacture MegaMan*, *Package MegaMan*, and *Ship MegaMan* all are on the critical path, with DRAG, and have potential DRED gains that make them attractive targets for additional resources. By contrast, notice that *Acquire Materials* is not at all resource elastic—its 2 weeks of DRAG cannot be removed by doubling the resources (although, of course, it may be possible to shorten the activity by changing resources: New suppliers, especially with additional dollars going to early delivery incentives, might do wonders).

It's time for a conference with the activity managers of all the resource-elastic critical path activities, and if necessary, their subject matter experts. The project manager should start by displaying the current network schedule, showing the scheduling and EMV implications, and explaining how the DRED estimates of these particular activities offer possibilities for improving the current scenario.

In looking at the *Design MegaMan* activity, we see that all the DRAG is in the first 5 weeks, where the work is that has to be performed in order for the next critical path activity, *Build Prototype*, to start. We might be able to use the DRED to save 2 weeks, thereby shortening the SS lag value to 3 weeks. Is this feasible? The activity manager for *Design MegaMan* says no—he doesn't have any additional resources available to put on this activity. Immediately the project manager stops him:

You don't understand. Leave me to worry about the resources. What I'm asking is, if we were able to double the resources on this activity, would we be able to shorten it by 2 weeks and shorten the SS lag to 3 weeks? And if we got you even more resources—never mind from where—would you be able to knock any more time off it?

One interesting thing about this approach is that activity and functional managers are often so delighted at the prospect of hiring additional resources that they will eagerly collaborate in the project optimization process. It may be important for the project manager to stress that the additional resources can only be purchased through the confident promise of the forecast time savings. It would be most unfortunate if additional resources were hired at exorbitant expense, only to discover that the activity's DRAG is left unchanged.

After more careful thought, the activity manager replies that bringing on a bunch of additional people to the *design MegaMan* activity would only muddle things, but that the DRED reduction might be accomplished by using one additional design engineer, and having the entire activity team other than the drafter work 80-hour weeks. There may be a risk, he warns, in that tired brains do not operate as imaginatively, and are more subject to errors. He suggests to the project manager that a nice project bonus for good work and on-time completion will keep the brains sufficiently fresh. The activity manager narrows his eyes and nods, but now stresses that this really is all he can offer—further reduction is not feasible. The project manager agrees, and the change is implemented.

The reduced duration of 6 weeks also reduces the SS lag to 3 weeks and the DRAG to 3 weeks. This in turn increases the project's EMV from $4 million to $6 million. Since the activity duration is now just 6 weeks, we don't need an SS7 relationship with *Design Packaging*; a simple FS relationship will do. The adjusted network logic diagram is shown in Figure 8.3, with a duration of 32 weeks (correlating to an EMV of $6 million).

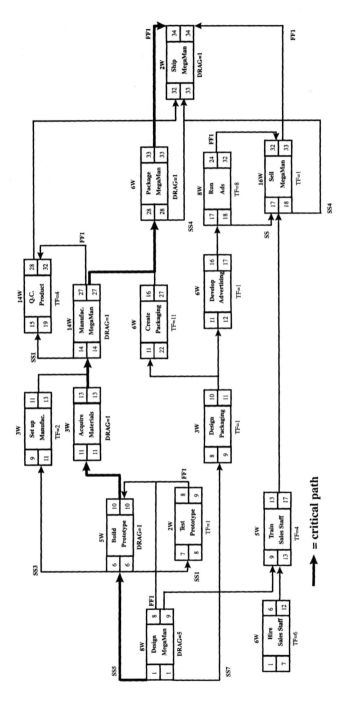

Figure 8.3 A DRED-reduced CPM Schedule for the MegaMan Project, Showing New Completion Date

➤ = critical path

With the increased EMV, the DIPP, previously 0.52, now grows to more than 1.0; how much more we won't know until all the resource and availability premium decisions have been made. But at least we now have a schedule that suggests the project will be profitable. It's important to recognize that this whole remedial process would be quite impossible in the typical organization where the budget is capped up front; if the project manager's mandate is to spend no more than, for example, $3,880,000, then there would be no room for this kind of maneuvering—we would have had to cancel the project by now. The concept of "spend money to make money" is alien to that environment.

Now the conference discussion turns to the other critical path activities where time might be saved. The DRAG on the other resource-elastic critical path activities *Manufacture MegaMan* and *Package MegaMan* (as well as the inelastic *Acquire Materials*) remains at 3 weeks. This is particularly fortuitous in the case of *Package MegaMan*, since its DRED shows it to be so resource elastic (1:1 in terms of time gained for doubled resources) as to also be 3 weeks. Is this indeed the case? The activity manager confirms that this is so, although he warns that the number of in-house packagers is limited and that the Human Resources Department has been particularly reluctant to approve the hiring of additional packagers. It seems that a booming economy has made the going rate for these unskilled laborers more than some cost-cutting maven is willing to pay. The project manager nods absently, mutters what sounds like: "Leave that to me," and changes the duration of *Package MegaMan* to 3 weeks, and its lag relationship with *Ship MegaMan* to SS2. This produces the following network logic diagram (Figure 8.4).

Now we have a schedule that not only meets the original requirement of allowing our product to reach the retail outlets by the start of the shopping season at the beginning of week 31, but we have also built in an extra week. That week may represent contingency time, or management reserve, in case anything slips. But remember, it is also worth an addi-

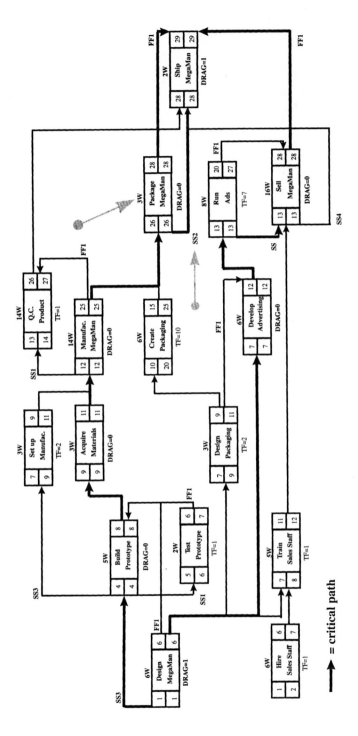

Figure 8.4 A Second DRED-Reduced CPM Schedule for the MegaMan Project, Showing an Even Earlier Completion Date

➤ = critical path

231

tional $400,000, according to the TPC Business Case projections. Our project EMV is up to $10,400,000.

In looking at the latest network logic diagram, three things should stand out:

1. There are now two separate critical paths, which means two paths of the same length.

2. The DRAG of almost all the activities (all except the source and the sink activities) on both critical paths is zero. This makes sense when you realize that an activity's DRAG is equal to the total float of the parallel activity with the least total float. Since the parallel paths are both critical, activities on each will have total float of zero, mutually limiting the DRAG of the parallel path activities to zero.

3. The total float of the activities that are not on the critical paths have also shrunk two small numbers, in most cases no more than 2 weeks.

All this is indicative of a project schedule that is being compressed to its minimum. Between the start of week 4 and the end of week 28, any further compression will require similar duration reductions on the parallel critical path. And if a 2-week compression is accomplished, even more paths will then become critical, making further shortening even more complex and less likely.

The two activities that still incorporate DRAG are the ones that have portions where little else is going on—the first 3 weeks of *Design MegaMan* and the last week of *Ship MegaMan*. We already know, from talking with the activity manager for *Design MegaMan*, that there is little hope of that activity being compressed further. However, that last week of *Ship MegaMan* seems to offer an opportunity. It has a duration of 2 weeks and a DRED of 1 week. Currently, it is on the critical path because of the FF1 relationships with *Package MegaMan* and *Sell MegaMan*.

But it seems somewhat wasteful to have to take a whole extra week to ship the packaged product. Because of the DRED, we know that all the actual work of shipping could be accomplished in 1 week. Yet we're adding a week of DRAG, at a cost of $400,000, for that 1 week. This requires a discussion with the activity managers of all three activities. The managers of *Package MegaMan* and *Ship MegaMan* are already present, so we send out and ask the activity manager for *Sell MegaMan* to join us.

The ensuing discussion soon makes it clear that the 1-week lags have been input as a sort of safety valve. Just in case there are any problems with any of the three activities, the three activity managers want to make sure there is time to coordinate things and work the kinks out. Which is fine, except it's going to cost us $400,000.

When this cost factor is explained to the activity managers, they understand the implications and are only too eager to work around the problem. The activity manager for *Sell MegaMan*, who is also the marketing manager assigned to that activity, agrees to hire an administrative assistant whose job it will be to coordinate the selling, packaging, and shipping. In going to the DRED level of resources, the activity manager for *Ship MegaMan* adopts a 3-shift, 6-days-a-week schedule that will allow shipping to continue for 32 hours after both selling and packaging are complete. This means that the last shipment will leave the loading dock at midnight Saturday night, still in time to reach the stores by 9 o'clock Monday morning. At a savings of $400,000.

Our completed CPM schedule looks as displayed in Figure 8.5.

The budgets of a few of the activities will have changed to generate the new durations. The new data is displayed in Table 8.5 in bold.

Notice that even though the DRED was used by the project manager to determine which critical path activities were resource elastic, in only one case was the activity duration reduced by doubling the resources. In the two other

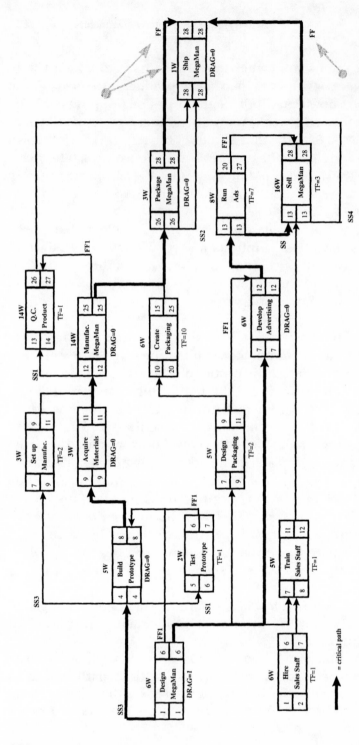

Figure 8.5 A Completed CPM Schedule for the MegaMan Project, Showing Completion Date of Week 28

234

Table 8.5 Effort and Cost Due to Using DRED

Activity	Duration	Resource @ Rate	Effort (WD)	Budget ($)
Design	6W	1 Prod Mgr @ $600/D	60	36,000
MegaMan		2 Prod Dsgners @ $500/D	120	60,000
		2 Dsgn Engrs @ $350/D	**120**	**42,000**
		1 Drafter @ $250/D	10	2,500
		Original Total Labor Budget		80,500
		Original Total Budget		107,333
		New Total labor Budget		**140,500**
		New Total Budget		**187,333**
		Total Budget Increase		**80,000**
Package	3W	2 Pkging Mgrs @ $350/D	30	10,500
MegaMan		2 Pkging Spvrs @ $250/D	30	7,500
		20 Packagers @ $150/D	**300**	45,000
		Original Total Labor Budget		63,000
		Original Total Budget		126,000
		New Total Labor Budget		**63,000**
		New Total Budget		**126,000**
		Total Budget Increase		0
Sell	16W	1 Sales Mgr @ $400/D	80	32,000
MegaMan		5 Telemarketers @ $250/D	400	100,000
		5 Field Sales @ $350/D	400	140,000
		Original Total Labor Budget		272,000
		Original Total Budget		1,360,000
	ADD:	**1 Admin Asst @ 200/D**	**80**	**16,000**
		New Total Labor Budget		**288,000**
		New Total Budget		**1,440,000**
		Total Budget Increase		**$80,000**

instances, once the activities were identified as being resource elastic, better and more precise ways were found of applying resources in order to shorten the activity.

Table 8.5 shows that the total budget for *Package MegaMan* was unchanged, while those for *Design MegaMan* and *Sell MegaMan* both increased by (coincidentally) $80,000. The total budget for the project has been increased (so far as we can determine at this stage) by $160,000 to $4,036,783, while the projected duration has gone from 34 weeks to 28 weeks, and the EMV from $2 million to $10.8 million. The DIPP analysis now looks much healthier:

$$\text{DIPP} = \$10,800,000 \div \$4,036,783 = 2.68$$

■ TPC VALUE SCHEDULING

Earlier we developed a value breakdown structure, which drove the concept of managing the project's EMV down to the activity level, by determining the value that each activity was adding to the project's EMV. The updated VBS is displayed in Figure 8.6, with activity value-addeds translated into percentages of the overall project EMV of, now $10.8 million.

We have been planning this project using the TPC methodology, and so have been able to optimize our project's schedule and, ultimately, EMV, without cutting scope. But this is not always the case. Nor will it necessarily remain the case with our MegaMan project.

In order to justify its inclusion in a project, an activity must add more value than it costs. This might seem like a banal concept, except that we have learned that the cost of an activity is often much greater than the price of the resources it uses—the delay cost is usually much greater. The fact that so many projects are scheduled without using CPM almost guarantees that activities with net value-added (NVA) that is negative will be included. Even projects that use CPM are prone to such inclusions if they do not incorporate the concepts of

1. The TPC Business Case
2. DRAG
3. DRAG cost
4. The VBS and activity value-added

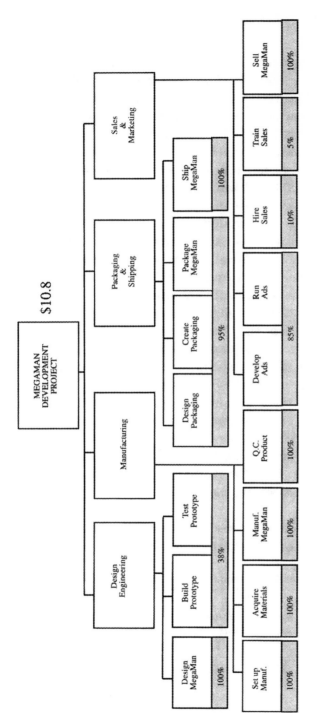

Figure 8.6 Current VBS of the MegaMan Project

As we said, right now the MegaMan project does not need to trim scope because all of its activities are adding more value than they are costing. This is primarily due to the fact that there is now only one activity with DRAG: *Design MegaMan* has 1 week of DRAG at a DRAG cost (given the current projected completion date) of $400,000. Add its budget of $187,333, and its net cost is nowhere close to its value-added of (now) $10.8 million. In fact, since *Design MegaMan* is a mandatory activity, we can never cut it from the project. *Design MegaMan's* value-added is always 100 percent of the project's EMV because we can't make and sell MegaMan without designing it (however we actually do the design).

But what about the optional activities? Three of them are so valuable that it is unlikely we would ever remove them unless we canceled the project. But three others are of sufficiently low value that they *might* become candidates for the trash at some point. (They are shown in Table 8.6.)

Currently, all of the optional activities are adding significantly to the value of the project. The two *Sales Staff* activities are currently insulated from DRAG cost by a week of float. But what would happen if it took an extra 3 weeks to hire the sales staff? Suddenly, *Train Sales Staff* would be pushed onto the critical path with 2 weeks of DRAG. That would carry with it a DRAG cost of $800,000, versus the $360,000 that the training has been estimated to add to the revenues.

The negative net value-added should not immediately cause the training to be abandoned; but it should cause an

Table 8.6 Net Value-Added of Three Optional Activities

Activity	Value-Added (%)	Value-Added ($)	Budget ($)		DRAG Cost	Value-Added Added ($)
Prototyping (Comb.)	38.0	4.10M	42,000	0	$0	+4.05M
Hire Sales Staff	10.0	1.08M	82,500	0	$0	+1.00M
Train Sales Staff	5.0	0.54M	177,500	0	$0	+0.36M

immediate and careful analysis of the situation. Are the numbers really accurate? Is the value of trained versus untrained salespeople really so small? Is there some other way we could accomplish this training, perhaps more expensively but utilizing less time? Can we trim some of the training, and accomplish it in 1 or 2 weeks?

The key to all this is that, with a project of 1,600, or 16,000 detail-level activities, rather than 16, even if the project manager notices the slippage, she will not notice its full significance in terms of project value, nor the likely remedy of erasing the training activity, until it's too late to do so. The training will occur, and other, more drastic, methods of pulling the project back on schedule will be analyzed. Scope trimming will occur, though often invisibly and in ways that harm both the product EMV and the good reputation of the company. Other projects will be delayed in order to shovel resources over to MegaMan. Finally, the project will probably never regain that lost week.

What is needed is a project management software package that will take the input from the TPC Business Case and VBS, and then apply it to the working schedule at the activity level. In this way, if low NVA activities start to slip, the software package would immediately generate an exception report to the effect that the following activities have negative (or very low positive) NVAs. Then it would be up to the project manager to analyze the data and implement the most satisfactory solutions.

Unfortunately, no such software exists currently. One would almost think that there is no relationship between project activities and profits.

■ SUMMARY

So what ABRA has done, so far, is to generate a budget for the project. This is done by pulling the required resources from the resource database and assigning them to the project, activity by activity. The resource database contains cost rates for the usage of each resource, and this allows us to develop the budget for each activity, and for the overall project.

What we now have is a project plan that includes the following information:

1. Total project duration = 28 weeks
2. Total project budget = $4,036,783
3. Project EMV = $10,800,000
4. Project profit = $6,763,217
5. Project DIPP = 2.68

We also have:

➤ A budget for each activity
➤ A schedule for each activity
➤ The precise resources that will be used on each activity

The combination of the budget and the schedule will allow us to generate a tentative cost accrual schedule, reflecting how the resource utilization and dollar expenditure would accumulate, if the current schedule were implemented. But we don't yet know if we will be able to implement the current schedule, because we still don't know if we will have the necessary resources when we will need them.

But we do have the data we need in order to find out. A combination of this schedule for each activity and the list of precise resources that each activity will use provides us with a schedule of our resource needs. Now all we have to do is compare a calendarized schedule of our resource needs against the calendar of resource availability. That database called a resource library that each department should be maintaining. This brings us to the final chapter of the TPC planning process.

Chapter

Resource Scheduling and Leveling

In the last chapter, we said that there are three items of information regarding resource requirements that need to be determined for each activity.

1. *What* resources are needed?

2. *How much* of each resource is needed in order to complete it within its estimated duration?

3. *When* will each resource be needed?

The first two of these allow us to develop our budgeting and costing information. But the third is at least as important as the other two. Without it, you can never know that you will, in fact, have the resources you need in order to meet your schedule. If you don't have the resources, and if it's real important that you meet that schedule, then either the project should be cancelled or the *What?* and the *How much?* have to change.

The three data elements listed above are entered into a project management software package and matched against the database consisting of the OBS of internally available resources, as shown in Figure 9.1.

■ THE PARAMETERS OF RESOURCE AVAILABILITY

The database of the internal resources should contain information regarding:

1. *What* resources are available?
2. *How much* of each resource is available?
3. *When* will each resource be unavailable?
4. *What is the unit cost* of each resource?

The last item, the unit cost, allows the resource usage to be translated into a budget that is stated in a common unit. This not only allows comparison of one type of resource with another, but also the results of one decision with another, in terms that are usually (though not always) directly related to the organization's reason for existence—profit. (The fact that companies are often so fastidious about budgetary caps and other cost controlling measures, yet so cavalier about revenue forecasts, is a strange dichotomy. Surely someone realizes that the two sides of the profit equation are closely linked, and should be closely linked and monitored, from the activity level up.)

The other three items combine to assist us in performing the last of our scheduling functions: Making sure that we have a work schedule in which the resources will always be there when we need them.

Most modern project management software packages have the functionality to incorporate one or more databases for resource availability as well as multiple project schedules, complete with resource assignment lists. As each project is assimilated, it reserves the resources it requires during

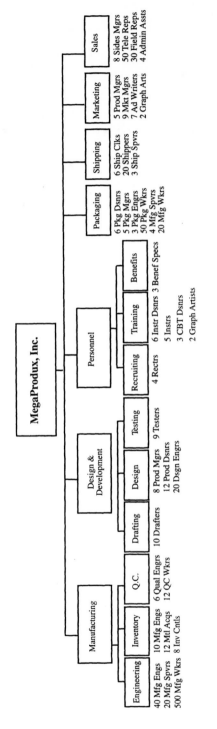

Figure 9.1 OBS of MegaProdux, Inc., Showing Internal Resources

the time that it's scheduled to need them. Then, when a new project is entered into the software, the resources that the previous project took are displayed as already assigned and thus no longer available. The software then matches the project data against the availability data and does two things:

1. It draws attention, through exception messages or online reports, to resource bottlenecks, where there is not a sufficient resource to meet an activity's requirements during its scheduled time.

2. It applies a set of alternative methods, some preprogrammed and some user-defined, designed to "get around" the bottleneck. Optional methods might include:

   ➤ Splitting an activity into one or more parts.

   ➤ Delaying an activity until sufficient resources become available.

   ➤ Utilizing a priority field, at either the activity or the project level, to steal resources from another activity or project to which they had previously been assigned.

This process of sliding the schedule around in order to reduce a project's peak resource requirements and eliminate resource bottlenecks is called resource leveling. The ability to perform this function easily, transparently, and effectively (in the sense of rescheduling activities with minimum delay or extra cost) is a very important feature of a good project management system, and one in which there is tremendous variation between the best and worst packages.[1]

It is also most important to be able to level resources across the organization's entire portfolio, on a multi-project basis. Just because another project was entered into the software first, and snatched up all the available resources, this should not mean that those resources cannot be reassigned to a newer, higher priority project if they are "vital" to that project.

First let's look at how resource leveling works (or is intended to work), and then we can discuss how it should work.

■ RESOURCE LEVELING OFF THE CRITICAL PATH

Two activities, *Set Up Manufacturing* and *Design Packaging*, require the following resources (Table 9.1).

The first hint that there may be a problem comes from the fact that the two activities are scheduled to occur at the same time, and both require manufacturing engineers. This can be displayed nicely in the Gantt chart format (Figure 9.2).

With 40 manufacturing engineers assigned to the Engineering Department, the project manager (and the activity manager) might well feel that there should be no problem getting the necessary resources to perform both activities simultaneously.

Unfortunately, this is a dangerous assumption to make. There is a reason the Engineering Department has 40 manufacturing engineers; it's because they're busy. This is exactly the kind of resource and department, that desperately needs a carefully maintained resource library. And it's exactly the kind of department that never has one.

Fortunately, we at MegaProdux, Inc., understand the value of resource libraries. Senior management has mandated that

Table 9.1 Resources Needed for Set Up Manufacturing and Design Packaging

Activity	Duration	Resource @ Unit Cost	Effort	Budget
Set Up	3W	2 Mfg Engrs @ $400/D	30WD	$12,000
Manufacturing		1 Mfg Spvr @ $300/D	6WD	$1,800
		4 Mfg Workers @ $200/D	60WD	$12,000
Design	3W	1 Pkging Dsnr @ $400/D	15WD	$6,000
Packaging		1 Pkging Engr @ $350/D	15WD	$5,250
		1 Mfg Engr @ $400/D	**5WD**	**$2,000**

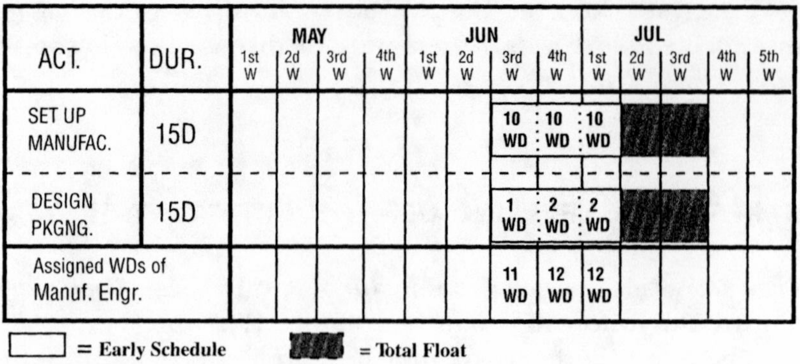

ACT.	DUR.	MAY				JUN				JUL				
		1st W	2d W	3rd W	4th W	1st W	2d W	3rd W	4th W	1st W	2d W	3rd W	4th W	5th W
SET UP MANUFAC.	15D							10 WD	10 WD	10 WD	▓▓	▓▓		
DESIGN PKGNG.	15D							1 WD	2 WD	2 WD	▓▓	▓▓		
Assigned WDs of Manuf. Engr.								11 WD	12 WD	12 WD				

▢ = Early Schedule   ▓▓▓ = Total Float

Figure 9.2 Gantt Chart of Two Activities in the MegaMan Project, Showing Required Levels of the Manufacturing Engineer Resource

every department will have one. So when we load our project into the software, we receive an exception message, informing us that there is insufficient availability of the manufacturing engineer resource to meet our needs for the two activities *Set Up Manufacturing* and *Design Packaging.*[2]

Many software packages will then allow us to examine the overloaded resource and the bottlenecked activities. First

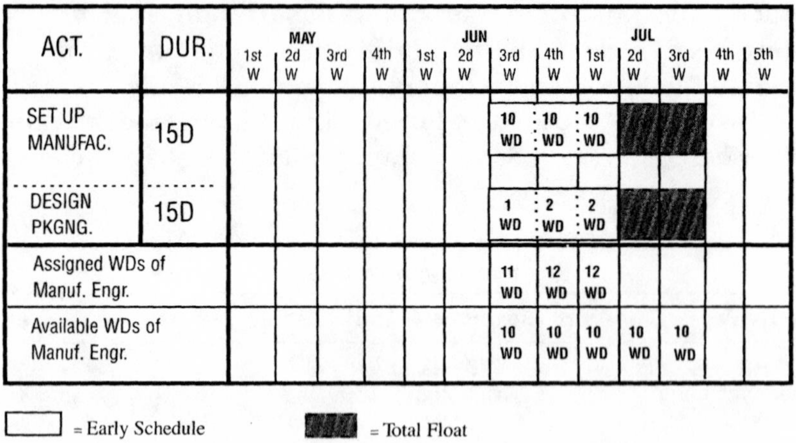

ACT.	DUR.	MAY				JUN				JUL				
		1st W	2d W	3rd W	4th W	1st W	2d W	3rd W	4th W	1st W	2d W	3rd W	4th W	5th W
SET UP MANUFAC.	15D							10 WD	10 WD	10 WD	▓▓	▓▓		
DESIGN PKGNG.	15D							1 WD	2 WD	2 WD	▓▓	▓▓		
Assigned WDs of Manuf. Engr.								11 WD	12 WD	12 WD				
Available WDs of Manuf. Engr.								10 WD	10 WD	10 WD	10 WD	10 WD		

▢ = Early Schedule   ▓▓▓ = Total Float

Figure 9.3 Gantt Chart of Two Activities in the MegaMan Project, Showing Required Levels of the Manufacturing Engineer Resource vs. Available Levels

on a Gantt chart as shown in Figure 9.3, and then on a histogram as in Figure 9.4.

We can readily see that we have good alternatives for solving the problem because we used CPM in scheduling this project. The 2 weeks of total float that each activity enjoys is the key; how we choose to employ that float in scheduling the activities and resources is a matter of preference. We can give priority to *Set Up Manufacturing* (Figure 9.5), which allows *Set up Manufacturing* to finish in 16 days, but pushes *Design Packaging* out to the end of its float (so that it becomes critical), or we could give priority to *Design Packaging* (Figure 9.6).

By giving *Design Packaging* that priority, we would leave it unchanged, but stretch *Set Up Manufacturing* out to 18 days. Whatever schedule is deemed preferable (and, without additional information, my feeling would be *not* to eliminate all the float on *Design Packaging*), the important factor is that the planned completion date for the entire project will not be

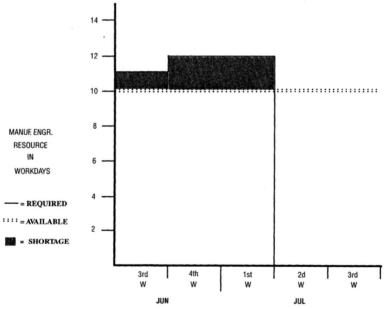

Figure 9.4 Histogram Showing Required Levels of the Manufacturing Engineer Resource vs. Available Levels

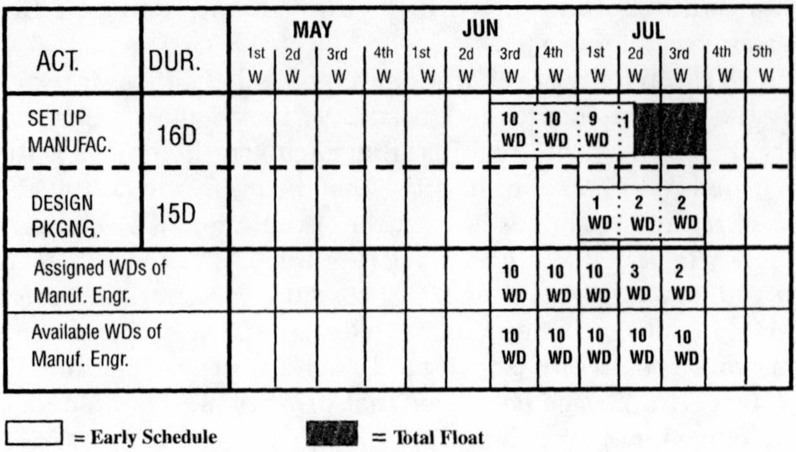

ACT.	DUR.	MAY				JUN				JUL				
		1st W	2d W	3rd W	4th W	1st W	2d W	3rd W	4th W	1st W	2d W	3rd W	4th W	5th W
SET UP MANUFAC.	16D							10 WD	10 WD	9 WD	1			
DESIGN PKGNG.	15D									1 WD	2 WD	2 WD		
Assigned WDs of Manuf. Engr.								10 WD	10 WD	10 WD	3 WD	2 WD		
Available WDs of Manuf. Engr.								10 WD	10 WD	10 WD	10 WD	10 WD		

☐ = Early Schedule ▓ = Total Float

Figure 9.5 Gantt Chart Showing Resources Leveled with *Set Up Manufacturing* Receiving Priority

delayed because of the float, and therefore its EMV will be unaffected. It is possible that there could be a ripple effect, with a successor activity also now being pushed through its float to a period of time when there is another resource bottleneck. And that new bottleneck might not be resolvable off the critical path.

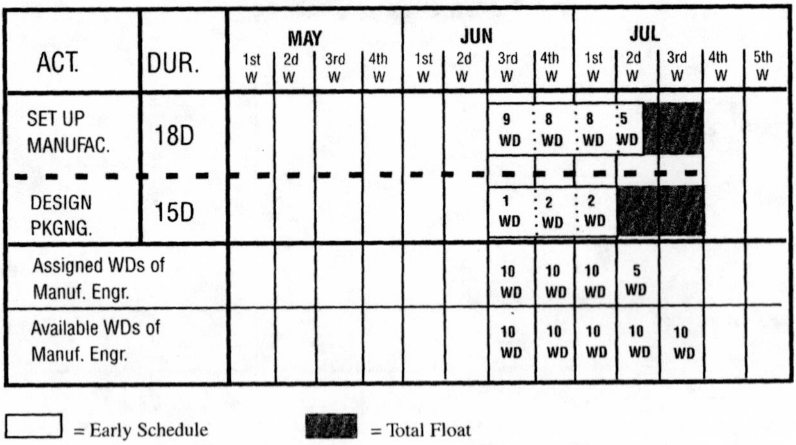

ACT.	DUR.	MAY				JUN				JUL				
		1st W	2d W	3rd W	4th W	1st W	2d W	3rd W	4th W	1st W	2d W	3rd W	4th W	5th W
SET UP MANUFAC.	18D							9 WD	8 WD	8 WD	5 WD			
DESIGN PKGNG.	15D							1 WD	2 WD	2 WD				
Assigned WDs of Manuf. Engr.								10 WD	10 WD	10 WD	5 WD			
Available WDs of Manuf. Engr.								10 WD	10 WD	10 WD	10 WD	10 WD		

☐ = Early Schedule ▓ = Total Float

Figure 9.6 Gantt Chart Showing Resources Leveled with *Design Packaging* Receiving Priority

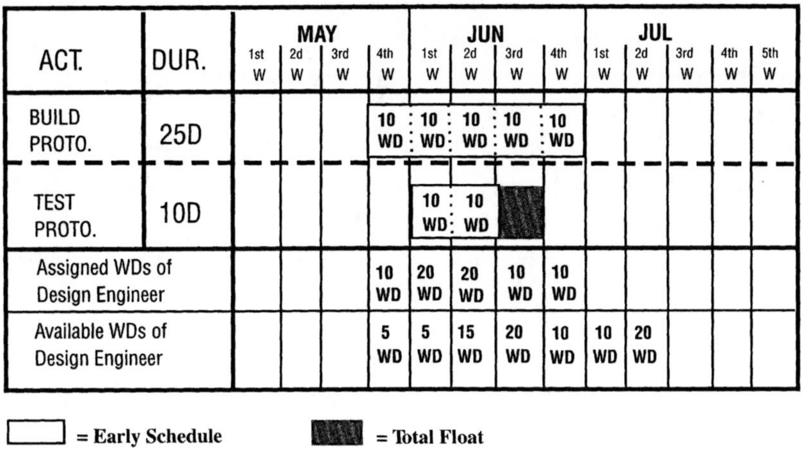

ACT.	DUR.	MAY				JUN				JUL				
		1st W	2d W	3rd W	4th W	1st W	2d W	3rd W	4th W	1st W	2d W	3rd W	4th W	5th W
BUILD PROTO.	25D					10 WD	10 WD	10 WD	10 WD	10 WD					
TEST PROTO.	10D					10 WD	10 WD		▓▓					
Assigned WDs of Design Engineer						10 WD	20 WD	20 WD	10 WD	10 WD					
Available WDs of Design Engineer						5 WD	5 WD	15 WD	20 WD	10 WD	10 WD	20 WD			

☐ = Early Schedule   ▓▓ = Total Float

Figure 9.7 Gantt Chart of Two Activities, One Critical, Showing Required Levels of the Design Engineer Resource vs. Available Levels

However, in general, if two activities are competing for the same resource, and one is on the critical path and one is not, whichever is on the critical path should have priority, delaying the other activity within its float.

■ RESOURCE LEVELING ON THE CRITICAL PATH

What happens when we cannot eliminate resource bottlenecks off the critical path? When, for example, two critical path activities are competing for the same resource, or when the float of the one off the critical path is so little that the resource delay will make it critical?

Let us look at the two prototyping activities, which are somewhat in parallel and share the need for certain resources:[3]

Build Prototype	5W	weeks 4–8	TF=0	2 Design Engrs	50WD
Test Prototype	2W	weeks 5–6	TF=1	2 Design Engrs	20WD

Again the software generates an exception message: We have a bottleneck due to insufficient design engineers. This can be shown on a Gantt chart (Figure 9.7), and on a histogram (Figure 9.8).

Build Prototype is on the critical path, and *Test Prototype* has only 1 week of float. In Figure 9.9, we show how trying to schedule these activities within the current resource limits pushes *Build Prototype* to 30 days, and therefore will push out the project completion date.

Again, this is one activity, but what would be the ripple effect, over a 1,600 activity project? Only a computer could wrestle through all the possible permutations and give an accurate picture of what our schedule might be within our resource limits.

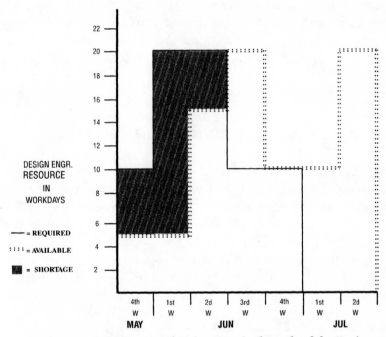

Figure 9.8 Histogram Showing Required Levels of the Design Engineer Resources vs. Available Levels

ACT.	DUR.	MAY				JUN				JUL				
		1st W	2d W	3rd W	4th W	1st W	2d W	3rd W	4th W	1st W	2d W	3rd W	4th W	5th W
BUILD PROTO.	30D					5 WD	5 WD	10 WD	10 WD	10 WD	10 WD			
TEST PROTO.	15D						5 WD	10 WD	5 WD					
Assigned WDs of Design Engineer						5 WD	5 WD	15 WD	20 WD	15 WD	10 WD			
Available WDs of Design Engineer						5 WD	5 WD	15 WD	20 WD	15 WD	10 WD	20 WD		

◻ = Early Schedule

Figure 9.9 Gantt Chart of Two Activities, One Critical, Showing Required Levels of the Design Engineer Resource vs. Available Levels

■ TIME-LIMITED VERSUS RESOURCE-LIMITED RESOURCE LEVELING

Most project management software packages have two completely different algorithms for resource leveling. They are called time-limited resource leveling and resource-limited resource leveling. Most of the time, there is a "toggle" within the software that allows you to select the algorithm you want to use.

The resource-limited resource leveling algorithms that come with certain software packages are close to useless. One very popular package simply pushes to the end of the project all those activities for which there is not sufficient resources available. This helps identify bottlenecked activities, but does nothing to resolve the problem. Other software packages can be tremendously helpful, trying to compute the shortest schedule they can. But a word to the wise, none of the packages produces a truly optimized schedule, in terms of either duration or cost. A slight change in the user-defined parameters, such as priority assignment, can cause the computer to generate a schedule that is much more or less efficient. That is because the number of variables on anything more complex than a very short project would introduce so many possible permutations that it would take hours for even the fastest computer to optimize fully.

In talking about time-limited versus resource-limited leveling, it is important for the software user to realize that these are not really two different tools, nor two different schedules. Rather, it is two alternative pictures of the same set of criteria, treated first in one manner and then in the other.

In the first instance, we will toggle the software so that it produces a time-limited schedule. What this means is that the computer may delay activities within their float, split activities in two, and obey any of the preset parameters as defined by the user. The computer may even schedule activities for which there are not enough resources. But the one thing the computer may not do is delay the project beyond the completion date that the user has specified.

Now, although the software manuals will not state this, and the software itself will allow you to specify any date for completion, it is crucial that the initial snapshot of the time-limited project schedule be based on the project completion date from the CPM schedule.

This is the completion date for which we know we can plan if we don't run into resource shortages. Thus we need to know what the completion date will be if we don't have to delay the project because of shortages, versus if we do. Because resource shortages are things we might be able to do something about.

We now have a schedule generated by the computer dealing simultaneously with all the resource restrictions on all the different activities, but without pushing any activity beyond its late finish date. Next we toggle the software so that it will produce a resource-limited resource schedule. Just as it sounds, this will be a schedule in which the software will once again try to resolve resource bottlenecks, but this time it will not schedule any activity unless and until the resource requirements are fulfilled. And that can mean only one thing: If the resources for an activity do not become available within that activity's float, then it has to be delayed beyond its float. That means that the project completion date may have to be delayed.

A or B, you get your pick. You can go out and get the additional resources you need, and finish the project on time; or you can hold the line on the budget and finish it late.

I have found that the best way to look at this information is in the form of two histograms, one placed immediately above the other so that the schedule implications can be easily seen. Figures 9.10 and 9.11 display these types of histograms.

In one case, we need more resources in order to meet the project completion date. In the other, the resource limitations are accepted as rigid, and the project completion date slips. Again, this is A and B. If we like, we can analyze A1 and B1, where we add more of this resource during that period; or A2 and B2, with more of that resource during this period. But ultimately the resource-limited resource schedule will be our project's working schedule; we are going to

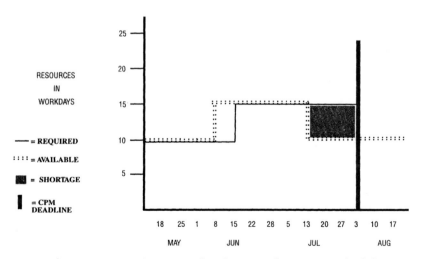

Figure 9.10 A Histogram of a Time-Based Resource Schedule

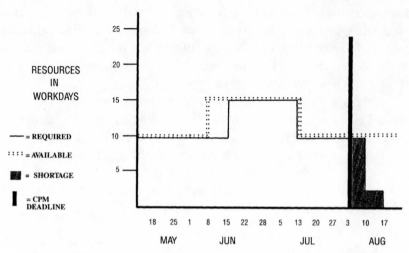

Figure 9.11 A Histogram of a Resource-Limited Resource Schedule

have to live with whatever resource limitations remain in our project plan at the end of this process. The project schedule must reflect those limitations, because they are reality. The project manager must always make of reality an ally, not a foe—that means *using* reality to improve reality.

All the information and formats above have long been a standard part of the traditional project management methodology (even if often ignored in practice). For decades, project managers have been trying to acquire additional resources by showing senior management the kind of data displayed above. "If we don't get two more electrical engineers (or one more plumber, programmer, or widgeter), the project's going to slip by 3 weeks." Most of the time the response is something like: "Your budget's already too much. You're going to have to make do without. Do the best you can."

Is it that senior management doesn't believe the data? Perhaps. But if the project has been planned, utilizing WBS, CPM, ABRA, and all the other standard project management techniques, then the data, while not infallible are certainly reliable. But what is missing is crucial information that will tie together the two sides of the issue in a way that will allow comparison and decision.

On the one hand, the project needs more resources if it is to finish on time. Those resources have an important negative impact on the project (and on the entire organization). That impact is cost measured in dollars.

On the flip side, if the project does not get the resources, it will not finish on time. Time is measured in days, weeks, and months—time is merely an abstraction. Corporations don't work for time, they work for *dollars*. Any time a corporate disagreement occurs, with one side arguing in dollars and the other in time units, the side arguing dollars is going to win.

This is, and always has been, the weakness of traditional project management. It has failed to provide true cost/schedule integration, and it has failed to justify itself, because it deals in time and not in dollars. Of course at some level, every corporate executive appreciates that time is money. But how much money? And how deeply do they appreciate it? The cost of one electrical engineer for 3 weeks is $5,000. You can see it, touch it, count it. There it is, in black and white on the spreadsheet, with a $ in front of it. What is a 3-week delay? You can't see it and you can't touch it. The fact that everyone knows it may be worth a lot more than $5,000 doesn't mean a thing if it ain't got that $ and number on the spreadsheet.

That's the big advantage of TPC. The TPC Business Case allows the schedule overrun to be monetized based on the resultant reduction in EMV. In previous chapters we saw how the delay cost of the project completion could be charged down to the activity level through DRAG and DRAG cost. Now, with the resource-limited schedule, we have further delay costs. These delay costs should be charged down both to the activities being delayed and, even more important, to the resource shortages that are causing the delays. In other words, TPC will allow us to list the cost of a resource shortage on the same spreadsheet as the electrical engineer's $5,000, also in black and white and with a dollar sign before it. Then we can subtract one number from the other and see what action is preferable, and by how much.

■ THE CLUB

The difference between the project completion date of the CPM schedule and that of the resource-limited resource schedule may be 3 weeks; but, if the project is our MegaMan development project, and the two dates are week 28 and week 31, the difference is also $2.8 million: $400,000 apiece for weeks 29 and 30, and $2 million for week 31. This difference is the result of resource leveling without first resolving the resource bottlenecks. So the TPC term for this reduction in project EMV is the Cost of Leveling with Unresolved Bottlenecks. It is the CLUB to be used for getting additional resources—pay now or pay later.

The CLUB is based on the reduction in value of the entire project due to resolving all the resource bottlenecks. But if we are employing ABRA, resources are not assigned to the project; they are assigned to each activity, during the time that the activity is scheduled to occur. Therefore, just as we charged the CPM schedule delay cost down to each activity's DRAG, so too we need to charge the project's CLUB down to the activities and resources that generate the delay.

■ RESOURCE SCHEDULE DRAG

On the CPM schedule, DRAG is a function of the logic of the work, that is, the way the work must be done. The DRAG calculation quantifies the amount of time that could potentially be saved by eliminating an activity, or by reducing its duration to zero. This is of great value when trying to determine where, and by how much, one can shorten the project duration on any given activity.

When we load resources and generate the resource-limited schedule, however, another delaying factor comes into play: Delay due to the lack of sufficient resources on a timely basis. This type of delay also should be tied to the activity that is being delayed, but when figuring out where and by how much we can shorten the project, we need to take into account both types of delay (in combination). Ultimately we must be able to separate out the two different types of delay, because one can be addressed by adding more resources and the other can't.

What this means is that on the resource-limited schedule, we need to quantify two different types of DRAG. The first is the combination DRAG, or what we will call resource schedule DRAG. It is the same type of DRAG as we had on the CPM schedule: It is the amount of time that could *potentially* be saved by shortening an activity, before the critical path changes. The actual number (indeed, the entire critical path) may change in going from the CPM to the resource-limited schedule; but it is still calculated in the same way— by determining the total float of the parallel activity with the least total float.

Once the raw total of each activity's resource schedule DRAG has been computed, we then need to determine how much delay is due to which of three different causes:

1. Delay due to the logic of the work, (i.e., CPM schedule DRAG),

2. Delay due to other ancestor activities, which unavoidably push out the schedule of the successor, and

3. Delay due to this specific activity having to wait for resources, which we will call resource availability DRAG or RAD (notice that it is still part of the Removed Activity Gauge—if the activity is removed, the resource delay will go with it).

■ RESOURCE AVAILABILITY DRAG (RAD)

It is this third type of delay, the resource availability DRAG, that we particularly need to isolate, because it is the one we can really do something about. Furthermore, by tying an activity's RAD to the CLUB, we can see how much it would be worth to reduce or eliminate the portion of the DRAG due to resource availability. This would allow us to arrive at the maximum availability premium that it would make sense to pay for a given resource.

The formula for calculating the RAD is complex, and not one that can easily be used mentally. But for a computer, it would be simple and very valuable. What follows is the formula for computing the RAD. (If you are not interested in how the formula works, but merely in the value of its output, feel free to skip it.) Here are the three important things to remember about the RAD:

1. An activity can only have RAD if it has resource schedule DRAG. The fact that an activity is delayed because of resource availability does not give it RAD unless the delay pushes out the critical path.

2. An activity can never have more RAD than the amount of its resource schedule DRAG. RAD is a subset of resource schedule DRAG. If activity X is being delayed by 5 weeks because its resources aren't available, but the parallel path has only 1 week of total float, then activity X has only 1 week of resource schedule DRAG and therefore can't have more than 1 week of RAD.

3. As always, DRAG is found only on the critical path—an activity may not have resource schedule DRAG even though

    ➤ It was on the critical path, with DRAG, on the CPM schedule, and

    ➤ It is further delayed on the resource schedule.

If another path on the resource schedule is being delayed even more (so much more as to negate the total float that it had on the CPM schedule), then the old CPM critical path activities no longer have DRAG—they are no longer delaying the project, so you would gain no time by shortening or deleting them.

■ COMPUTING RAD

The RAD for activity X can be calculated by using the following formula:

Resource availability DRAG = Late finish (resource-limited schedule) – late finish (CPM schedule) – (largest difference between any predecessor's CPM late finish and resource-limited schedule late finish)

OR

the resource schedule DRAG, whichever is less

The first part of the formula measures the amount that the activity is being delayed in going from the CPM to the resource-limited schedule. The second part of the formula determines the delay due to lack of resources on this activity by subtracting out the amount of the above delay that was caused by ancestor activities. The third part of the formula ensures that the amount of time that will be gained on the project completion date is not overstated. The resource delay may be reduced from 10 days to 0, but if this only shortens the project by 2 days, 80 percent of the reduction would be of little value.

■ THE VALUE OF RAD

Resource availability DRAG is a vital metric to the project, the functional department, and the overall organization, because it is a delay factor that we can do something about. Much of the time, we might be able to correct the problem right on this project and activity. If the RAD due to insufficient programmers is 2 weeks, and the project's EMV is being decreased by $50,000 for each week of duration, that computes to $100,000 that we would save by removing the RAD. That makes $99,999 we can spend to get additional programming help and still be 1 dollar better off than we were before. Do you know of a programmer who can be hired for $49,999.50 per week?

I bet you do! In fact, I bet you know a programmer who would work for 2 weeks at a mere $10,000 per week. Or $2,000 per week. Fifty thousand dollars is simply the *maximum* availability premium (MAP) we should pay. When quantified in the right way, on a project delay and EMV basis, the resource availability premiums are almost always *so enormous* that it makes the whole process seem ludicrous. (After all, we aren't really going to pay a programmer $50,000 a week! That would blow up our salary structure and ultimately our entire organization. Everyone would soon be blackmailing us for exorbitant wages.) But those kinds of numbers are real. This is what it's really costing a project like this not to have sufficient programmers available.

And that's just one project. Where else is the lack of programmers hurting us? How many projects across the entire organization would finish 1, 2, or 3 weeks earlier if we had 1, 2, or 3 more programmers? How much do those weeks add up to, in dollars, in the course of a quarter? In a year?

This is where the functional manager comes into play. Functional managers are responsible for maintaining the resources that support the projects, and usually find themselves with departments and subordinates that are grossly overworked. Every time a functional manager tries to hire additional resources, he's told that he has to hold the line on head count. As a result the head count numbers keep becoming even more grotesquely unbalanced.

One trouble is that most functional managers really don't understand project management. WBS, critical path, total float, that's all project manager stuff. When corporations run training seminars on project management, the functional managers don't even attend. After all, they're not project managers. They don't have to manage projects. They just get to damage projects by not fully understanding the relationship between the project and the resources that they control. They don't know how to get the project data they need in order to justify the additional resources that are required to better support the projects.

One company with which I have worked often is an international organization that puts communications satellites into space. Every penny of revenue that this organization generates is related to projects: building satellites, building ground stations, developing telemetric software, changing orbits, selling broadcast time, and so on. Yet, until very recently, this company did not use CPM; did not assign resources to projects, never mind activities; and never charged work hours to projects or activities. The board of directors had mandated a budget cap, and additional expenditures and new hires had to be rigorously justified. As a result, everyone throughout the organization complained bitterly about being underresourced.

What is wrong with this picture? How can you possibly justify additional resources in a project-driven company when you have absolutely no data to indicate what impact the lack of such resources is having on projects? Never mind the fact that the data was not quantified in dollars; it wasn't even quantified in time units. Two departments, human resources and the controller's office, understood the problem and attempted, despite great resistance, to introduce project management techniques and project-based time reporting. However, functional managers were the most resistant individuals because they could only see that more data would make the inefficiencies of their departments more visible—not how these project management techniques could benefit them.[4]

➤ The Resource-Leveled Schedule for the MegaMan Project

The resource bottlenecks due to the lack of sufficient design engineers for the prototyping activities causes the *Build Prototype* activity to take 6 weeks instead of our estimated duration of 5 weeks. To compound matters, when we look at the entire resource-limited schedule, it turns out that we have slipped not 1, but 5 weeks. We knew when we went to the DRED for the *Package MegaMan* activity that we were going to need additional resources—well, they have not yet been hired. Additionally, the resources to *Ship MegaMan* in 1 week are there for weeks 28 or 29, but thereafter they'll be needed on other activities, forcing *Ship MegaMan* back to it's original two-week duration. Our resource-limited schedule looks like Figure 9.12.

Notice that the duration of *Package MegaMan* is back to 6 weeks, its SS lag with *Ship MegaMan* is 4 weeks, and the two FF predecessors for *Ship MegaMan* again need a week of lag. Additionally, *Test Prototype* cannot start until week 6, a RAD of 1 week, and so its float has disappeared and it is now critical. As we discussed earlier, *Set Up Manufacturing* has had its duration increased by a week. *Design MegaMan's* start remains critical, but its finish now has two weeks of total float.

If we have to adopt this resource-limited schedule, our duration will be 33 weeks and our EMV will decrease to $4 million, a point at which our DIPP would indicate that it is probably no longer worth undertaking. On the other hand, it would be worth $6 million to shorten it by 3 weeks, and another $800,000 to get back to where we know we can be without resource delays, the CPM schedule duration of 28 weeks. Surely we can use some of this money to find a way to shorten the schedule.

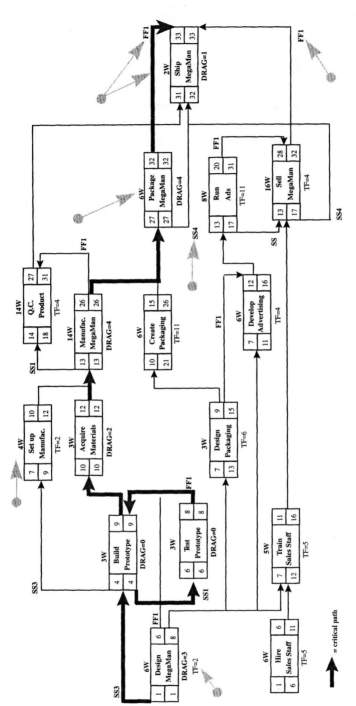

Figure 9.12 Resource-Limited Resource Schedule for the MegaMan Development Project

■ AVAILABILITY PREMIUMS

It's time for a meeting. All the data we have assembled thus far show that the net result of our company being short 1 design engineer and 10 packaging workers for the few weeks that we need them, will be a profit reduction in excess of $6 million. The activity manager for *Package MegaMan* shrugs, and reminds us that we had said that we'd get the approval for hiring the additional packagers through the human resources department. "I've told them we need more people until I'm blue in the face. They won't budge."

A quick phone call gets the director of the human resources department to drop in on the meeting. Once again the data are laid out. The lack of 10 packagers for 3 weeks is about to cost us $6 million, which we explain to the director of human resources.

The director of human resources looks at our charts. Clearly, he is concerned that the blame for lost revenues is going to be laid at his doorstep. He'd like to hire more packagers, he explains; several other project managers have been asking for them as well. But there just aren't any packagers available out there. The economy is very good right now, and it's difficult to attract even unskilled workers for $10 an hour.

Our first reply is, "let's offer $20 an hour."

We can't do that, comes the response. "When you add in benefits and other overhead, it would push the cost of a packager from $150 per day to almost $300. It would throw the entire corporate salary structure out of whack."

At this point we draw a vertical line down the middle of the white board. On one side we write the heading: "Cost Due to HRD's Refusal to Hire 10 Additional Packagers for 3 Weeks." On the other side: "Cost of Paying 10 Additional Packagers for 1 Year." Then, on the first side we write "$6,000,000."

Now we offer the director of human resources the marker and ask him to write in the additional cost of the packagers. He doesn't do so, but it's okay—the point has been made. When the meeting ends half an hour later, he has agreed to work with the packaging manager to ensure that sufficient additional packagers are hired to complete the activity in 3 weeks. He has also agreed to approve the hiring of an additional design engineer that will allow the prototyping activities to return to their CPM durations.

We, in turn, have agreed to charge the project budget for 12 weeks worth of 150 percent of the burdened wages of each of the 10 packaging workers, plus the design engineer. These will be charged to the specific activities under the line item "Availability Premium." The 150 percent is to make sure the resources can be obtained. The 12-week charge is in case the functional departments are not able to keep the additional employees sufficiently busy and have to lay them off with appropriate separation packages. The charges work out to $27,000 for the packagers and $6,300 for the design engineer.

With the *Ship MegaMan* activity once again scheduled for week 28, the resources are again available to complete it in 1 week. We're back to our 28 week schedule, and to our $10.8 million EMV. Not bad, at a cost of $33,300!

Before we go home that afternoon, we send an e-mail to the CEO explaining how "the proactive support of the human resources department is saving the organization $6.8 million." And, of course, we cc the director of human resources.

Unfortunately, the process does not always go that smoothly. There are even occasions when $6.8 million opportunities must be passed up, due to cash flow or other considerations. But, under any circumstances, the numbers that are involved must be computed and made crystal clear. To make a decision to forego $6 million is one thing; to do so without even recognizing the issue is gross incompetence. Unfortunately, it is precisely the sort of incompetence that the corporate world engages in thousands of times a year.

■ RIGHTSIZING A PROJECT-DRIVEN ORGANIZATION

The impact of insufficient resources can only be monetized by tying it to project delay in the following manner:

➤ Project delay costs money by reducing the project EMV.

➤ Project delay can be assigned to specific activities through CPM and DRAG.

➤ The difference between an activity's DRAG on the CPM schedule and on the resource-limited schedule is RAD, the delay due to resource availability.

➤ Through ABRA, both project delay and its cost can be attached to the resource whose lack of availability is its cause.

The connection can be shown on one project, and on all the projects in the organization which share resources. But that information needs to be collected at the resource level, which is to say by the functional department. By maintaining the resource library and assisting project managers in resource scheduling and leveling, functional managers can collect data on the schedule impact of the scarcity of each resource. Through the projects' TPC Business Cases, this impact can be monetized, and additional resources and availability premiums justified. Ultimately a staffing level can be attained that is optimized, on the basis of profits, for each resource.

It is crucial to realize that this is an entirely different definition of optimized and rightsizing. It is a definition that is driven by the total, integrated, nature of a project, and of a portfolio of projects. It is a definition that is impossible to codify without an integrated concept of the project, a concept that has at its root the monetized value of the work scope.

Previous approaches to rightsizing included some idea about keeping people busy. If people weren't busy all the time, resources weren't being used to full capacity and thus were being wasted. This concept is an anachronism, left over from the days when business consisted almost exclusively of steady, repetitive work. With projects, that paradigm is out the window. Projects *don't* have steady and even work requirements and therefore don't have steady and even resource requirements. Instead, they have a dominating need to finish at a certain time, and a subsidiary need to have those individual items of work of which they are comprised occur at specific times. That means that they need to have the resources to do those individual work items only at specific times. If those resources aren't there, that original dominating need is compromised.

This may seem relatively obvious, but now there is a corollary, one that many managers and management consulting companies that specialize in downsizing refuse to recognize: As long as you've got those resources when you need them, it doesn't much matter what they do when you don't.

Consider the following: Henry comes to work every morning at 8:30, puts his feet on his desk, slips on the headphones from his CD player, and pulls out a good book. About every 2 weeks, a project lands on his terminal. He grabs his mouse and keyboard, works feverishly until he's finished, forwards it to the next person, then picks up his book again. Are there any Henrys where you work? I sure don't ever see them. In most companies, they'd be fired the first week. Certainly, they'd be laid off as soon as the first management consultant walks through. Yet there is nothing wrong with Henry's behavior. Maybe the good book is about HTML programming, or project management. Or that new corporate concept, the learning organization.

Henry's value *must* not be determined by what he's doing when he's not working—his value comes from what he's doing when he *is* working. If we decide that we don't need Henry goofing off 4 days out of every 5, and give him the pink slip, we also lose him for that fifth day, when he works. And to not have him there when our projects need him might cost us 20 days of resource availability DRAG over the course of the year, and those 20 days might be worth $400,000. But that's okay, right? Because at least we've got

Henry's salary off our books, which, including overhead, is $75,000. Right? No?

Of course, if we can get Henry's $400,000 work for less than $75,000, so much the better. Perhaps we can lay him off and then utilize him as a consultant 1 day a week. We'll undoubtedly have to increase his hourly wage, but since we won't have to pay him when he's not working (we'll also save something on health insurance, worker's comp., etc.), we'll be much better off.

This example is precisely why the labor force of consultants, freelancers, stringers, temps, and so on, has burgeoned so greatly in the past 2 decades. These individuals owe their careers to projects, the numbers of which have also burgeoned. Projects make temp workers extremely valuable, because they can be brought on board just when they're needed, targeted to the right work, and then their cost eliminated when they are no longer required. It's worth paying a premium for this flexibility and targeted effort, so the busy freelancer's income can be significantly larger than that of the permanent employee.

Unfortunately, sometimes that freelancer you've been counting on can grab an assignment with someone else's project, just when you really need her. By the time you discover this, and either replace her or make her an offer she can't refuse, your project has slipped by $150,000.

Some jobs you just *can't* use temps for. The worker needs to be thoroughly familiar with the organization, the specific product, or the type of product. If he isn't, there is a ramp up time that must be factored in. For some types of work, there simply is not a sufficient supply of that resource in the labor force to be able to depend on it being available on a temporary basis when you need it.

In such cases, you have to maintain the resource on staff, even if you only utilize it a small percentage of the time. The downside of not having it, the reductions in EMVs all across the board, is just too great. The dollars you shell out to Henry for him to sit and listen to Mozart are just a different form of that availability premium you have to pay to keep that resource on call. If it grieves you, or Henry's colleagues, or senior management, to watch Henry sitting there every day, tell him to go sit at home instead. Just give him a beeper so you can get him as soon as you need him. And, whatever you do, don't irk him too much. If you do, he's liable to realize that the 4 extra days a week he spends listening to Mozart could very profitably be rented out to other employers. A consulting business might allow him to retire years earlier and devote all the more time to Mozart!

■ HRD AND THE CLUBS

Every 3 or 6 months, the human resources department of project-driven companies should assemble a CLUB meeting. This would be for all the functional managers, who would bring the data regarding the collected CLUBs of each of their department's resources during the previous period. These should be arranged into Pareto charts listing in descending order the delay costs due to the shortage of each resource. Human resources should then present the information to senior management, showing which resource shortages, across the entire organization, are costing the most, and outlining a plan for lessening the problem. This plan should include:

➤ Which and how many of each resource will be added to the permanent staff?

➤ What will be done to make sure that temps and freelancers are available when needed?

➤ What availability premiums will be paid to accomplish each of these goals?

➤ What will be the long-term dollar benefit as a result of human resources' proactive vigor?

There are few things that human resources could do in a project-driven organization that would be of greater "visible" value.

In general, human resources departments, like functional managers, do not have sufficient knowledge of how projects and project management work to be able to support such an organization properly.

Sometimes this ignorance can be extremely damaging. A classic example occurred a few years ago in a very large international computer company. This company had announced that it would be bringing out a new version of its software by the end of the year. Knowledgeable individuals in the computer industry and on Wall Street smiled knowingly, remembering that each previous release of the software had come out months late. "Not this time," said the company, "we're going to have it in the stores by December 31." Word was passed to all key members of the project team: Don't plan on seeing much of your families after October; this project is too important to slip.

Unfortunately, the corporation had been suffering through some hard times and had been watching its market share and its revenues slip for many months. Cost-cutting mandates had gone out to all parts of the company; travel was being restricted, supply cabinets were being locked, and all the other classic symptoms of a management that doesn't know what to do were evident.

Late that summer, a memo was released from human resources was distributed internationally. It said something like:

> We are aware that, in past years, many employees have elected not to use their vacation time, allowing it to accrue instead. Unfortunately, this is a cost liability on our books, and, in these financially strapped times, we cannot allow this to occur any longer. Henceforth, employees will only be allowed to carry 2 weeks of vacation time into the new year. All previously accrued vacation time must be used up by the end of this year or else it will be forfeited.

You can imagine the effect of such a memo on the critical path activities of all the company's projects, including the software release. Employees who had not taken vacation in years did so, starting the next Monday. When they returned, in early January, their projects had already slipped by weeks. The new software version came out months late, as usual, just in time to be destroyed by its major competitor. The cost, in both revenues and market share, was considerable; in terms of credibility and stock price, it was even worse.

Sure, the vacation time was a liability on the corporate ledger. But this is a classic example of snapping at pennies while dropping millions, and is typical in organizations that have zero knowledge of the implications of project work and project management techniques.

The concentration on work is an essential part of the project management process. This can sometimes cause those whose job it is to deal with the people side of things, both functional managers and human resources, to feel diminished in significance. Nothing should be further from the truth. If performed properly, project management should actually *increase* the importance of resource management. Not only are resources the only way to get the work done, but projects introduce a tricky new dimension in managing them successfully—*time*. It's fine to know that you've got 10 good people in your department, but

➤ When do you have them? And when do you not have them?

➤ When is each assigned to other projects?

➤ When will only seven be needed, and what will you do with the other three at that time?

➤ When, and for how long, will you need 12 people?

➤ What will the cost be, to projects, to your own department, and to the entire organization, if you don't get them? If you only get 11?

➤ How much of an availability premium should you be willing to pay?

➤ How long before the extra two people are actually required will you need to hire them and train them?

All these questions are TPC issues. They all require that resource managers understand project management. They all require a well-maintained resource library. They all require project managers who utilize a TPC Business Case and critical path planning, and include the functional departments in the project planning process.

■ MULTIPROJECT RESOURCE SCHEDULING

Among project management software packages, the ability to perform multi-project resource leveling is the functionality that really separates the megs from the bytes. Some packages (especially the inexpensive and more popular ones) are incapable of performing this vital function. Such packages should be regarded strictly as single-project scheduling tools.

But now here is the bad news: even the best software packages are abject failures at performing multi-project resource leveling. The reason is simple: they don't have the information to level projects properly.

Many years ago, when I was first delving into project management theory, I worked for one of the leading distributors of project management software. At the time, they were developing a new product for the Unix environment. I was still quite naive about, and intimidated by, the software and could not understand why changing the "Priority" field should randomly reduce or increase the resource-leveled duration. I went and asked the product designer for the new software if the new leveling algorithm would produce an "optimized" schedule. He looked at me pityingly and said:

There are two things. First of all, with a complex project, the computer would have to run for a year, to explore all the possible permutations for activities and resources in order to produce any sort of 'optimized' schedule. [This is pretty accurate. At the time, I underestimated the complexity of a large project plan.]

But even more important is the question: What is an 'optimized' schedule anyway? Are you talking about optimizing for time? Is the shortest schedule what you want? Or are you talking about cost? Is the cheapest schedule the optimized schedule? Don't you see? It all depends on what you want.

I walked away from that meeting feeling a bit embarrassed, but even more, confused. I sensed that somehow there should be more to it than that. A human being can tell which project schedule is better, so a computer should be able to figure it out also. Yet I could not decide: Was it a shorter schedule or less cost that should take priority?

That problem idled at the back of my brain for several weeks. Then, slowly and with much associated self-doubt, the answer took form: revenues, profit, cost reduction, and value! That should be the criterion for determining the best project schedule. That was the whole reason we were doing the project in the first place! But that was also an item of information that the software did not have. Project management software deals with cost and schedule—value just ain't important on a project!

On a single project, you can often get away with the assumption that a shorter schedule means greater value. Sometimes this assumption is invalid, but overall it's not a bad rule of thumb.

But when the issue is multi-project resource leveling, the short-is-better rule becomes incomprehensible. Shorter *which*? Shorter *what*? Shorten one project and you lengthen another. Complete them *all* in less time? But each has a different delay penalty or acceleration premium—some may be able to slip a month without serious impact, while others may cost a half-a-million dollars a day. Applying all the different parameters and constraints is a job for a computer, yet project management software doesn't accept that kind of input.

But what about the caveat that a computer, even if the right data were input, doesn't have the capacity to compute an optimized schedule? If a computer that can beat Gary Kasparov at chess can't figure out the best way to distribute the resources, what chance do *you* have of doing it? (Okay, so you've never in your life lost a game to Gary. Still.)

The computer may not be able to compute an optimum schedule, but it can generate a pretty good one. If the right data are entered, and the software has the right algorithm to manipulate the right metrics in the right way, then, given enough time, it should be able to isolate the multi-project schedule that, over the course of, say, 50,000 tries, gets the highest score. Or maybe the three highest scores. And it should be able to tell you exactly what those scores are.

What units should those scores be in? If you've read all these pages, and still can't guess the answer, I'm moving back to the West Indies and becoming an obeah man! Dollars, of course. Measured by the EMV across all the projects, adjusted for net present value, and minus costs. Profit, quoted either in raw dollars or, because it's simple and convenient, the Simple DIPP.

Every night before going home, the portfolio manager of all the organization's projects should go to the computer and access the project management software application with its entire portfolio of current and forthcoming project files. Then a click of the mouse, and the software should spend the night clackety-clacking through the activities and resources, assigning first two programmers to this project and one to that, then two to that and one to this. At 8:00 the next morning, the portfolio manager should be able to see the current schedule and its EMV numbers, as well as the top three new schedules the software has been able to generate, with their EMV numbers. If there's not much of a difference, the portfolio manager can decide to stick with the current schedule. Indeed, if there is a chasm between the different schedules, the portfolio manager may still eschew the changes. Management remains the province of human beings, but a computer that has the right data can be an indispensable tool.

Notes

1. Indeed, the most popular of the inexpensive software packages is quite hopeless in the way it handles resource leveling. However, this is not as much of a drawback as might otherwise be the case, because most users of this package hardly ever bother assigning resources or maintaining a resource library in the first place.

2. Different software packages perform this function differently. Some are better than others at pinpointing where the potential trouble lies. Some packages will identify the activities, the resources, and the dates of a bottleneck; others may simply flash a message that a problem exists. In either circumstance, decisions about resolving the bottleneck will have to be made. It's a lot easier to do this if we don't have to go hunting for the problem.

3. Here we are ignoring the fact that *Design MegaMan*, the predecessor of *Build Prototype*, also utilizes design engineers and, being an SS3 predecessor, is partly in parallel with the two prototyping activities. For simplicity's sake, we will simply assume that we have already decided to assign the necessary resources to *Design MegaMan*, and are now dealing with the remaining activities and resources.

4. The underlying problem, of course, is a fundamental part of the human condition: In order to improve a situation, we first have to be willing to admit that there's a problem. In a corporate hierarchy, where we need senior management to approve the necessary fix, we have to demonstrate, in the clearest terms possible, just how inefficient we are being. That's a tough requirement to ask of anyone.

Tracking and Controlling the Project

Theory divides the process of managing a project into two parts: Planning and tracking. Project management, it is said, is about planning the work and then working the plan.

There is value to this way of visualizing a project. But, in another sense, it introduces a false dichotomy. The planning process does not stop when the project begins. In fact, the tracking process is more about planning than anything else. It's about *re*planning—over and over again.

However, there is one big advantage in the replanning; we should never have to go back to square one. The original plan (A-I-M F-I-R-E in Chapter 2) should be a vital tool for facilitating the replanning. Indeed, making the process of replanning easier is a major goal of the original planning process, and a big part of the reason for such formats as WBS, CPM network, ABC, and so forth.

The "A" of A-I-M F-I-R-E, you may recall, stands for *aware*. Awareness that a change has occurred. That means a change from the original plan. So the original plan had better be good, and had better be detailed, and had better be closely tracked.

We have now the elements of the plan for the MegaMan development project. Next we need to submit all these elements to the project review process for the next phase, prior to the final gate of project approval. This you may recall, is the third gate of the process. The first gate approved funding through completion of the project plan, which is where we are now. In order to proceed with the project, we need further funding, and in order to get that funding, the entire plan, including budgetary requirements, must be submitted.

■ THE FINAL PROJECT APPROVAL GATE

Figure 10.1 shows all three phases, through the gate signifying approval for funding of the detailed plan.

The elements of the plan that must be approved, and that will be used to track the project, are:

1. The TPC Business Case: $10 million if completed by the end of week 30.

                                           $2 million less for each week later.

                                           $0.4 million more for each week earlier.

2. The project work scope document, including the assumptions appendix.

3. The project WBS (Figure 10.2):

4. The resource-limited schedule: Total duration of 28 weeks for EMV of $10.8 million. Through the securing of resources by the payment of availability premiums, the project baseline schedule is essentially the same as the CPM schedule. The only resource delay is off the critical path, where the *Set Up Manufacturing* activity has been stretched from 3 to 4 weeks, and its total float reduced from 2 weeks to 1.

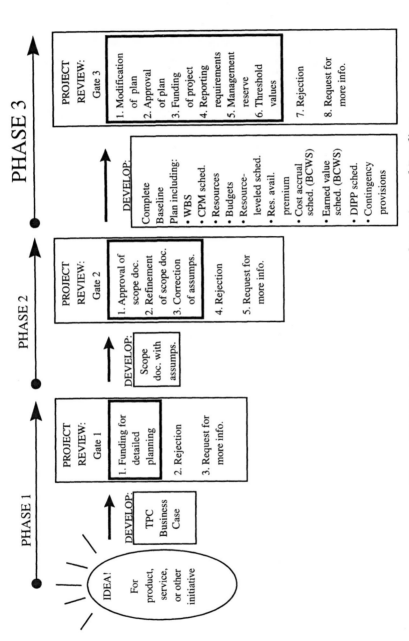

Figure 10.1 The Project Review Process for Gating and Funding

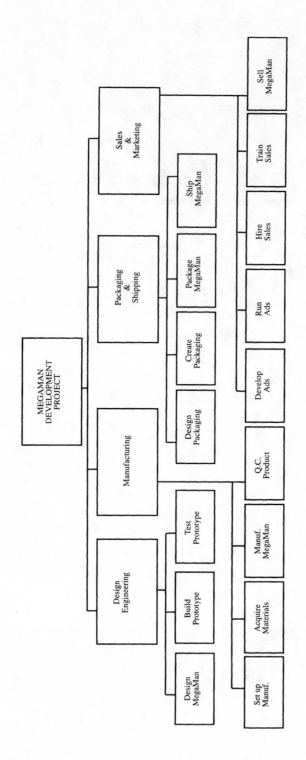

Figure 10.2 WBS for The MegaMan Development Project

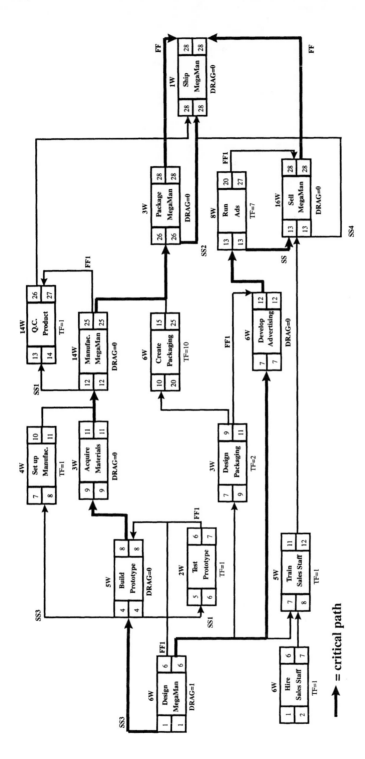

Figure 10.3 Baseline Schedule for MegaMan Development Project

5. The activity-based budgets (Table 10.1).

6. The project budget:

Project Name	Labor Budget	Availablity Premium	Total Budget
MegaMan Development Project	$1,067,600	$33,300	$4,070,083

7. The project DIPP: $10,800,000 ÷ $4,070,083 = 2.654

8. The project VBS (Figure 10.4).

Table 10.1 Activity-Based Budgets

Summary Activity	Activity	Labor Budget ($)	Availablity Premium ($)	Total Budget ($)
Design and Prototyping	Design MegaMan	140,500		187,333
	Build Prototype	21,500	6,300	34,967
	Test Prototype	10,000		13,333
	Design Packaging	13,250		17,667
	Total:	185,250	6,300	253,300
Packaging and Shipping	Create Packaging	51,000		102,000
	Package MegaMan	63,000	27,000	153,000
	Ship MegaMan	6,100		12,200
	Total:	120,100	27,000	267,200
Manufacturing and Q.C.	Set Up Manufac.	25,800		86,000
	Acquire Materials	1,600		5,333
	Manufacture MegaMan	357,000		1,190,000
	Q.C. Product	12,600		42,000
	Total:	397,000		1,323,333
Sales and Marketing	Develop Advertising	20,250		101,250
	Run Ads	5,000		425,000
	Hire Sales	16,500		82,500
	Train Sales	35,500		177,500
	Sell MegaMan	288,000		1,440,000
	Total:	365,250		2,226,250

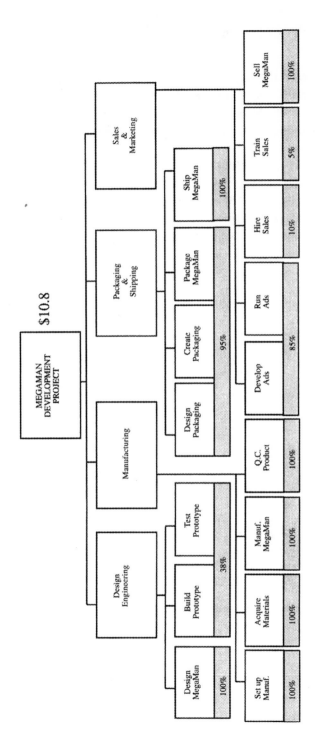

Figure 10.4 VBS for the MegaMan Development Project

There are two other elements, both traditional project management documents, that should be a part of the baseline plan. The data to assemble these two documents have already been generated through the planning process. They are:

9. The cost accrual schedule. Since we have planned the cost that each activity will incur, and we have scheduled each activity, we also know when the cost for each budget item will be incurred and how that cost will accumulate. We can therefore assemble two histograms:

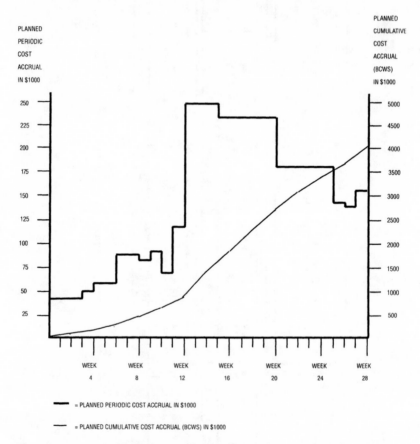

Figure 10.5 Periodic and Cumulative Planned Cost Accrual Histograms

➤ A periodic cost accrual histogram, showing how much cost will be incurred in each time period.

➤ A cumulative cost histogram, showing how that cost will accumulate as the project work is performed.

Most project management software packages will extract the data from the plan and allow us to generate both these cost functions on the same histogram display by simply using different x-axes for the different dollar totals.

An example of such a histogram is shown in Figure 10.5.

10. The earned value schedule.

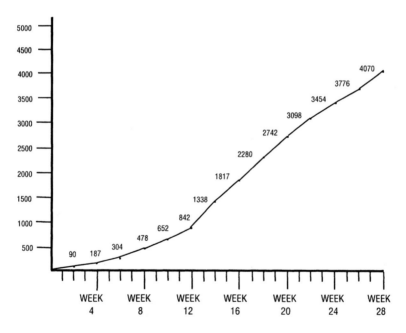

Figure 10.6 Budgeted Cost of Work Scheduled, or BCWS (It is identical with the Cumulative Planned Cost Accrual Curve Shown in Figure 10.5.)

Earned value is a very simple, yet a very misunderstood technique of traditional project management. It's the sort of thing that software users and business school students don't like to deal with because they're somewhat intimidated by it. Needlessly.

■ THE EARNED VALUE SCHEDULE

Not long ago, I outlined the basic approach of TPC to the senior management of an international construction company based in Boston. After listening to a description of such techniques as the TPC Business Case, the DIPP, and the VBS, one of the executives said, "Well, this is basically just earned value, right?" That told me (and several others in the room) that not only had he not understood TPC, but he also did not comprehend earned value.

Earned value is this: Every activity in the project is "weighted" by some attribute that is common to all the activities. Then, as each activity is completed, our project is said to have "earned" the value of that pre-determined "weight."

The attribute used for weighting activities may be anything (work hours, miles of highway, schedule risk, even value-added), but the most common "weight" is budgeted dollars. Each activity is assigned the earned value equal to its budget for resources. As each activity is completed, the earned value of the project will increase by the amount of dollars originally budgeted to that activity, irrespective of how much it actually costs to perform the activity. In other words, the schedule along which the earned value should mount, as shown in Figure 10.6, is identical to the cumulative cost accrual schedule shown in the histogram in Figure 10.5.

The standard name for the earned value accumulation schedule has been adopted from U.S. Department of Defense procedures, and is called the Budgeted Cost of Work Scheduled (BCWS).

When work begins on the project, two types of data get plotted against this one schedule (whether called planned cumulative cost accrual, BCWS, or earned value plan). They are:

1. Earned value, equal to the original budgets for all activities completed. This is also called (again from U.S. Defense Department procedures) the Budgeted Cost of Work Performed (BCWP).

2. Accrued cost, or the amount of money that was actually spent to complete those activities (the Actual Cost of Work Performed [ACWP].

Those three four-letter acronyms have done more than anything else to scare people away from using the very useful technique of earned value. So here they are with their common language synonyms:

BCWS = schedule of planned cumulative cost accruals (as in Figure 10.4).

BCWP = earned value achieved, or the budgets of the activities accomplished as the project is performed.

ACWP = actual accrued costs as the project is performed.

Notice that the BCWS (Figure 10.4), is the only one assembled during the planning stage; the BCWP and ACWP accumulate during the performance of the project and are reported against the curve of the BCWS to see how the project is being performed compared to what was planned.

■ REPORTING PROGRESS

As the project is performed, every attempt should be made to stick to the plan. The most important guiding aspect of the plan is the schedule. Activities should start, as well as finish, according to the schedule. If finishing an activity on schedule means using additional resources, and thus exceeding an activity's budget, it usually makes sense to do it. Again, it usually takes plenty of resources to balance out the cost of a week's delay.

Project tracking, like project work, must be performed on a delegated basis. A project manager simply does not have time to check all the work taking place on a major project. Therefore the activity managers must check the work (or, of course, on a very large activity, get reports from their subordinates) and report how it's coming against the work scope document requirements, the schedule, and the budget.

A reporting schedule of once a month is often used when dealing with customer projects, such as Defense Department programs for the U.S. government. However, a monthly reporting schedule is inadequate for trying to manage a project. The cost of a month's delay is almost invariably six figures, and usually seven. If the project is being delayed, we need to identify the problem and resolve it long before it has had such a huge impact. On nuclear plant refueling projects, the cost of each day that the plant is shut down can be worth up to $1.2 million. On this type of project, a single week's delay would be worth almost $10 million. Therefore refueling projects are sometimes scheduled with activity estimates measured in quarter-hours, and with schedule updates following each 8-hour shift. If nuclear plant refueling can be managed in such an online, real-time manner, then the same could be done for any project.

This, however, may not be necessary for most projects. For most product development projects, my recommendation would be that progress be reported by the project manager to senior management at least every 2 weeks, and that activity managers should update the project manager at least once a week.

That would be the regular schedule. Obviously, there should also be a mechanism by which ad hoc updates are both required and submitted. The project manager may be aware that a portion of the project is especially risky, and demand daily updates. Or an activity manager might suddenly realize that his activity is going to take 3 weeks longer than planned. That information must be passed on to the project manager immediately, and the project plan updated to reflect the bad news.

■ THRESHOLD LEVELS

Project management, at any level, must depend on management-by-exception—there is simply too much going on, on one project or across the portfolio of projects, to waste time checking on things that are just fine. In addition, the time-sensitive nature of a project demands that a problem must not only be identified as early as possible, but also resolved as quickly as possible. Wherever possible, a problem should be dealt with by the person immediately responsible. However, if that person is unable to resolve the issue without either changing the work scope, slipping the schedule, or exceeding the activity budget by more than a stipulated amount, then the problem may have to be escalated to the next highest level. This is true whether we are talking about activity to project level, or project to portfolio level.

A common management tool is to incorporate procedures that fix a certain threshold level on the schedule or cost of the work. It is the job of the project review process, at this last gate, to set the metrics and threshold levels for escalation. In less sophisticated organizations, not used to earned value metrics and analysis, the threshold level is usually a raw number: The schedule can slip 4 weeks, or the cost exceed the budget by $200,000, before the project manager is required to submit to a senior management review. If earned value metrics are being used, the threshold levels are usually set on those values: Escalation is required if the work performed falls 10 percent behind the work scheduled; or if the actual costs for work done thus far (ACWP) exceed the BCWS by more than 10 percent. (The earned value metrics have the big advantage of identifying potentially disastrous trends long before the catastrophic point has been reached.)

➤ Threshold Levels on the DIPP

The trouble is that none of these thresholds is really on the right data item. Schedule and cost are only indirectly important, or by inference, as it were. What's really important is the three-way interaction of work scope, schedule, and cost—the EMV of the project, as measured by the DIPP. The project's DIPP is what project manager and team should, at all times, be working to maximize. It's when the DIPP descends below a certain level, indicating a specific reduction in profits, that senior management should get nervous, and involved.

The project's DIPP can shrink for several different reasons:

1. The schedule could slip, causing delay costs to shrink the EMV.

2. The accrued costs could grow, forcing the project over budget and generating less profit.

3. Work scope could be pruned, to preempt either schedule slippage or cost overruns, and result in a less attractive and valuable product.

All three of the above are caused by the project work, and project team. Close supervision of the project might make any of the three visible. But there is a fourth reason why the

DIPP could shrink, and no amount of project supervision would ever be able to tell, because the reason for the DIPP shrinking would be totally unrelated to the project work:

4. External forces, such as the retail market, could cause the EMV of the final product to shrink. In fact, such external factors can impact the project value in any number of ways:

➤ The delay costs of $400,000 and $2 million, could change up or down.

➤ The date of the switchover, the last week of November, could change.

➤ Product features, which had been omitted in the original specs, could suddenly become very valuable.

➤ Other features, which had been included, might become of no importance.

➤ The entire market for our forthcoming product could disappear.

All of the above are changes about which the typical project manager, doing a project manager's job, would normally never become aware. Yet they are factors that are crucial to the success of our project. The individuals who should be aware of them are the product manager, marketing manager, or whatever title you want to give to the individual whose job it should be the track the market. Remember, the market side is at least as important as the project side.

The TPC Business Case, with its forecast of EMV and its estimate of the impact of different variables on the project plan, is the driving force at the start of the project. But the TPC Business Case, however, must not be abandoned once the project starts; it too is a working document, intended to be tracked, updated, and modified when changes occur in its data. The product manager should be responsible for checking the data and ensuring their accuracy as often as the project manager is required to report on the project. The product manager and project manager need to work together as closely as possible with the goal always being to maximize the DIPP. If they are not one and the same person (an innovation that has been tried recently, although both functions may be too much for any one human being), then perhaps they could be surgically joined at the hip. Whatever the solution, close interaction between these two roles is mandatory.

Of course, placing a threshold level on the DIPP requires more than simply choosing a number that's 10 percent less than the starting DIPP. As the project goes along, work gets done, money is spent, and the amount that it will take to finish the project decreases while, presumably, the EMV remains the same. Remember, the formula for calculating the DIPP is:

$$\text{DIPP} = \frac{\text{EMV (as of current completion date)}}{\text{Estimate-to-complete (ETC)}}$$

As the last item of work on the project is done, and the last dollar is spent, the ETC becomes zero, and the DIPP rises to infinity. Long before that, however, the DIPP will have risen far above its original level (or so we most fervently pray!). Understand, this is not a distortion, or something for which we have to make allowances. It's reality. When we have completed half the work of the project, we must no longer factor into our decisions the money we've already spent. Those are sunk costs, gone no matter what decision we make. All that we can affect is the future. All that we can, for example, save on the project by canceling it is the money we have yet to spend. Our major concern now is the ETC, what we have to spend to finish the project and get its EMV.

What is needed is a forecast of the periodic DIPP, not dissimilar to the histogram of the accrued costs. For the MegaMan project, the DIPP curve would start at 2.91 and rise to the level it should be at during week 28, when the last $150,000 or so on the *Package MegaMan, Sell MegaMan,* and *Ship MegaMan* activities is scheduled to accrue. At that point, the DIPP should be:

$$DIPP = \$10.8 \text{ million} \div \$150,000 = 72.0$$

At 14 weeks, halfway through the project, our accrued costs (from the BCWS curve) should be approximately $1,168,000. Therefore, if we are on schedule and budget at that point, our ETC would be:

$$
\begin{aligned}
ETC &= \text{project budget} - \text{accrued costs} \\
&= \$4,070,083 - \$1,168,000 \\
&= \$2,902,083
\end{aligned}
$$

Therefore at the end of 14 weeks, if everything is on target, the project DIPP should be:

$$DIPP = \$10.8 \text{ million} \div \$2,902,083 = 3.721$$

Suppose that senior management feels that anything more than a 5 percent reduction in profits should not be routinely accepted. Currently, profits on the MegaMan project are expected to be $10,800,000 minus $4,070,083, or $6,729,917. 95 percent of $6,729,917 is $6,393,421. Therefore we want to put a threshold on the MegaMan project's DIPP so that if it ever shows the forecast profit slipping beneath $6.39 million, senior management will immediately be notified.

In order to make a profit of $6,393,421 on a budget of $4,070,083, the project EMV would have to be $10,463,504. The initial DIPP would therefore have to be:

$$DIPP = \$10,463,504 \div \$4,070,083 = 2.571$$

This DIPP (reflecting a profit that is 95 percent of the current planned profit) is 3.12 percent less than the current baseline DIPP of 2.654. This means that the DIPP would have to be at least 96.88 percent of what it was at the 100 percent profit figure in order to maintain a 95 percent profit.

At the halfway point in the project, after 14 weeks, if our schedule and budget are on target, and the EMV is at the 95 percent profit level of $10,463,504, our DIPP would be higher, due to the work completed and the corresponding reduction of the ETC.

$$\text{DIPP} = \$10,463,504 \div \$2,902,083 = 3.605$$

Remember, this is as opposed to the DIPP of 3.721 at the 100 percent profit figure. Once again, the DIPP at the 95 percent profit rate is 96.88 percent of what it was at the 100 percent rate.

A pattern has emerged. Let's try it one more time, at the last week of the project. At that stage, you may recall, we had an ETC of $150,000, giving us a DIPP, based on the $10.8 million EMV, of 72.000. If the EMV fell to the 95 percent profit level of $10,463,504, our DIPP would be:

$$\text{DIPP} = \$10,463,504 \div \$150,000 = 69.757$$
$$96.88 \% \text{ of } 72.000 = 69.753$$

So now, in addition to the DIPP, we can set a *DIPP threshold*. For this project, senior management has decided that profit reduction of more than $540,000 is unacceptable. For other projects, different threshold levels might be suitable. But whatever the threshold level, it can be attached to the DIPP, ensuring that the profit forecast remains high, or that the project is escalated for review. Figure 10.7 is a histogram of the forecast DIPP for the MegaMan development project, with the threshold-level DIPP drawn 3.12 percent beneath it.

Any time, at any stage of the project, that the profitability of the project dips (if you'll pardon the expression!) below a predetermined floor, alarm bells will sound, signaling the

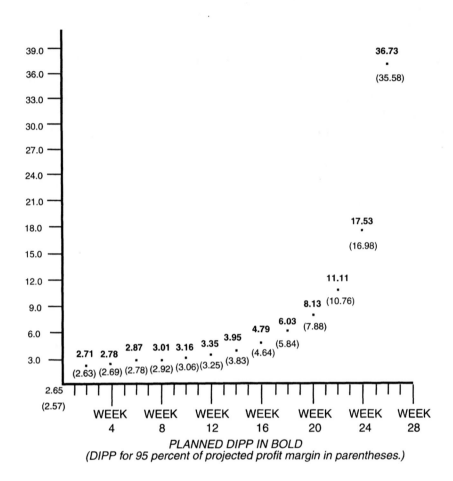

Figure 10.7 Histogram of DIPP and DIPP Threshold Curve for the MegaMan Development Project

need for senior management intervention. Remember, the alarms are triggered not because the schedule slips, not because of budget overruns but because of any of the myriad possible causes for the project being less profitable than we can accept. Why, at the third gate of the project review process, do we choose to invest our limited resources in this project rather than any other?

■ SUMMARY

Project tracking consists of checking the project to see where you are and then checking the plan to see where you should be. When the two don't jibe, or don't jibe well enough, the plan must be changed.

Changing the plan means replanning those parts of it that might allow the project to get back on the right track. This is almost identical to the process we went through in developing the initial plan, except this time we have a head-start: The baseline plan, with its identified critical path and CPM metrics; the breakdown structures with the attached cost and value data; and ABRA and resource library, with identified bottlenecks. All these assist the project manager in finding alternative ways of maximizing the project's EMV.

The project plan allows us to track, compare, and look for ways to improve whatever it is that we've planned. If we've planned schedule, resources, and cost, we can track the data on all those items, and attempt to adjust their courses as soon as they start to go askew.

The TPC approach to planning brings three new aspects to the tracking process:

1. It allows us to track the most important part of the project, namely its value.

2. It allows us to set threshold levels on the project value that will automatically trigger alarms if the value sinks below preset levels.

3. It allows us to modify all the other parts of the project plan with the goal of maintaining or maximizing its value.

What we do for one project, we can do for the entire portfolio of projects—the value of the organization's entire portfolio is ultimately the measure of how well we are managing our projects. One project finishing early or slipping, another project finishing under or over budget, may be insignificant, but only the big picture, the value that the organization gets from its investment in projects, can determine that. It's precisely that picture that TPC is designed to both display and improve.

Chapter 11

Conclusion

Despite having been around, with most of its techniques and benefits, for more than 40 years, traditional project management is still largely ignored. The only exceptions are in those industries and applications where either it is mandated, such as NASA or U.S. Department of Defense projects, or where its value is overwhelmingly clear, such as nuclear power outages, where the delay premium is easily computed and can be in excess of a million dollars a day. The vast majority of the business world, however, is ignorant of the techniques, and continues to assume that project management is equal parts magic, luck and testosterone. (As one senior manager said during a recent client conference: "What we really need here as project managers is a bunch of Alpha male dogs!" The facial expression of the only woman present caused some of the other men in the room to add hurriedly: "Or Alpha female dogs!" But the message was clear.)

So if even traditional project management has trouble gaining a toehold in the corporate world, why should TPC have any better luck? The answer is because TPC is tied to what's really important to the organization—value and profit. Even in nonprofit organizations, there are divergent values among the various projects. How should one judge between them? The resources that are assigned to them are paid for in dollars. If we decide to pay more for resources on one project than another, aren't we hinting that one is "worth" more dollars than the other? No matter what the value systems are that are generating the two projects?

Everything in life requires prioritization. Getting the most value from the resource usage is the goal, even if that value is measured not in profits, but in reduced infant mortality rates, or elderly people made comfortable, or numbers of distant stars examined for radio signals. The fewer resources we can use to do good, the more we have left over to do better. By "dollarizing" that good, we can make decisions about the targeting of our resources. The link is made between the project and that which everyone wants: "value," however determined.

At every organization I have worked with in the past decade that has tried to implement project management, someone invariably makes the point: "In order for this to work, senior management has to understand it and get behind it." They're absolutely right. But, more often than not, executives regard project management as something to be done by their underlings. After all, they never studied this in their MBA programs (and in the few cases where they did, it was with professors who also did not completely grasp the material), so obviously it's beneath a professional executive with an MBA.

TPC changes all that by providing a way to tie the lowest adminstrivia of project management directly and visibly to what matters to executives: the bottom line that's used to determine how they are doing their jobs. If the relationship can be clearly drawn between a programmer getting a $7,500 bonus for working 80 hours a week for 2 weeks, and an extra $992,500 in profits, that will get their attention. If they can leave their computer running all night, and early next morning there's a multi-project schedule that offers an extra $2.7 million in revenues, *that's* worth buying into. Maybe mandating a standardized project methodology, with project managers being required to produce a WBS and CPM schedule, and functional departments being forced (and given the necessary resources) to maintain up-to-date resource libraries, isn't beneath the notice of top executives at all.

The time has come to change the way that corporations are organized and run. If 90 percent of a company's revenues are generated by projects, then that company's business is project management. The entire management structure and personnel should be steeped in project management methodologies. Whatever steps are needed to manage projects should be taken: procedures, software, and organizational hierarchies. Steps should also be taken to eliminate whatever interferes with the ability to manage projects.

Business schools too are going to have to alter their curriculum. Much of what they teach is far less relevant than would be the rudiments of CPM. Yet students at the best business schools in the United States continue to obtain Masters' degrees without being required to take so much as a single course in project management. The fact that business school professors often don't understand CPM, with all its functionality and benefits, is a problem. Business schools, and their faculty, would much rather teach the sorts of things that future executives of Fortune 500 companies (the alumni who are likely to make big donations) like to play around with. But when the relationship between scheduling a project and making a profit is demonstrated to be inextricably close, it's amazing how glamorous project management suddenly becomes.

Within recent years, a handful of universities have started offering M.P.M. degrees (Master of Project Management). Others offer a project management specialization as part of their MBA program. This trend will have to continue with greater velocity because the alternative is a higher bankruptcy rate. Those corporations that are first to make significant improvement in their management of projects are simply going to put the competition out of business.

A final word about project management software. About 6 years ago, I had the good fortune to speak with the president of a company that made one of the better and more sophisticated project management software packages. He observed that in the decade or so that he had been in business, project management sophistication had actually decreased. While at the time I was not sure he was right, I have since noticed exactly the same trend. And simultaneously, another trend has run parallel: The number of commercially available project management software packages has declined precipitously, from several hundred to about 20. Of these 20, 1 has gained almost a 50 percent market share.

I do not believe that these two trends are unrelated. The software that has taken over the market is a package that provides the least functionality, the least sophistication, and allows the greatest number of "shortcuts" that short circuit the techniques of good project management. Nine times out of 10, the software is being used as nothing more than a graphics package to draw Gantt charts. Companies that utilize this software package and claim they're doing project management are the equivalent of a seven-year-old jumping on an airbag that shoots a plastic rocket up 30 feet claiming he's in the space exploration business.

Yet this software package controls almost 50 percent of the market. That's because for the way most companies are currently doing project management, this software is more than enough. But that's only because they aren't really doing project management! Anyone using it who tries to do real project management hits the wall real fast. There are add-on software packages that do improve the functionality, but they cost money that management sometimes is not willing to approve. ("We pay a lot of money to have that project management software on our network, and projects are still late; what do we need to spend more money for?") Even the best project management techniques can't make a silk purse out of porcine aural resources. Resource scheduling is precisely where this particular software package is most inadequate.

If individuals in a company with this package start trying to do real project management, they will either become frustrated and give up, or they will need better software. Either the company that produces it (a very large and famous corporation for whom project management software is a very small sideline) is going to have come out with a brand-new package that really does project management, or the organizations that use the current package are going to have to invest in something worthwhile. Any of the other packages would be an improvement.

Ultimately, there will be a package that ties projects to profits, that calculates DRAG, and that performs the other TPC functions. Then senior management may start getting excited. But until then, traditional project management methods have a great deal to offer. Any company not using them is sacrificing a huge competitive advantage, because their competition probably isn't using them either.

Index

Printed in the United States
67215LVS00002BA/295-312

9 780471 328599